silentselling

look

compare

innovate

silentselling

SIXTH EDITION

best practices and effective strategies
in visual merchandising

judy bell

FAIRCHILD BOOKS

NEW YORK · LONDON · OXFORD · NEW DELHI · SYDNEY

FAIRCHILD BOOKS
Bloomsbury Publishing Inc
1385 Broadway, New York, NY 10018, USA
50 Bedford Square, London, WC1B 3DP, UK
29 Earlsfort Terrace, Dublin 2, Ireland

BLOOMSBURY, FAIRCHILD BOOKS and the Fairchild Books logo are trademarks of Bloomsbury Publishing Plc

Fourth edition published 2011
Fifth edition published 2017
This edition published 2022

Library of Congress Cataloging-in-Publication Data
Names: Bell, Judith A., author.
Title: Silent selling : best practices and effective strategies in visual
    merchandising / Judy Bell.
Identifiers: LCCN 2021038242 (print) | LCCN 2021038243 (ebook) | ISBN
    9781501367977 (paperback) | ISBN 9781501368004 (pdf)
Subjects: LCSH: Display of merchandise. | Fashion merchandising.
Classification: LCC HF5845 .B35 2022 (print) | LCC HF5845 (ebook) | DDC
    687.068/8—dc23
LC record available at https://lccn.loc.gov/2021038242
LC ebook record available at https://lccn.loc.gov/2021038243

ISBN: 978-1-5013-6803-5

Typeset by Lachina Creative, Inc.
Printed and bound in India

To find out more about our authors and books visit www.fairchildbooks.com and sign up for our newsletter.

contents

extended contents

Part Four
VISUAL PRACTICES FOR NONTRADITIONAL VENUES **252**

10

Grocery and Food Service Stores **255**

11

Nontraditional Retailing **275**

preface

Wisdom is a blend of knowledge, experience, and good judgment. It can be expanded by knowing yourself, standing up for what you believe in and listening to other's ideas and collaborating. In this new edition of *Silent Selling*, you, as a future visual merchandiser, will be

invited to learn the basic design principles and best practices of visual design along with the latest technologies in augmented reality, artificial intelligence, and advances in customization and sustainability in mannequin design.

What is next after you have begun to practice and master these strategies in a workplace setting? Is there a way for you to reach for a taste of wisdom that will empower you to develop your own unique signature? Yes, there are many, and new ideas will be revealed to you from philosophers like Aristotle and psychologists like Eric Fromm, as well as the Creative Wizards active in the retail design industry today. By stretching your thinking through the lens of these experts and opening your eyes to new advances in neuroscience, you will begin to **build your own brand identity**. This book is not just about design techniques, it is expressly written to encourage you to think creatively about your own destiny in a vast field of opportunities.

Silent Selling: Best Practices and Effective Strategies in Visual Merchandising presents the industry at its finest and provides a practical view of the activities that go into creating store environments that sell. This book serves as an introduction for aspiring visual merchandisers and a handy reference for current practitioners. This is a complete learning resource for instructors teaching fashion design, fashion merchandising, or visual merchandising students in visual merchandising, store planning and design and window display courses that focus on how to create visual displays and present merchandise effectively.

About the Author

Retail design strategist and author Judy Bell finds the heart of her inspiration in an artful blend of music halls, museums, and theatres in Minneapolis, New York, and

Paris. Earlier in her career, Bell's love of writing and speaking landed her a job at Target for 22 years, where she traveled throughout the United States and Europe to seek out presentation trends. She offered her photographs and commentary to 3000 team members annually in colorful and often humorous presentations in venues that included the Guthrie Theatre and Target Center. At Target she served on several national boards for which she received numerous awards, including the coveted Markopoulos Award "in recognition of extraordinary achievements and outstanding contributions in the visual merchandising and store design industry." The award honors Andrew Markopoulos, the late, legendary senior VP of visual merchandising and store design at Dayton's. Other recipients include past design executives at Barney's New York, Bergdorf Goodman, Neiman Marcus, and design firms nationwide.

Today Bell is CEO, Chief Energetic Officer of Energetic Retail, where she offers half-day workshops that incorporate her life-long study of human behavior, and where retailers and design firms can envision a fresh perspective on retail environments. The process leads to novel and eloquent ways to engage and inspire shoppers. Active in the industry as a freelance writer and speaker at events like the World Retail Congress in London and Fortress REIT in Johannesburg, she stays informed about up-to-the-minute developments in retail globally. Decades of hands-on experience in innovation and continuing membership in FGI, RDI, and Shop! Association fuel her desire to engage students to strive for a career in visual merchandising and join her in the world of creative expression in the retail community. www.energetic-retail.com

Organization

Silent Selling's organization consists of six parts divided into fifteen chapters. **Part One: Preparation for Visual Creativity** introduces the field with a unique opening chapter that explores the path to wisdom in creativity, an artful blend of knowledge, experience, and good judgment. Part of that journey involves the practice of Judy Bell's model of Thinking Outside the Box, a theme that is carried throughout the book. This chapter focuses on the creative and artistic mindset of visual merchandisers and features "Creative Wizards" in the industry from past and present day. The second chapter discusses the practical application of the visual merchandiser's creative talent in the retail setting. Chapter 3 shows how design elements and principles are put to work to produce effective visual presentations.

Part Two: Practices and Strategies for the Selling Floor focuses on the presentation of fashion goods, with attention to the basics of floor layout and fixtures in Chapter 4, wall setups in Chapter 5, and apparel and accessory coordination in Chapter 6. Chapter 7 discusses the presentation of home fashions.

Part Three: Communicating Retail Atmospherics shows how signage (Chapter 8) and lighting (Chapter 9) support the presentation of fashion merchandise and communication of the retailer's message.

In **Part Four: Visual Practices for Nontraditional Venues**, the practices discussed in earlier chapters are applied to grocery and food service stores in Chapter 10 and to other retail outlets, including online retailers, in Chapter 11.

Three chapters comprise **Part Five: Tools and Techniques for Merchandise Display**. Chapter 12 features the Window Show, an on-location exhibition organized under the auspices of the Cooper-Hewitt Museum in New York, to demonstrate the magic of display windows. Basic techniques underlying the magic are fully explained. Chapter 13 provides instructions for dressing mannequins complete with step-by-step illustrations and offers advice on using mannequins together with display fixtures to present fashion merchandise to its best advantage. In Chapter 14, the threads of earlier discussions are woven together in a description of the organization and management of the visual merchandising function. **Part Six: Career Strategies** concludes the text with advice on building a career in visual merchandising. Leading practitioners share their success stories in their own words.

Parts 1 through 5 conclude with installments of the applied Capstone Creative Project.

Features to Enhance Learning

Throughout each chapter, special features reinforce the content of the text. The emphasis is always on practical advice from the real-world experience of industry professionals, advice that readers can apply in their own careers. Brief quotations from authoritative sources open each chapter and appear periodically in the text. Technical terms of the trade are highlighted in boldface in the text and defined in the margin at their first mention. Succinct tips and observations in **Retail Realities sidebars** point out practical concerns that affect visual merchandisers on a daily basis. Within the text, boxes call attention to safety concerns related to the verbal instructions and practical explanations. This edition features over 200 full-color photographs of cutting-edge displays from stores around the world to demonstrate how creative visual merchandisers use outside-the-box thinking in their interpretations of standard strategies and practices. Detailed illustrations offer a journeyman's guide of the best how-to techniques for everything from outfitting store fixtures with apparel, home, and grocery products, to building in-store and window displays, to dressing mannequins and positioning and lighting them properly.

A series of end-of-chapter features offer further opportunity to relate the text to real-world experience. First is **Shoptalk**, a statement in which a visual merchandising expert shares his or her observations about the aspect of the field discussed in the chapter. Next is the **Design Gallery**, with an analysis of why the store windows and interiors pictured were award-winning presentations. Following are **Review Questions** that will allow the reader to examine and go over what they have learned in each chapter. The three types of assignments that follow provide hands-on experience. In the **Outside-the-Box Challenge** section, the challenge is to generate ideas for creative, attention-getting presentations by following author Judy Bell's look-compare-innovate process.

This assignment is followed by **Critical Thinking** activities and a **Case Study**. Both are written to improve analytical thinking as it relates to the world of visual merchandising. Visual merchandisers must "think on their feet" and be strategic when developing their aesthetically successful, retail-business–enhancing designs. These two sections will allow the reader to understand the varieties of tasks that many visual merchandisers must do in order to incorporate the world of retail operations into visual merchandising for successful silent selling.

Throughout the book leaders in the field offer words of advice and inspiration through personal quotes and career stories. A comprehensive glossary and a list of references and resources are also provided.

New to This Edition

This sixth edition has been extensively revised with the following new features and content to enrich the readers' learning experience:

- A new opening to the book unlocks a path for students to achieve wisdom, an artful blend of knowledge, experience, and good judgment. Philosophers like Aristotle and psychologists like Eric Fromm along with four Creative Wizards, active in the retail design industry today, offer guidance and inspiration. This new opening to the book will provide a way for students to investigate the seeds of creativity, learn how to plant them, nourish them, watch them grow, and in the process define their own personal brand identity.
- Neuroscience Pop-Ups! will open students up to the world of how and why consumers think the way they do. Knowledge of these patterns will broaden the scope of creative strategies to engage and inspire shoppers.

- Designers' Pet Peeves call out unsettling visual merchandising faux pas and offer suggestions on how to turn one-star displays into five-star winning presentations.
- A system of signage hierarchy is offered in Chapter 8 Signage, to provide a framework and a sense of order in positioning signs in the retail store environment. A case study at Lowe's Home Improvement is included in a new Shoptalk feature, with a photograph illustrating the five-tier signage hierarchy system that is expertly employed.
- Augmented reality, artificial intelligence and robots are introduced in Chapter 11 Nontraditional Retailing, with photographs of examples in retail store settings.
- The latest developments in customization and sustainability are explored in Chapter 13 Mannequins and Mannequin Alternatives.
- A complete list of current retail design publications, industry organizations, markets and conferences with descriptions has been added to Chapter 14 Building a Visual Merchandising Department.
- Ten new or revised Shoptalk features and Case Studies refresh chapters through the text.
- Over thirty-five new resources in the form of books, magazines, agencies, and associations are introduced to allow students to see a broad range of inspiration as they begin to develop their own brand identity.
- Over sixty new color photographs have been introduced to the text from around the globe. Many of the images represent new and innovative concepts that won awards in the Retail Design Institute's 2019 49th International Design Competition. Others come from the vast library of WindowsWear, an international subscription service that photographs the best windows in retail. New additions include global retailers from London, Paris, Singapore, Honolulu, Minneapolis, and New York; all bring more retail design theories in the text to life. Students are asked to examine every aspect of the retail store environment in the prototypes, including fixtures, signs, and merchandise presentation. By using Judy Bell's Look, Compare, and Innovate model, they have a tool to evaluate where opportunities lie. When they take on their new roles in the workplace, they will have laid the groundwork for developing visual merchandising strategies that are effective, differentiated, and brand-right.

- Searchable resources in every chapter have been updated. In a field that demands constant change, the text offers new places to go and new things to discover beyond the covers of this book.
- The **Capstone Creative Project** inspires learners to apply their best ideas from each chapter's reading and activities to a hypothetical store design. The resulting project could become a practical portfolio piece, could take the place of a comprehensive final examination, or both. Capstone assignments follow the end of Parts 1 through 5 and task learners to synthesize the information from each multichapter part to an application in the hypothetical store they have chosen to design.

Student Resources

Silent Selling STUDiO

- Study smarter with self-quizzes featuring scored results and personalized study tips
- Review concepts with flashcards of terms and definitions

STUDiO access cards are offered free with new book purchases and are also sold separately through www.FairchildBooks.com.

Instructor Resources

- Instructor's Guide provides suggestions for planning the course and using the text in the classroom, including supplemental assignments and lecture notes
- Test Bank includes sample test questions for each chapter
- PowerPoint presentations include images from the book and provide a framework for lecture and discussion

Instructor's Resources may be accessed through www.FairchildBooks.com.

acknowledgments

I would like to express my thanks to the following individuals who made outstanding contributions to this textbook: Janet Groeber, Director, Retail Design Institute, for trophy winning photos from their 2019 49th International Design Competition; Bruce Barteldt,

chairman, for award-winning photographs from Shop! Design Awards events; Jon Harari, chief executive officer and Raul Tovar, co-founder and creative director at WindowsWear for their assistance with images; and all of the retailers, designers, manufacturers, and architects who offered their quotable insights and Shoptalk letters so willingly.

At Bloomsbury, thanks to Emily Samulski, senior acquisitions editor, for her creative insights and support of new features like Neuroscience Pop-Ups! and Designers' Pet Peeves, and Joseph Miranda, editor, for his guidance, sharp eye, and generous support as he cheered me on every time I submitted more chapters: it made a difference! Edie Weinberg, Art Development Editor, thanks for her endless enthusiasm in creating an engaging new art program.

Thanks to my agent, George Harper, for initiating my partnership with Fairchild/Bloomsbury. Thanks also to Kate Ternus, retired marketing instructor at Century College, for her robust contributions to the 2nd and 4th editions of *Silent Selling*. Her talent, enthusiasm and passion for the visual merchandising industry is evident in her work on the original instructor's guide, test bank, and references, in addition to chapter exercises including critical thinking and case studies. Kate also shared her knowledge throughout the book by contributing real-world thinking from her rich background in retail environments in New York City and Minneapolis. Bravo to Kate!

To the people I worked side by side with during my twenty-two–year career at Target: John Pellegrene, for his brilliant, from-the-heart marketing style; Bob Giampietro for his contagious enthusiasm for innovation; Greg Duppler, for his incredibly motivating and appreciative management style; Joe Perdew for his friendly, supportive partnership; Michael Whittier, for his design brilliance and high standards; and Tracy Tommerdahl and Cheryl Campbell, who share the same excitement and love for the work that we did together. I also want to thank my dear friends and colleagues in the retail design community, who have inspired me through the many board meetings, events, and conferences we've attended over the years.

I am also grateful to the memory of Andrew Markopoulos, for his advice and support during our lunches in the Oak Grill Room at Dayton's, and to the memory of Peter Glen, for his support and inspiration, a man who could present his findings and insights with theatrical delight.

From the Publisher:

Fairchild Books wishes to gratefully acknowledge and thank the reviewers who have contributed to this revision: Holly Lentz-Schiller, Stevenson University; Suzanne Scholz, Cal Poly Pomona; April Elisha Stanley, Kirkwood Community College; and Leslie Browning-Samoni, Texas Christian University.

Bloomsbury Publishing wishes to gratefully acknowledge and thank the editorial team involved in the publication of this book:
Senior Acquisitions Editor: Emily Samulski
Development Manager: Joseph Miranda
Editorial Assistant: Jenna Lefkowitz
Art Development Editor: Edie Weinberg
In-House Designer: Louise Dugdale
Production Manager: Ken Bruce
Project Manager: Courtney Coffman, Lachina Creative

This book is dedicated to Andrew Markopoulos, former senior vice president of visual merchandising and store design at Dayton Hudson, who moved visual merchandising from the display window to the boardroom, establishing it as a valued profession and an integral part of the magic and delight of the retail store environment.

Every year in his honor an individual in the store design industry is recognized for their outstanding achievements and contributions in the visual merchandising and store design industry. They join the ranks of former recipients in The Markopoulos Circle and together they continue Andy's legacy of mentoring the next generation of retail talent.

At Andy's funeral (1999) the priest told what might be a familiar story about a man passing away and when he gets to heaven, St. Peter is showing him around God's mansion. He noticed another man running around, moving art and putting everything in its place. The man on the tour asks St. Peter, "Is that God?" St. Peter replies, "No, that is Andrew Markopoulos."

The Markopoulos Circle, Jenny S. Rebholz,
design:retail, April/May 2016

Part One   PREPARATION FOR VISUAL CREATIVITY

1 Creative Thinking: Getting Outside the Box

The Wisdom in Creativity

What is wisdom? It is an artful blend of knowledge, experience and good judgment. In this book you will explore design principles and creative retailing practices. To absorb this knowledge, it must be put into action. Through time spent in trial and error, success and failure, you will gain experience and learn to use good judgment in making design decisions. This approach combined with paying attention to what is happening globally in economics, demographics, politics, and technology leads to a degree of wisdom. And then, by giving your strategies a unique twist, you can create your own "Secret Sauce." But there is even more to consider. The greatest historical authorities of philosophy like Aristotle said, "Knowing yourself is the beginning of all wisdom." And later came the psychologists like Eric Fromm who held that "Man's main task is to give birth to himself." In other words, in addition to gaining the wisdom to cultivate your own strategies, you must develop a sense of "self" and take a stand for what you believe in. But you must also learn to listen to the ideas of others and collaborate to reach an even deeper level of wisdom. Winston Churchill said, "Courage is what it takes to stand up and speak; courage is also what it takes to sit down and listen." How can you learn to do that? Who are the authorities of wisdom in Visual Merchandising and Store Design who can act as mentors to inspire and guide you?

First we'll take a look at the genius of the late Gene Moore, famous worldwide for his captivating Tiffany windows, and Tom Beebe who befriended Moore and became his protégé. Then you will be introduced to four creative wizards of today. Early in their professions these highly regarded individuals focused on absorbing the knowledge of design principles and put them into practice in a variety of retail professions. Along the

> "Creativity is seeing what others can't see, saying what others won't say. It's a juicy awareness that can be triggered by pausing and turning your attention away from the challenge you are facing—to create space for a new idea to emerge."
> *Judy Bell for* design:retail *magazine*

AFTER COMPLETING THIS CHAPTER, YOU SHOULD BE ABLE TO

- Identify characteristics inherent in wisdom
- Discuss a variety of processes for creative thinking
- Develop strategies for overcoming creative blocks
- Identify a variety of resources for idea development
- Explain the process of getting new ideas accepted

Figure 1.0 Bergdorf Goodman's captivating Gold Award–winning "Wild Card" window, Fifth Avenue, New York, December 2019.

way they identified significant mentors, and working alongside them, they were able to shape their own unique models of creativity—and that takes wizardry. As Francoise Gilot, French modernist painter and former wife of Pablo Picasso and Jonas Salk said, "You know, most teachers want to tell you that this is the way things are. There is only one correct approach, and so you must do it that way. But that's not the case at all. You can approach a subject in any conceivable way if it's the right way for you."

The Wisdom of Two Iconic Mentors

Gene Moore, vice president and artistic director at Tiffany & Co. for nearly forty years, made an art form of creative thought in his company's world-famous store. When he died in November of 1998, he left a rich legacy of window design that included wit, brilliant merchandising savvy, and notoriously unconventional methods for getting people to stop and enjoy his visual merchandising creations. He is best known for combining exquisite pieces of fine jewelry with everyday objects like eggs, keys, gumdrops, dolls, and ice cream cones. Moore's windows themselves became tourist destinations. See Figure 1.1.

"When it comes to Gene 'The Mentor,' there are many artists who can thank him for their own successful careers. He recognized the talents of artists, such as Jasper Johns, Robert Rauschenberg and Andy Warhol, to name a few. Moore's windows offered a platform to launch their artistic careers." (*design:retail*, Jenny S. Rebholz, April–May 2015, "The Lost Archives of Gene Moore")

Tom Beebe, New York–based creative consultant-stylist-window wizard, says he was fortunate to have Gene Moore as his mentor. Their decades-long friendship began while a younger Tom was doing windows at Paul Stuart. The two men didn't know one another, but were both habitual window shoppers

strolling Fifth Avenue, eyeing the displays in all the stores. Then Tom wrote Gene Moore a letter of admiration for a particular set of Tiffany windows and Moore, ever the Southern gentleman, replied. What followed was a long correspondence with many two-hour lunches in between.

Many years later, Tom still treasures the letters and his place in Moore's life. He became part of Moore's family and even worked with him at Tiffany. Tom later became the champion for preserving and sharing Moore's archival materials with visual merchandisers worldwide. When Moore retired from Tiffany & Company in 1994, after thirty-nine years and more than 4700 windows, he donated his collection of sketchbooks and photographs to the Cooper Hewitt Smithsonian Design Museum. In 2012, the collection was transferred to the Archives Center, National Museum of American History, Smithsonian Institution. Through the funding of donors William Rondina and Daniel Gelman, and the perseverance of Tom Beebe, the seventy-eight black-and-white albums have been indexed and are now available online to retailing students and graduate researchers. Tom Beebe expressed his involvement in this effort:

> "We can't lose this information. It needs to be shared with students, designers and display professionals. There isn't a thing I do that isn't affected by Gene Moore. I am passing along what I learned to students. It is a payback in your career to pass on knowledge, and it's my time to help and to pay back."

Tom Beebe, whose efforts over a 20-year period to make Moore's collection available worldwide, is himself clearly an iconic mentor of wisdom. His own genius was lauded by trade magazine *vmsd (Visual Merchandising + Store Design)*, when they dubbed him a "window

Figure 1.1a Gene Moore used everyday objects like a pitcher, glass, and a knife arranged in an "after the party" manner to showcase exquisite jewelry.
National Museum of American History/Smithsonian Institute

Figure 1.1b Gene Moore, Tiffany and Co.'s famed visual icon.
Photo by Lucy-Ann Bouvman, provided by Tom Beebe.

magician" known for his flying ties. Gene Moore once said of Beebe, "He's taken men's clothes out of being dull, dreary nothings to real excitement." See Figure 1.2 for examples of his work with W Diamond Group.

Tom Beebe is passionate about sharing his visual ideas with young people just starting their careers. Under Tom's direction, and with his eye for detail, the mannequin's gown in Figure 1.2a was crafted by FIT design students:

> I wanted it to look like the sheet music had just blown into the vignette to form that garment—and might disappear just as easily with the next breeze. I loved getting the students involved and we talked about Gene Moore and his windows the entire time we worked together.

The results? "I always track sales from the windows and we sold that white tuxedo by 10 a.m. the next day . . . and 13 others before we changed them out."

Those apple barrels you see behind Tom in Figure 1.2c contained real apples, and in keeping with his "full speed ahead" mantra, he filled the store with autumn atmospherics, right down to the aroma:

> They were real. Imagine walking into the store and smelling that aroma. By the time we changed the window over to pumpkins a few weeks later, we had refilled the barrels several times. Shoppers ate the apples, staff ate the apples, and we ended up making apple juice at the end.

Figure 1.2a Tom Beebe collaborated with the Fashion Institute of Technology in his Hickey Freeman holiday window. Students from FIT created the whimsical dress out of sheet music. This window exemplifies Tom's philosophy: "The goal of any store window is to stop people in their tracks and get them to look." Richard Cadan Photography, Brooklyn. Photo by Richard Cadan.

Figure 1.2b Tom Beebe's trademark "flying ties" in his spring season window at Hickey Freeman in Manhattan. Photo by Tom Beebe.

SPRING TIME

"If you feel safe in the area that you are working in, you're not working in the right area. Always go a little further into the water than you feel you are capable of being in. Go a little bit out of your depth. And when you don't feel that your feet are quite touching the bottom, you are just about in the right place to do something."
David Bowie

The Creative Process in Visual Merchandising

In nearly every retail store there are a few people who seem to have an unusual flair for presenting merchandise. They coordinate trend-right fashion looks effortlessly, set up attractive displays without seeming to think about what they're doing, and arrange effective department layouts with precision and speed. They are highly valued employees because of their special talents. When they "set the floor," merchandise moves and profits grow.

What do these talented retailers have that others may not? They have a solid understanding of retail design principles and of company presentation standards, and they use a creative approach to merchandise presentation. Design principles and company standards can be learned, but what about creativity—that extra twist or new approach which is, in effect, a unique signature?

Are you creative? The answer is always a resounding YES. To be human is to be creative. No matter what profession someone chooses, creativity is always at the core. Lawyers use creativity when presenting their cases to juries in the courtroom. Landscapers use creativity when selecting and arranging colorful flowers when designing garden retreats. It is true that some people are born with more creative ability than others. Elkhonon Goldberg, PhD, in his book *Creativity*, asks the question: "Is the gift of innovation and creativity inherited? Today the likely answer to this question is 'sometimes and to some degree.'" He goes on to give examples of creative clustering in

Figure 1.2c Tom Beebe, former VP Creative Services, W. Diamond Group, in his window of fragrant apples that celebrates the fall fashion season at Hickey Freeman in Manhattan. Photo owned by Tom Beebe.

families, like Marie and Pierre Curie and their daughter Irene, all three Nobel prize-winning physicists. To contrast, Goldberg writes: "most famously creative individuals were born into unremarkable, ordinary families." He goes on to explain that creativity "is a product of many moving parts: biological, cultural, and social."

Therefore, whether or not you have the genes, clearly you can further develop your creativity. What creative people do is open their minds to idea generation through various brainstorming processes. The more often these processes are used, the easier it will be to find creative solutions to problems. You can give yourself a boost of confidence by reading *The Dot*, by Peter H. Reynolds, an illustrated children's book. In the story, Vashti sits in class with a blank sheet of paper and with much frustration informs her teacher, "I just can't

draw!" Her teacher smiles and says, "Just make a mark and see where it takes you." That "mark" is the beginning of Vashti's journey to discover her creative spirit, a simple but profound path to confidence.

Most dictionaries use the word *productive* as a second meaning for the word *creative*. Being productive means getting results. If your creative work produces results that meet your merchandising objectives, you are on your way to developing your creativity at a professional level.

Outside-the-Box Thinking

The term *outside the box* has found its way into today's business language as a buzz phrase for creative thinking. Another phrase, *coloring outside the lines,* means much the same thing. "Stay inside the lines!" Remember hearing

"Working is not grinding but a wonderful thing to do; creative power is in all of you if you just give it a little time; if you believe in it a little bit and watch it come quietly into you; if you do not keep it out by always hurrying and feeling guilty in those times when you should be lazy and happy. Or if you do not keep the creative power away by telling yourself that worst of lies—that you haven't any."
Brenda Ueland, author of If You Want to Write

Four Creative Wizards' Secret Sauce

Our four Creative Wizards hail from a full scope of the visual merchandising and store design industry: retail, media, conferences, and events, marketing and visual merchandising agencies, along with sales in design and manufacturing. As part of the process in developing their own secret sauce, our four creative wizards collaborated with others in the retail design industry in ways that encourage all to grow and expand. Participating in national conferences and fund-raising galas, these warm-hearted, approachable visionaries all share in their desire to give back in appreciation of their own fulfilling careers. They all have one thing in common: they love the day-to-day interactions with their teams and colleagues throughout the design industry. Psychologist Mihály Csikszentmihályi, writing in *Creativity: Flow and the*

Creative Wizard Alison Medina, Vice President Content, RetailX, Atlanta. Retail trends expert, thought leader, content disseminator and former editor-in-chief, *design:retail* magazine.

What is your background? Eighteen years as an editor at *design:retail* magazine, where I tracked trends, aggregated ideas and covered retail design, and translated those ideas into public speaking and editorial content.

What is your creative process? In my view, creativity comes from keeping my eyes and mind open to the conversations, designs and ideas around me, and converting those swirling ideologies into a digestible form that other people can react and relate to. I have visited amazing retail the world over and use that as a basis for my perspective on current trends. I am a translator, in a sense, and view my purpose as an aggregator of content and being able to share that content in a format that retailers and designers can use now.

Who did you look to for wisdom? I find the design world is full of mentors that inspire me daily, and the content world is full of data and numbers to validate the story. Just making the design innovations and ideology marry up with the data around us is how we make sense of the present happenings, which enables us to build the future.

How have you shared your wisdom with the design community?
Each year, I develop a new trend talk that dives into the current state of the retail community, and deliver said talk in some 20 invited speaking engagements both domestically and internationally. I also participate in podcasts and interviews regularly, and am now enabling our live content—RetailX—with a 365-day-a-year virtual content strategy to get information out to the market year-round.

What is the most inspirational book you have ever read?
A Whole New Mind by Daniel H. Pink.

Creative Wizard Joe Baer, Founder and CEO of ZenGenius, Columbus. Visual merchandising, special events and creative direction, serving international clients from Fortune 500 companies to small businesses.

What is your background? Visual Merchandising at Lazarus, Macy's, Victoria's Secret, Chute Gerdeman and Adjunct Professional in Art Direction and Fashion Merchandising at Columbus College of Art & Design.

What is your creative process? At ZenGenius we use a five-phased approach:
Ideation: Identify and explore goals, objectives and options for solutions.
Mock-ups: Refine ideas and build test samples.
Sourcing: Shift from right brain to left brain to budget and coordinate logistics.
Installation: Solve challenges that require flexibility, perseverance and patience.
Edits: Observe how shoppers respond to the presentation and make adjustments.

Who did you look to for wisdom? Denny Gerdeman and Elle Chute. Observing their daily actions on how respectfully and warmly they treated their team, each other, and the retail design community has provided the most wisdom.

How have you shared your wisdom with the design community?
I developed the annual Iron Merchant Challenge for the IRDC (International Retail Design Conference) in 2006 to celebrate Visual Merchandising and to show that creativity is a magic that has no timelines or limits. Also led a Master Class for students to create centerpieces for the PAVE Gala (Planning and Visual Education Partnership) which I co-hosted in 2019.

What is the most inspirational book you have every read? *The Prophet* by Kahlil Gibran. "to love life through labor is to be intimate with life's inmost secret."

Psychology of Discovery and Invention, describes creative people this way: "Creative persons differ from one another in a variety of ways, but in one respect they are unanimous: They all love what they do. It is not the hope of achieving fame or making money that drives them; rather, it is the opportunity to do the work that they enjoy doing." Consider that well over one-third of your time during your career will be spent working in your chosen profession. If you are passionate about what you do, those around you will notice and interesting doors will open.

> *"Your work is going to fill a large part of your life, and the only way to be truly satisfied is to do what you believe is great work. And the only way to do great work is to love what you do.*
> *If you haven't found it yet, keep looking. Don't settle. As with all matters of the heart, you'll know when you find it."* Steve Jobs

Creative Wizard Reginaldo Reyes, Vice President Brand Experience and Environmental Design at KNOCK, Minneapolis, a full experience creative agency driven to cultivate love and loyalty for brands through the understanding of art and science. We serve clients from Fortune 500 to startups and nonprofits.

What is your background? Interior Architecture at Kansas State. Creative teams at Hallmark Cards and Marshall Fields. In my 15 years at Target, I broadened my experience in a wide variety of design positions that stretched my creative thinking and led to valuable business and operational knowledge. I started in Store Planning and Design, moved to Product Development and Design, and finally to In-Store Marketing. While at Target I also provided creative and design direction for a 7-year pro bono project at MIM, the Musical Instrument Museum in Phoenix, which was founded by Bob Ulrich, former CEO of Target Corporation.

What is your creative process? My creative process begins with listening and understanding the needs and expectations of the client. From there I move into researching, synthesizing, designing and prototyping ideas.

Who did you look to for wisdom? I have had many, but the most profound are the students and peers that I myself mentor. They open my eyes to see things in a new way, both professionally and personally.

How have you shared your passion and wisdom with the design community? Communicating through sketching ideas and nuggets of wisdom. Teaching and mentoring as an adjunct professor at MCAD, Minneapolis College of Art and Design, and volunteer work as a board member at both Art Buddies and Theatre Mu, the second largest Asian American theater in the U.S.

What is the most inspirational book you have ever read? *Walking in Wonder* by John O'Donohue.

Creative Wizard Lena Lim, Vice President of Business Development, B&N Industries. Serving the Retail, Hospitality + Commercial Architecture + Design Communities to realize their visions with physical products. We elevate the transformation of spaces and places.

What is your background? Propaganda, a supplier of props for retail stores, Sales Exec & Showroom Manager at Bay Area Display, Account Exec at LOOK, a retail store designer of store fixtures and graphic frames.

What is your creative process? I work with clients to actively listen and communicate between our teams to realize a 3D solution for their design and creative vision.

Who did you look to for wisdom? Brad Somberg, B&N Industries CEO, for his drive, compassion and deep thinking. Linda Lombardi, industry veteran and extraordinary leader, on how to put on a PAVE show. A former boss, Keith Walton, taught me how to have fun and be a serious businessperson at the same time.

How have you shared your passion and wisdom with the design community? I've volunteered to join committees throughout my entire career.

As NY chapter secretary for both NEWH (The Hospitality Industry Network) and RDI (Retail Design Institute), I have learned how to listen and share focused messaging.

When elected to be PAVE's (Planning and Visual Education Partnership) Event VP, I wanted to celebrate our fabulous retail community with the next generation of students, and also introduce these amazing and talented young people coming up the ranks to retail design industry executives. It has given me such fulfillment and joy in my life!

What is the most inspirational book you have ever read? *I Know Why the Caged Bird Sings* by Maya Angelou. It shares the incredible arcs of life.

BOX **1.1** ▶

judy bell's thinking outside the box

1. Look. Visit two or more stores and look at the merchandise presentations.
2. Compare. Compare the merchandise presentations.
3. Innovate. Combine the best presentation techniques from stores you visited with those in your own store and create a unique presentation that fits your store's brand image.

"The pursuit of truth and beauty, is a sphere of activity in which we are permitted to remain children all our lives."
Albert Einstein

"Part of what I am in some ways is a traffic cop, ultimately deciding what's going to get into the film. Everyone who wants to be a filmmaker will have to face, that you will have to kill, as they say in journalism, all your little darlings."
Ken Burns

those words? Your kindergarten teacher wanted your earliest artistic efforts to conform to those of your classmates. Coloring inside the lines was your behavioral task; developing eye-hand coordination and following rules were the learning objectives the teacher set for you.

Once you had those basic skills mastered, you were allowed to advance to more creative freehand artwork. However, by the time that happened, you may not have cared about being creative because the desire to do unique things had been "schooled" right out of you. As a five-year-old, your wildly creative urges— curbed for the sake of orderly learning in the classroom— may have been temporarily inhibited.

For a retailer, creativity means you must color outside the lines again in order to find new solutions for merchandising problems you encounter. Being able to move beyond your usual way of thinking about things is essential in today's competitive retail environment.

According to Kurt Hanks and Jay Parry (*Wake Up Your Creative Genius*), "Creation isn't making something out of nothing. Instead it's organizing existing elements into new and different wholes." That is good news; it implies that you don't have to come up with totally new ideas, provided that you do some "editing" along the way.

What is editing? It's a term borrowed from journalism, the news industry. News editors don't normally write the stories you see in print or online. Instead, they assign and oversee the

work of staff reporters who actually gather information, interview people, and write the news articles you read. Just before the newspaper is printed or the story is uploaded, editors inspect and edit, or fine-tune, them for content, accuracy, grammar, spelling, and length.

Sometimes reporters think their original story is compromised by editing, but most will admit that editorial changes—shortening a sentence here, changing a word there—make the resulting story or article clearer, tighter, and better overall. This is similar to the process that takes place when visual merchandisers modify ideas they've gotten from other retail sources. Presentations become more focused, more dynamic, and more effective. New (and better) ideas can come from the ideas of others.

▌JUDY BELL'S CREATIVE PROBLEM-SOLVING PROCESS: LOOK, COMPARE, INNOVATE

To author Judy Bell, thinking outside the box consists of three simple action steps that can jump-start creativity and enable you to explore, edit, and expand on current ideas and practices.

Look

The first step is to look at what your retail competition is doing. Visit both direct competitors and other categories of retailers. A home fashion retailer may find inspiration in the way colors are coordinated in the window of a fashion apparel retailer. A toy retailer may find inspiration in a bookstore that carries puzzles and games. If you see that your retail competitors are doing something right with their store's merchandise presentation strategies and techniques, you will have a head start on doing something even better with your own.
How will you know what works for other retailers? You might watch their customers

and note how they react to displays in those stores. You can observe which displays appear to be ignored and which seem to have "traffic-stopping power."

Compare

The second step to thinking outside the box is to compare. Once you gather ideas from other retailers, you're ready to compare them with your own company's presentations. For example, you might compare a presentation at a competitor's store entrance with the presentation at your own store entrance. You might observe whether the competitor used any mannequins or props to draw customers into and through the store. You'd read the directional signage and determine whether it assisted customers to locate departments. You'd read signage on merchandise fixtures and ask yourself whether it seemed to encourage customers to make buying decisions. You'd ask yourself about the effectiveness of the merchandise displays. You'd decide whether merchandise presentation overall seemed to give customers fresh ideas about how fashion or home apparel products could be combined or coordinated. You'd make note of what types of lighting were used to spotlight items or add to the overall atmosphere of the store. You'd wonder about the general feeling of the store—whether it felt good to be in the store or which specific merchandise areas invited you to stay and browse.

Innovate

The third step, innovate, will be much easier as a result of your observations and comparisons. In this phase of the outside-the-box process, you become an editor. You start planning your store's next merchandise presentations based on effective things you've seen elsewhere. However, instead of just copying what you've seen, you'll put your own spin, or interpretation, on the strategy or technique. You'll be able to look at the original competitive presentation and analyze it—compare it to an ideal display (evaluate its strengths and weaknesses)—and, finally, innovate by creating some new alternatives to the original.

■ THE SCAMPER MODEL

You often see visual merchandisers carrying toolboxes as they go about their duties. They may need rubber mallets, screwdrivers, pins, and wrenches—the mechanical tools of their trade—as they set up shelving and fixtures, hang signs, and dress mannequins. What you won't see is the "mental toolbox" that visual merchandisers reach into for inspiration every day—the creative tools that they've acquired as they've developed professionally.

In retailing, the creative thinking process can follow several useful problem-solving models. You've already learned about five in this chapter. The important thing is finding the outside-the-box method that works for you.

Some visual merchandisers use Robert Eberle's creative thinking model SCAMPER (a mnemonic for ways to brainstorm for an unusual solution) to solve the merchandising problem at hand. This classic model for creative thinking offers seven options to give your thinking a creative boost. These SCAMPER options are as follows:

SUBSTITUTE
COMBINE
ADAPT
MODIFY, MINIFY, MAGNIFY
PUT TO OTHER USES
ELIMINATE
REVERSE OR REARRANGE

SCAMPER MODEL CREDIT: *Eberle, Robert. SCAMPER: Games for Imagination Development. 1977. DOK Publishers, Buffalo, NY.*

Substituting strategies involve exchanging one expected element of a visual idea for another. It might mean borrowing an accessorizing strategy from the fashion department for use in the home furnishings area. A fully accessorized fashion mannequin might wear several layers of fashionable clothing, plus jewelry, hosiery, shoes, hat, and handbag. To use a substituting strategy in the home furnishings area, you might apply the fashion accessory strategy to create a formal-occasion table top in the housewares department. Showing fine linens (tablecloth, placemats, and napkins), place settings of fine china, crystal stemware, silver service, candles, candleholders, a centerpiece, and handwritten place cards in sterling holders for each guest at the table creates a strong—and fully accessorized—home fashion statement.

Combining strategies may mean seating a pair of elegantly dressed and fully accessorized mannequins at the table you have just set. Substitute Valentine cards for the place cards and the scene is set for a romantic Valentine's Day dinner party for two. The fashion and home furnishings tie-in also gives you a presentation with **cross-merchandising** impact.

Adapting strategies will find the visual merchandiser taking the rainbow-hued progression of colored merchandise used often on women's fashion department walls and applying it to a wall of bedding or bath linens, a display of shower curtains, or an assortment of children's toys. Or, adapting might involve using a stepladder, paint buckets, and brushes as props to display half a dozen pairs of brightly tinted tennis shoes. You simply take an item intended for one use and adapt its purpose to suit your sales presentation.

Modifying strategies—magnifying (making something larger) or minifying

(making something smaller)—provide an imaginative counterpoint to otherwise routine presentations of any merchandise. One effective display employed a toy action figure to prop a jewelry display window featuring cultured pearl necklaces. Dressed in full scuba diving gear, he appeared to be swimming underwater (the backdrop and sides of the window were covered in sea-blue fabric). The pearl necklaces became a trail of bubbles streaming toward the surface of the water in which the figure swam. Using the toy miniature made the small pearls seem much larger and more important in scale than they would have been in a conventional display window. That's an example of minifying. Using a gigantic golf ball and wooden tee in a men's sportswear display surely attracts attention—if for no other reason than making shoppers take a second look at what magnifying a prop fifty times does to perspective and scale. That second look is the visual merchandiser's opportunity to focus customer attention on the merchandise.

Putting to other uses is a strategy that finds the visual merchandiser dressing a mannequin in a crisp white apron but inverting a stock pot on its head in place of the chef's traditional white toque. This is a fun, eye-catching way to focus shopper attention on a cooking vessel. The pot's general shape and undeniable link to the professional cook could make shoppers stop and rethink their cookware choices! The unexpected other use can be entertaining, thought provoking, and attention getting— three good elements to employ in any display.

The **eliminating** strategy is an amazingly useful tool to prevent a creative visual merchandiser from becoming too clever. It is always a good idea to "quit while you're ahead" in a presentation. In the stockpot example, you could easily get carried away with the fun of it all and keep on reaching for even more obvious tie-ins to the chef concept. It might be tempting to dangle cookie cutters

cross-merchandising refers to moving merchandise across traditional department or classification lines to combine elements in a single department or display. For example, books of poetry, romantic novels, candles, bath salts, terry cloth robes, and oversized bath towels could be brought together in a single display.

A **prototype** is the original model on which later types are based. For example, before rolling out a dozen retail stores, a prototype is built so that design features may be tested and refined if necessary. The same process is used in the development of custom merchandise fixtures and visual fixtures.

retail realities

Retail stopping power makes casual passersby focus attention on the visual presentation and really consider the merchandise. Once focused, they become potential customers and the presentation becomes a "silent seller."

from the mannequin's ears as another kitchen-related accessory, but it would be far better to use restraint and retain the impact of the inverted cooking pot. A useful adage: When in doubt, leave it out.

The **reversing** or **rearranging** strategy is another method of presenting merchandise in an unexpected way. Mannequins that normally stand on their feet can stand on their heads (if you have a sturdy and reliable way to suspend them from the ceiling grid in a display window). Things normally arranged from smallest to largest can be reversed in order. Mannequins dressed back-to-front can stop traffic. You can have a great time devising new ways to do the opposite of what's expected.

BOX **1.2**

🪢 Neuroscience Pop-Up!

Why does the scent of warm-baked bread appeal to so many? How can that familiar aroma in a grocery store actually change shoppers' intended traffic patterns and draw them over to the bakery? Because the sense of olfaction may be one of the earliest senses developed in human beings. That leads us to the study of neuroscience, the knowledge of which clearly offers a competitive advantage to retailers. As you begin to develop your own creative process, you will find it valuable to consider how and why consumers think the way they do. Neuroscience Pop-Ups will appear throughout this textbook to inspire you and encourage you to consider how brain function links with consumer behavior.

You will need to keep a watchful eye out for new technology as it emerges in this field of many moving parts. Matthew Cobb's book, *The Idea of the Brain: The Past and Future of Neuroscience*, offers this description, "The brain is the most complicated object in the universe. The attempt to understand it has been one of science's greatest challenges." Long-held theories are sometimes washed away and replaced with new thinking, so it is important to keep up to date with the latest developments. In our Neuroscience Pop-Ups, we will look at how today's findings are used to create presentations that stimulate the senses of shoppers in a variety of ways and invite them to try and buy new products.

Fresh baked!
Alexander Spatari/Moment via Getty Images

Best Practices and Practical Applications

Retailers worldwide use creative thinking strategies. Some very competitive (and successful) retailers actually hire individuals whose principal assignment is to look at what other retailers are doing and develop new presentation concepts based on industry trends and the best current practices.

Highly professional visual merchandising managers make local comparison shopping a regular part of their working week, with occasional trips to different locations in the country to look at the latest store **prototypes**. Visual merchandisers at any point in their careers (from window design specialist to vice president) must use their powers of observation to build professional skills and creative muscle. In all cases, the ability to look, compare, and innovate should really be part of any visual merchandiser's formal job description.

◼ VISITING COMPETING STORES

As you begin this course, visit your favorite store's direct and indirect competitors. If you currently work for an independent junior fashion store in a local mall, you'll want to keep an eye on other junior shops in the mall. In today's fast-paced junior fashion market, you'll also want to shop for presentation ideas in international chains like Free People, H&M, Madewell, Uniqlo, and Zara, if they are located in your community. You always want to know what the leading specialty and department stores in the retail industry are doing, whether they are your direct competitors or not. Recognized leaders are usually the trendsetters for product presentation.

It is also a good strategy to keep in touch with noncompeting stores that have interesting themes, décor, or merchandise. If your store carries only junior footwear, for example, you may find ideas at stores such as Anthropologie, Bath & Body Works, and Urban Outfitters, which feature other products targeted to the junior customer.

One-of-a-kind stores often provide a wealth of creative ideas. They can quickly develop and implement new ideas without dealing with the top-down bureaucracy that sometimes slows change in a larger operation. The one-of-a-kind store can often change direction and react immediately to a developing retail merchandise trend. You may find more highly innovative ideas for merchandise presentation there than anywhere else. Once you make store observations part of your retail routine, you can begin to compare and improve upon the techniques you see to create new and more effective methods of presentation for yourself and your employer.

◼ TRENDSPOTTING

As you explore applied creativity and other topics in this text, you will notice that there is a recurring theme throughout. It refers to **trends**, the direction in which things like demographics, economics, politics, and technology are moving. Fashion trends are greatly influenced by these categories that drive nearly everything we see, do, and think as we go about the business of being human.

The term *trend* is going to appear again and again in this text and in your life. Retail language uses the word as a noun, as a verb, and sometimes as an adverb or adjective. You'll want to add it to your professional vocabulary right away.

To be successful in recognizing and analyzing trends as a retailer, you must understand something about people—who they are, how they live, what they value or believe in, and what they want versus what they need. To a retailer, every trend relates in some way to people and the things they buy. Consequently, you must become aware of trends in:

- **Demographics**—age, sex, income, geographic location

---

trends are the direction in which things like demographics, economics, politics, and technology are moving. These influencers drive fashion trends in all categories of retail.

- **Economics**—the financial state of the country influences what we purchase for everyday basics, leisure, entertainment, travel, etc.
- **Politics**—the role government plays globally affects our feelings of security and safety
- **Technology**—the effect of the Internet and social media on communication patterns, attitudes toward information, and entertainment

Professional retail trend analysts make brave predictions that translate those factors into behaviors that you see at work in your world today . . . and tomorrow, if they're correct. Robyn Waters, former vice-president of trend, design and product development for Target, is a trend expert well worth reading. Her first book, *The Trendmaster's Guide: Get a Jump on What Your Customer Wants Next,* outlines an A–Z range of insights for understanding and anticipating trends. As the title implies, it's a practical book written with the retail marketplace in mind. She identifies skills for all readers:

> *Anyone can use the tools in* The Trendmaster's Guide *to become more aware of the world around them. Even if you weren't born with a trendspotting bone in your body, you don't have to be a follower forever. Recognizing and reacting to trends is a learned skill as much as it is an art. If you've ever witnessed a trend unfolding and said to yourself, "I should have seen this coming," there's hope. You too can become a Trendmaster and get a jump on your competition.*

Her second book, *The Hummer and the Mini: Navigating the Contradictions of the New Trend Landscape,* goes several steps further and recognizes the contradictory nature of today's

consumer, saying that there is more than one right answer. A dictionary definition of the term *paradox* might say that two things may be totally opposite, yet both could be true.

An example? Waters writes about the fashion mavens who wear Chanel jackets (ultra-chic and expensive) over worn denim jeans, gold chains of Chanel bling, and high-heeled shoes. Trend and counter trend, that's what Robyn Waters believes is happening in the retail world today. And that's what well-prepared visual merchandisers must be ready to implement in their workplaces.

Another top-notch resource, Sphere Trending, is a Detroit-based group of futurists, technologists, and strategists who gather design intelligence. "We study the present, learn from the past and apply our unique expertise to connect the dots for limitless future opportunities." They gather over 75,000 images every year and research over 450 monthly resources to track, analyze, and deliver trend insight. Visit their website www.spheretrending.com to learn more about their offerings and sign-up for their free Innovation Trends Newsletter.

Reading Trade Websites and Periodicals

Don't limit yourself to visiting retailers to find ideas for what's new and exciting in current practice. You have many additional sources of information available—as close as your computer, mailbox, bookstore, or public library. For example, some retailers offer tours on the Internet, virtually walking you through their stores. Subscribing to monthly trade magazines is an excellent way to visit other retailers and compare. The magazines *design:retail, vmsd* (*Visual Merchandising + Store Design*), and *shop! retail environments* can all keep you updated on the latest visual techniques and fixturing trends because they target retail design and presentation professionals. All magazines are available online, and both vmsd.com and shopassociation.org offer a career tab with job postings. In addition to showcasing current window displays in brilliant color and articles detailing current trends and strategies, these publications offer the addresses of hundreds of fixturing and display manufacturers nationwide. They also offer information on seasonal market weeks in Chicago, New York, and Las Vegas, where manufacturers and representatives gather to display their products at annual conferences.

To see international stores you can find the world's largest database of windows and displays at WindowsWear.com, a subscription-based online service. Their worldwide coverage includes cities from their home base in New York to Paris, Tokyo, and beyond. They also feature an exclusive archives collection dating back to 1931, which is certain to delight and inspire. There are four levels of memberships; learn more at www.windowswear.com.

Based in London, GDR Creative Intelligence (gdruk.com), "combines investigative journalism with connections to more than 2000 global agencies." Their focus is empowering their clients to pinpoint where, why, and how they can achieve innovation. Click on BLOG and sign up to get news and insights delivered straight to your inbox.

Another excellent international resource is Echochamber (www.echochamber.com). Click on "Our Story" to learn more about their mission:

> Retailers need to keep on top of what's happening around the world. Our clients are hungry for knowledge but are often too busy running their businesses to look at the big picture. We created Echochamber back in 1998 to do just that: to feed our clients with information and inspiration, so that they can understand the fast changing evolution of retail and plan for the future.

To subscribe to their mailing list and receive free monthly updates, click on "Say Hello" and register your email address.

▍EXPLORING LOCAL ▍COMMUNITY RESOURCES

Closer to home, other resources for visual merchandising ideas are community events and local traditions. You can get ideas for retail signs from parade banners, ideas for lighting from theater productions, and inspiration for retail themes from seasonal events. Tapping into local celebrations, ethnic and cultural events, plus local lore or historical information can also trigger ideas for creative retail visual tie-ins. You can find visual ideas everywhere and anywhere, so it is important to be open and receptive to inspiration in any form.

▍FOLLOWING SOURCES ▍ABOUT CURRENT EVENTS

Knowledge of current events and cultural trends can also trigger your creative merchandising solutions. The *New York Times* Styles section, published on Sundays, features articles on consumer trends, fashion news, and the hottest new products from New York City shops. The *Wall Street Journal* offers the latest buzz in business and economics, plus articles on new gadgets and technologies. The Personal Journal section on weekdays and Off Duty on weekends are treasure troves of fashions straight from the runways. *USA Today* runs surveys called "*USA Today* Snapshots" on the cover page of each section that can be helpful in determining consumer insight. *The Week* magazine offers a digest of the best news columns of the prior week; worldwide events by country; plus recommendations for dining, television, theater, and music. Check it out at www.theweek.com. Television news programs like CNN and Fox News are well worth tuning into every day to get a perspective from different point of view. On Sunday mornings, Fareed Zakaria GPS,

Face the Nation, *Meet the Press*, *State of the Union*, and *This Week* all provide an excellent overview of the week's events, along with the opportunity to see and hear the people in the news. A free online subscription to the Daily Skimm will start your day with highlights of the top news stories, all thoroughly explained in simple terms. (theskimm.com) Another newer resource, Axios, also provides free newsletters, complete with "read-time" for each story, and promises "Axios gets you smarter, faster on what matters" (axios.com). Review these resources and others, choose your favorites, and build them into your routine. The more you see, hear, and read, the more ideas you will generate.

▌ RESEARCHING RESOURCES ▌ ABOUT HISTORY

Books and movies (new and old) will show you what the world looks like today and what it looked like in the past. They can tell you what people wore, what they looked like, and how they lived. Because fashion is cyclical in nature—and what goes around *does* come around—a working knowledge of fashion history and lifestyles from other eras can be a treasury of adaptable ideas. Don't overlook college-level electives; history courses, art history courses, and fashion history courses offer valuable insights into the past from which you can develop a view of the future by looking, comparing, and innovating! The book *How to Skimm Your Life* is a valuable read in that it covers past and current global politics and civic engagement, along with personal finance, career, and stress management. It is written in an easy-to-access format, similar to the Daily Skimm online newsletter by the same organization.

Top Innovative Thinkers

"Exploration is the engine that drives economic growth," says Edith Widder, an American oceanographer and marine biologist.

"Innovation drives economic growth. So let's all go exploring."

As a visual merchandiser, it is critical to have a vision that includes not only what you will create, but also what it will mean to your company's bottom line. Your goal in any presentation of merchandise is ultimately to sell products, and that goal should always be foremost in your mind. An artistic approach to visual merchandising will be much more effective when balanced with a business approach. Learning new creative-thinking techniques and business strategies will not only help you to innovate, but it will prepare you for management positions. Whether working for a small specialty store or for a major corporate retailer, you will advance more rapidly if you have a point of view that focuses your creative activities on a productive end result.

To help you develop a well-rounded style, you can find a list of Business Best Sellers in the *New York Times* Sunday business section. You can also search "best business books" at www.forbes.com for articles with lists of books that inspire motivation and leadership for graduates, entrepreneurs, and corporate teams. When you look over these lists and have a basic knowledge of the titles that are most current, it is also interesting to spend time browsing through the business section shelves in a bookstore. This is a practice that is wise to continue throughout your career. The insights you will gain and the techniques you will learn will help you to think outside the box and become a true innovator.

A summary of work from some of today's top innovative thinkers follows. Included are two books on creativity, a wildly popular young adult book series, a children's book, and a unique treasure of a film by a master filmmaker. While seeking innovative ideas, it is best to look at a wide variety of books, whether they cater to adults or children.

"Develop interest in life as you see it; in people, things, literature, music—the world is so rich, simply throbbing with rich treasures, beautiful souls and interesting people."
Henry Miller

"Being clever is the key, but it's much more than just putting merchandise in the window. Display needs to reflect the company's philosophy to make a true brand statement, yet do it in a way that makes the CEO smile. Even more than that, it has to be compelling, so that shoppers simply have to have the product."
Christine Belich Design, and former executive creative director, Sony

anyone can think creatively "once you know how to go about it and once you decide you want to." He cites five characteristics that make the difference for innovative and creative thinking:

- **Mental flexibility**—being free of preconceived interpretations and fixed opinions
- **Option thinking**—willingness to give problems further thought and reluctance to jump on the first idea that seems to be a solution
- **Big-picture thinking**—taking the "helicopter view" and rising above the landscape of everyday ideas to see all the factors involved at once
- **Skill in explaining and selling ideas**—being able to develop a concept and connect the facts and ideas involved so that others can understand and accept them
- **Intellectual courage**—willingness to advocate an idea or a course of action that you believe in that is unpopular with your peers

Shoptalk "Thinking Outside the Box" by Judy Bell

Early in my career as a visual merchandising director for a chain of women's apparel specialty stores, a vice president of the company made an unusual request. He asked me to look at our competitors, decide which had the most inviting presentation at their store entrance, and then copy it in our stores. I had a difficult time with the idea of copying someone else's ideas; not only did I want our stores to be fashion leaders, I knew that the presentation must fit our own brand image. But I made a trip to Southdale Shopping Center in Minneapolis to see what I could learn. Many of the women's specialty stores had positioned a table with value-priced sweaters in their entrance. I watched as nearly every female customer who passed by the store stopped at the table to look at the sweaters. Many also entered the store.

I compared those presentations to what we were featuring in our store entrances: two-way and four-way basic chrome fixtures with full-price fashions. These same types of fixtures filled the store, in addition to many simple round racks. I thought about how eye-catching the tables in front of our competitors' stores were because they were different from the basic fixtures in the store. I also thought about the appeal of showing a value item at the entrance to the store to engage the customers' interest as they passed by.

With those two ideas in mind, I met with a fixture manufacturer, and together, we designed a unique fixture for the store entrance. It fit the stores' brand image, was flexible and could handle both folded and hanging products, and it fit into my budget. Next, I met with a few of our company's merchants to discuss moving value product to this new fixture and then worked with them to write signage copy. I presented the concept to the VP who had requested the action, and he approved a two-month test in a few stores. I was pleased that I had decided not to interpret his request to copy our competitors' presentations too literally and, instead, took the opportunity to innovate. What was the end of the story? Sales went off the charts, and we ordered the new fixtures for every store in the company!

After this experience, I was sold on the idea of looking at the competition before developing new presentation strategies. The inspiration was invaluable. I still use the process of looking, comparing, and innovating every day of my career. I have broadened my base of research to include the Internet, the media, restaurants, and a wide variety of resources. I always begin with a direct look at my competition. I believe that in order to lead, you must be aware of what everyone else is doing. And I never, ever copy!

BOX 1.3

DESIGN GALLERY: "BERGDORF GOODTIMES"

Bergdorf Goodman was founded in 1899 as a purveyor of luxury goods and still proudly sits on Manhattan's Fifth Avenue in New York City. Known for its outstanding and award-winning window displays, a walk around Bergdorf is a must on any visit to Midtown. Their festive "Wild Card" window pictured here was crowned with a Gold Award in the 2019 Winning Windows competition in New York City, sponsored by *design:retail* magazine. One in a series of windows all befitting the theme of "Bergdorf GoodTimes," shoppers were offered a birds-eye view, as if they were looking down from above on colorful and curious scenes of party games. In the Wild Card window, notice the menagerie of animals in the bright green sculpture garden intermixed with oversized playing cards. A frog dives into the pool under the watchful eyes of a crocodile and a mannequin sits in the center of it all.

In *design:retail*'s long-running, twenty-one year competition, two editors, one associate professor from FIT, and Judy Bell, the author of this textbook, walked the streets of Manhattan touring storefronts that competed for three awards: Platinum, Gold, and Silver. The official judging criteria involved three categories, in which several desirable elements were called out. Look at how well this Bergdorf Goodman Gold Award–winner went above and beyond what the judges were earnestly seeking. In the first category, *Originality and Creativity,* the judges looked for "fresh ideas not seen before, an innovative and unique theme, an artistically executed idea or concept and attention to detail with well-selected props." In category two, *Captures the Spirit of the Season,* they evaluated whether or not the window "engaged emotions, was a show-stopper, appeals to all ages and captures a celebratory, holiday mood." Category three, *Professionalism: Execution and Technical Aspects,* considered such factors as "lighting,

Bergdorf Goodman's captivating Gold Award–winning "Wild Card" window, Fifth Avenue, New York, December 2019. Copyright WindowsWear Inc., http://www.windowswear.com, contact@windowswear.com

mechanics, signing and mannequin and/or merchandise presentation."

The Winning Windows Official Judging Criteria of *design:retail* is a valuable framework to keep in mind as we review other windows in the Design Gallery feature in each chapter. Use it on your own personal tour of storefront windows in your city or local shopping mall. Do you find any windows that would qualify for a Platinum, Gold, or Silver Award? Why or why not?

2 What Is Visual Merchandising?

Visual Merchandising Supports Sales

Visual merchandising, once called display, has evolved from its origins as a store's decorative arts department to its current status as a sales-supportive entity that impacts store design, store signage, departmental merchandise placement and display, store atmospherics, and store brand image. Where once the display department was charged with "making pretty," the visual merchandising department is now challenged with "making sales." In a large corporate retail operation, it is generally part of the retail advertising and in-store marketing department. In **mom-and-pop stores**, sales staff or freelance visual merchandisers may perform the visual merchandising tasks.

To begin our working definition of visual merchandising, we could refer to a dictionary and find that the adjective *visual* relates to images that are taken into the brain by way of the eye. One meaning for the verb form *merchandising* is "promoting the sale of certain commodities." Thus, *visual merchandising* could be defined as the process of promoting the sale of products by producing mental images that urge potential customers to make purchases.

The title of this text, *Silent Selling*, gives you a succinct sound bite to define for visual merchandising. Effective visual merchandising techniques establish and maintain the store's physical (and mental) image in the customer's mind, providing support for the rest of the store's selling effort. In other words, merchandise should be displayed and signed so effectively that it can sell itself, without the assistance of a sales associate.

The phrase **mom-and-pop stores** *comes from early retailing when many retailers were in family businesses and often lived in apartments above their stores. Today, it refers to small independent retailers.*

AFTER COMPLETING THIS CHAPTER, YOU SHOULD BE ABLE TO

- Define visual merchandising
- Explain how customers process visual merchandising messages
- Describe how retailers communicate through visual images
- Explain how visual merchandising efforts educate customers
- Identify why visual merchandising efforts increase sales
- Explain how visual merchandising efforts support retailing trends

"Visual merchandisers create the in-store environment that supports the retailer's marketing and merchandising strategies. They set the mood; highlight the merchandise; and invite, attract, welcome, and inform shoppers. They also, somewhat more subtly, make the store a wonderful, joyous place to be."
Steve Kaufman, Former Editor in Chief, vmsd magazine

Figure 2.0 Ralph Lauren on St. Germain in Paris focuses on its iconic polo shirt in this vividly colorful window which demonstrates outstanding visual merchandising precision. Photo by WindowsWear Inc., http://windowswear.com, contact@windowswear.com

Visual Merchandising Supports Retail Strategies

Successful stores have mission statements that describe how they will serve their **target markets**. They also have vision and goal statements that describe their ambitions— how they see their stores moving forward. In addition, they have strategies for reaching the goals and realizing their vision by utilizing a mixture of promotional methods. Their challenge is letting their target customer know who they are, what they stand for, and what they plan to do. Clear communication is the key to success.

A store's total **promotional mix** is a combination of marketing communication tools—online, print, broadcast, special events, and in-store visual merchandising, as well as personal selling—that tells targeted customers about merchandise. If each part of the mix accomplishes its goal, potential customers will be drawn to the store for a closer look.

Marketing tells customers that a store's merchandise is different, better, less expensive, or more fashionable than products offered by other retailers. When those ad-reading, viewing customers arrive at a store, they expect to see whatever it is that the marketing has communicated to them—in a setting that matches the promise of the marketing. The visual merchandiser's job is to make the advertised promise of a pleasant and productive shopping experience come true.

Visual merchandisers physically carry out a store's promotional selling strategies by:

- Designing and executing window and interior displays that support marketing goals
- Installing promotional signage for in-store selling
- Producing workable departmental layouts and interior décor
- Devising merchandise fixture layouts for day-to-day operations

- Placing and presenting merchandise on walls and fixtures
- Working as team members with the retailer's promotional staff

Visual Merchandising Communicates with Customers

Communication has three basic elements: the sender, the message, and the receiver (Figure 2.1). Unless all three elements are present, communication does not occur. If you call 911 and no one answers your call, for example, communication has not taken place.

If a retailer buys advertising space in a newspaper that is never delivered to the customer's doorstep, how productive do you think the ad will be? If a discount retailer designs an elegant storefront that discourages bargain hunters and annoys upscale customers once they have entered, has the design message reached the right customer?

The retailer is the message sender. The retailer's store, its interior design and selling floor layout, **atmospherics**, and merchandise presentation, plus the store's selling services, are the unique merchandising message. The retailer has chosen a specific person to send this message to in hopes of attracting that targeted individual to shop in the store. If that person is open to receiving the message and responds by coming to the store and making purchases, then communication is complete and can be judged successful. That's the retailer's communication goal—attracting customers and making sales.

Every tangible (seeable, hear-able, smellable, touchable) aspect of a store sends a message to shoppers. Whether a store is a stand-alone structure, next to other stores in a **strip mall**, or side by side with other stores in an indoor mall, the store's exterior must have a physical appearance that will identify it to its intended market segment and differentiate it

from its neighbors. The store's exterior must effectively communicate its message to the customer.

COMMUNICATING RETAIL BRAND IMAGE

Retail **brand image** is a combination of tangible and intangible factors that describe what a shopper thinks about his or her relationship with a store. Brand image describes not only how the store looks but also how it acts toward its customers. Target, for example, has guests rather than customers; Walmart stations "customer hosts" inside its doors to assist shoppers and deliver pleasant, personal, welcoming messages. What type of brand image do you think those retailers are trying to establish in their customers' minds?

THE MISSION STATEMENT COMMUNICATES BRAND IMAGE

A store's brand image is generally driven by the retailer's mission statement—a formal expression of the retailer's purpose for operating the business. Sometimes the mission statement is posted prominently in the store and incorporated into its print advertising as a slogan or identifying phrase. The mission statement summarizes what the company and its products or services are all about, whom it hopes to serve, and how it hopes to do it.

For example, Aveda's body product stores carry this message:

> Our mission at Aveda is to care for the world we live in, from the products we make, to the ways in which we give back to society. At Aveda, we strive to set an example for environmental leadership and responsibility, not just in the world of beauty, but around the world.

From this statement, you might guess that the company's management wants to build customer trust in the way that its products are

A store's **brand image** is the shoppers' perception of a retailer's identity. It encompasses not only merchandise but also store environment, reputation, and service.

developed and manufactured. You could also infer that the company wants the customers to know that by purchasing Aveda products, they are helping the environment.

In some cases, the retailer employs the store's name or another branded element on its private-label products, like Hermes signature "H" pattern on handbags, rings, belts, pocket squares, and dog collars.

A simple mission statement that clarifies the core customer and highlights an aspirational goal comes from Target:

Our Mission: "To help all families discover the joy of everyday life."

As you can see, retail companies develop mission statements that vary in length. Some have philosophies of doing business stated in three or four words. However, the number of words in the statement is not as important as how effectively the retailer is able to get that message across to the customer.

SALES ASSOCIATES' RELATIONSHIPS WITH CUSTOMERS COMMUNICATE BRAND IMAGE

Brand image is also portrayed by a retailer's interest in developing ongoing relationships between its sales associates and its shoppers. Members of the selling team in small stores may keep track of special clients' names, sizes, brand preferences, birthdays, etc. In large stores, this information may be accessed through a database. The idea that retail operations are interested in creating relationships with their customers says much about the value of brand image. Concern for reputation, responsiveness to customer needs and wants, easy-to-manage credit arrangements, convenient hours and locations, brand and service reliability, fashion leadership, and technological leadership are all intangible factors by which customers measure retail brand image.

STORE INTERIORS COMMUNICATE BRAND IMAGE

Smart retailers choose their target customers and build stores and advertising strategies that match their customers' values and self-images. Throughout the entire store—from the **lease line** to the back wall and everything in between—the environment should communicate the brand image. Every fixture, sign, and display in the store must fit the brand. The cashwrap (where customers go to check out), lighting fixtures, wall coverings, floor coverings, and even the restrooms should tell shoppers where they are. An exceptional example of a store with a well-defined brand image is Timberland, a retailer that clearly communicates its outdoor theme and in doing that calls out its corporate responsibility. "At Timberland, we strive to make the world around us better through our dedication to sustainable products and innovations, greening initiatives, and service to our communities" (Figure 2.2).

Fitting rooms are frequently overlooked when it comes to brand image. Often tucked away into a tiny space, they are difficult for shoppers to locate. Shoppers should never have to ask where the fitting rooms are. If they can easily see them, they may be more likely to try on an item. One successful retailer's mantra is: "The sale is one-half made when the customer is in the fitting room." Some retailers understand the importance of carrying their store brand image into the fitting rooms; they even call them "selling rooms." They are spacious, comfortable, and well lit. There is no gap in décor style or quality between the sales floor and the fitting rooms. Others, like Evereve, have cleverly created "Dressing Room to Go" where shoppers begin their journey online. They select a pickup store and date, and then answer questions about items they are looking for. A stylist pulls 12–15 pieces that fit these preferences and shoppers can pick the bundle up at the store. They have two full days

A **lease line** marks the boundary where store space begins and a mall's common area ends.

"Visual merchandisers are the creative conscience in communicating the product and brand with detail and flair that excites consumers and differentiates your company from others. They must understand the business objectives and go to places others have never been, as visual merchandisers live in and create the environment every day."
Tony Mancini, Chief Executive Officer at ThinkTank Retail Hospitality Group

NATURE NEEDS HEROES

PLANT THE CHANGE
WE'RE PLANTING 50 MILLION TREES IN FIVE YEARS

Figure 2.2 Clearly defined brand image in Timberland's Carnaby Street store in London, highlighting their "Plant The Change" goal to plant 50 million trees in five years." Photography: Giuliano Berarducci, London. Design: Dalziel & Pow, London. This Timberland store was recognized by the Retail Design Institute as a winning entry in its annual design competition.

to try on the fashions, check out online and return anything that they don't wish to keep directly to the store. That is thinking outside the box at its best!

STORE LOCATION COMMUNICATES BRAND IMAGE

Location of stores is also important when considering a store's brand. Have you ever seen a Victoria's Secret store adjacent to an Italian carryout restaurant in a shopping mall? Probably not. Why? Because the two entities have conflicting brand images and different atmospheric goals. It's hard to imagine shopping for luxurious lingerie in a shop filled with the aroma of a neighbor's garlic and tomato sauce. That's why Victoria's Secret is careful about selecting its locations. It wants to sell perfumes and bath products with its fine lingerie, not pizza. Retail communication is most effective when the message sent is clear and consistent with the image.

Shopping centers must also pay attention to their brand image. The Sevens shopping mall in Düsseldorf, Germany, is one of the best branded malls in the world (Figure 2.3). Seven stories of shops, each with its own identity, all fit under one umbrella because the architecture of the mall is so distinct. In general, shoppers do not like to travel up more than two flights to reach their destination. Malls with numerous floors must employ interesting architectural details to make traveling up irresistible. Sevens Mall does it best through innovative use of lighting and design.

Atmospheric elements influence how shoppers feel about being in and staying in a retail space. The longer they stay in the store, the more likely they are to buy.

retail realities

Figure 2.3 Exceptional architecture and lighting create a strong brand umbrella for shops in the Sevens shopping mall, Düsseldorf. Judy Bell.

Shopping Is a Form of Communication

The way people act in a certain environment is a form of communication, too. Retail merchants put the entire store on display, saying symbolically: "Here's what we have to offer. Here's our pricing. What do you think?" If customers respond by making purchases, they're saying: "This is quality merchandise at great prices. We like your way of doing business."

Over the years, retailers have studied shopping patterns and have passed them down from one generation to another. Have you ever wondered why the less-expensive, generic cereal products are on the lowest shelves in some grocery stores, while the premium-priced, kid-pleasing brands are on the middle shelves, and the "healthy" brands are on the top shelves? Grocers believe that the more expensive brands should be placed on a higher shelf with adult-level sight lines in mind, because they are the decision makers on these brands. Products placed on middle shelves catch the attention of the younger child riding in the shopping cart reaching out to grab at recognizable favorites. As a consequence, bottom shelves may be the least desirable spots for merchandise, but grocers know that bargain hunters don't mind reaching down to save money.

As retailing methods have become more scientific, formal research studies have been conducted in an attempt to quantify and formalize some of retailing's common wisdom. In these studies, experts study shoppers and their behavior. They watch how people act when they're shopping and then use the information to help retailers sell more profitably. One of the best-known researchers is Paco Underhill, founder of a company called Envirosell. Underhill's book *Why We Buy: The Science of Shopping* details the thousands of hours he and his team of "trackers" have spent observing and recording shopping behavior.

Underhill says:

The first principle behind the science of shopping is the simplest one: There are certain physical and anatomical abilities, tendencies, limitations, and needs common to all people, and the retail environment must be tailored to these characteristics. . . . You'd think it would be easy to get everything right. Yet a huge part of what we do is uncover ways in which retail environments fail to recognize and accommodate how human machines are built and how our anatomical and physiological aspects determine what we do. . . . The implications of all this are clear: Where shoppers go, what they see, and how they respond determines the very nature of their shopping experience.

For every truism about consumer behavior, there is a corresponding retail practice that uses the common (or highly scientific) wisdom contained in it. Retailers are learning how to make profitable use of this information and shoppers are the beneficiaries. For example, did you know that Americans tend to shop at a store in much the same way they walk and drive—veering to the right? When was the last time you pulled out a grocery cart and turned left to start your marketing? It's almost impossible to do. Smart retailers know to set up their traffic patterns and prime merchandise layouts to facilitate this preference.

Because certain shopping behaviors are fairly predictable, retailers can make use of the knowledge. That's why clearance racks are most often found at the rear of the store or department. Retailers know that experienced shoppers habitually check for bargains, but they also want to guide them through all their regular-priced goods on their way to the markdown racks.

Did you know that it takes furniture shoppers at least 20 seconds to become acclimated to the store's layout before they're ready to do any serious looking? That's why most furniture stores employ an "up" system. Salespeople take turns watching the entrance of the store from a discreet distance, then wait for those important seconds to tick by before approaching customers after they've entered the store. They are counting: "one, one thousand, two, one thousand, three, one thousand, four . . . ."

Those few seconds also equate to distance traveled. When shoppers enter a fashion store, they are so busy getting a feel for the retail atmosphere, they may not be able to process any fashion messages from merchandise positioned directly inside the doors. The best way to use this space is to create entrance presentations with traffic-stopping impact. If you've shopped in an Old Navy store, you know that its "Item of the Week" causes shoppers to pause. Without this strategy, shoppers might move into the store too quickly and fail to get the most important fashion message. As shoppers move the next ten feet into the store, Old Navy has their full attention.

In retailing, the expression "too close for comfort" really means physically too close for comfort. Americans are quite conscious (and protective) of their personal space and they're very uncomfortable in stores that force them to squeeze between fixtures or bump up against other shoppers. This has been a difficult concept for many retailers to grasp since they've been trained to make the most of every square foot of selling floor space. However, if shoppers are continually jostled by traffic moving through a department or down an aisle, they'll spend less time examining garments or reading labels on packaged products. They may even leave the store. With the advent of the global pandemic in 2020, and the introduction of guidelines to maintain six feet between individuals, the notion of personal space expanded to personal safety.

The Americans with Disabilities act (ADA) mandates that retailers create aisles that allow wheelchairs to pass safely between fixtures. Stores that comply with this far-reaching law improve shopping experiences for all. In 2020 the U.S. Census Bureau (www.census.gov) released the information that the 65 and older segment of the population has grown rapidly. People who cannot bend and stretch or see as clearly as they once did have special needs when they shop. Imagine what a store that does not accommodate this growing segment of the population will communicate to the shopping public. It would be wiser to listen and attend to customer preferences before they become major issues. Communication is a two-way process.

BOX 2.1

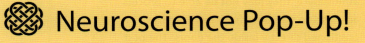 # Neuroscience Pop-Up!

Have you ever considered that you might think about a retail store as if it were an actual person? In his Mind & Matter column in WSJ, Robert M. Sapolsky, a professor of biology and neurology at Stanford University, called out: "Our Brains Say Corporations Are People Too." He talked about his realization that because he liked Pepsi, he liked the corporation too. He further revealed, "I wanted to give Pepsi a warm, appreciative handshake. And I have similar feelings about Apple, Quaker Oats and whoever makes duct tape—I imagine it as a corporation that wears flannel shirts and hiking shoes." To make sense of this, he looked at research undertaken at Baylor College of Medicine that compared subjects' response to human vs. corporate actions. Findings indicated that individuals use similar parts of their brain to understand corporate and human behavior. Now it made sense why Sapolsky expressed emotions about his favorite brands. In some ways, they were like people!

Look at the photo of Nordstrom's friendly "Hello" called out in large block letters next to a welcoming seated mannequin. At first glance you may imagine that Nordstrom—the store—is speaking directly to you, and the way your brain works has something to do with it! But there's more to the story. Humayun Khan, in Shopify Retail Marketing Blog wrote, "Ask anyone in the retail industry what the first words are that come to their mind when they think of Nordstrom, and they'll immediately tell you 'customer service.'" Nordstrom sales associates are trained in best practices like walking shoppers to the destination of a desired product rather than pointing to it. They can ring up purchases without shoppers having to wait in line. The list goes on, but what they are doing in a sense is "building relationships" with shoppers. Visual merchandisers can also encourage relationship building with conversational signs like Nordstrom's "Hello," accentuated with its placement next to a mannequin. What other ways can visual merchandisers contribute to a perceived "personhood" of a retail store?

Nordstrom's NYC flagship, on West 57th Street, greets shoppers with a friendly hello.
Photography: Connie Zhou, New York City. Design: Nordstrom Inc. Store Design, Seattle, in collaboration with James Carpenter Design Associates, New York City. This Nordstrom store was recognized by the Retail Design Institute as a winning entry in its annual design competition.

HOW DO CUSTOMERS PROCESS VISUAL MERCHANDISING MESSAGES?

Think about your last trip into a store that you had never shopped before. Ask yourself:

- Why did you decide to go to the store?
- Were you responding to a specific ad or were you just curious as you walked by?
- Did someone you know visit the store first and tell you positive things about his or her experience?
- What did you see as you walked up to the store's entrance?
- Did the store's exterior send you any messages about what would be inside?
- Was the view through the storefront appealing? Informative?
- When you entered, was the lighting pleasant to your eyes?
- Do you remember any particular scents or sounds?
- How welcoming did the store's interior feel once you'd stepped inside?
- Was it easy to tell what the store was selling?
- Did you get the impression that the store was selling merchandise that you'd want to buy?
- On the basis of your first impression, did you decide to explore further?
- Was it clear to you how to shop the store?
- Were you directed to or drawn to the merchandise?
- Bottom line, did you make a purchase?

If your answers were mostly positive, the store's visual merchandising probably played a large role in you going home with a package under your arm. There is a sequence or set of events that usually takes place for merchandise presentation to result in an actual sale. The retailer communicated something vital to you about merchandise through the store's presentation methods . . . and you got the message.

INFORMATION PROCESSING IN A VISUAL MERCHANDISING STRATEGY

Visual merchandisers expose merchandise to potential customers, who process the information in eight stages (see Box 2.2). Imagine that you're walking into an Anthropologie store to shop for a few new accessories. Immediately you notice a mannequin in a casual outfit with an attractive cotton jacket. That's *exposure* (Figure 2.4).

If the store's visual merchandisers have presented the merchandise in a way that shows how it could be used when purchased, you might say, "If I had that jacket, I could wear it with jeans." That's *attention*.

Figure 2.4 Mannequin forms accessorized from head-to-toe, Anthropologie, New York City. Eugene Gologursky/Getty Images.

If the visual merchandising message is clearly stated—by signage, by location in the department, by accessorizing, by vivid color, and by level of activity in the area—you will reach the *comprehension* stage. You may say to yourself, "The way this jacket is shown, I could wear it to work on casual Fridays. I wonder how it would look dressed up . . . ."

The next step, *agreement*, occurs if the product information you've just absorbed is credible and compatible with your values, and you mentally file it away—perhaps for future reference. If, at this point, you revert to looking for accessories, your *retention* of the mental image of the jacket and later *retrieval* of it will be very important to the store. Will the visual merchandiser's message about the jacket stay with you after you purchase the accessories you had in mind when you entered the store? Will you ask yourself, "Now where did I see that great cotton jacket? Oh, that's

right . . . it was near the entrance. It was on a mannequin, so it should be easy to find."

If the mental imagery of the presentation was strong enough and all the rest of the promotional elements supported the *consumer decision-making* process, you will probably take *action*. If your next step is to purchase the jacket, the consumer information processing model worked for you—and for the specialty store.

▌ VISUAL MERCHANDISING SUPPORTS SELLING

In the last scenario, there was no salesperson to suggest the cotton jacket to you as a shopper. The visual merchandiser's presentation of the jacket on a mannequin made the sale. Current trends in store staffing indicate that stores have reduced the number of sales associates on the selling floor to lower operating costs. Effective visual merchandising efforts can supplement and support the sales staff of any store.

Although they will never replace an alert and attentive sales associate, successful visual merchandising techniques may keep customers involved with a display until a sales associate reaches them and completes the sales transaction. If the cotton jacket had been presented on a floor fixture with eleven others in assorted colors, you may not have noticed it.

You were only looking for a few new accessories, a scarf or a bracelet, a simple purchase priced around $25, but the jacket on the mannequin caught your eye. Even though you'd been momentarily sidetracked, you resumed your original plan to shop for accessories, and purchased a new bracelet. The next move you made was to try on the jacket. The silent selling of merchandise presentation added $98 to your shopping bill—for a jacket that you sold to yourself!

According to Cotton Incorporated's Lifestyle Monitor research:

retail realities

An add-on sale of $2.89 for a pair of socks adds more than 10 percent to a $25 purchase of denim jeans. Ask people you know if they'd be happy to have a 10 percent increase in their paychecks this week . . . or if they'd like to be earning 10 percent interest on their saving accounts!

Retailers maintain that in-store displays should do the following: (1) communicate the latest trends in fashion and colors, (2) assist the customer in making a buying decision, and (3) create an exciting environment within the store. In addition, retailers are also faced with the challenge of a consumer who is spending less time shopping, making it all the more imperative that visual displays act as instruments of swift persuasion.

Visual merchandising can transform a shopper into a buyer. It can also increase the average dollar amount per sale. Effective displays teach shoppers about using multiple basic and accessory items to enhance and extend the use of their purchases. It's not uncommon to hear a shopper say "I'd like to purchase the entire outfit, just the way you have it on the mannequin." That's silent selling at its best.

A fully accessorized visual merchandising treatment educates customers about when and how to wear fashion and trend items. In this way, effective merchandise presentation provides fashion direction to customers who may not trust their own fashion savvy.

Imagine gift shopping for someone whose taste is different from yours. You may not know what kind of table linens to select for a wedding gift if the bride's china pattern is far removed from your own preference. You may not know what kind of socks to wear with a pinstriped suit and wingtip oxfords if you've spent most of your life in boots and jeans. Effective visual merchandising techniques can solve many buying problems for prospective customers who are looking for advice.

Shoppers don't have to have all the answers, but the store's merchandisers do. When shoppers can trust their favorite store's merchandisers to offer them advice, they can

It is possible for fewer sales personnel to manage more customers when the product presentation assists with the selling process.

Visual merchandising's effect on the presentation of goods builds add-on sales by suggesting coordinating items for the customer's selection—which creates a value-added transaction for both retailer and customer.

relax and enjoy the shopping experience. Educational and tasteful presentations can give confidence (and direction) to shoppers and save them time.

The visual merchandiser can stimulate customers' appetites for artfully presented merchandise in the same way that the gourmet cook stimulates diners' appetites for an artfully presented meal. Pick up any lifestyle magazine and look at the food in the photographs. You anticipate how good the food will taste because your senses are stimulated by the imagery on the paper.

An effective presentation of merchandise is a virtual recipe for making the most of the shopper's investment. The shopper tells others about your value-added services . . . and the shopper comes back again and again.

HOW DOES VISUAL MERCHANDISING SUPPORT RETAILING TRENDS?

A fashion apparel or accessory item becomes a trend when it is widely desired by consumers. Visual merchandisers have the tools to draw attention to the item and make it easy for shoppers to locate. Product placement, mannequins, props, signage, and lighting may all play a role in highlighting trend merchandise. Every retailer wants to be the first, the best, the leader. The visual merchandiser is the invisible force that is doing a lot of the pushing behind the trend.

"A fad gives us momentary joy, and part of the joy comes in knowing that it's momentary. A trend, on the other hand, satisfies a different human need. A trend gains power over time, because it's not merely part of a moment, it's a tool, a connector that will become more valuable as other people commit to engaging in it."
Seth Godin, Seth's Blog: Trends vs. Fads

THE TREND TOWARD EMPHASIZING INTERIORS

Store interiors have changed, presentation methods have changed, and shopping has changed. In the 1980s, trend reports indicated that interior store layout and wall and fixture merchandising had more impact on sales than store windows did. Many specialty retailers removed traditional street-side theatrical display windows and opened up the entire main floor to public view. Windows that once blocked the pedestrian's view of the inside of the store now created an opportunity to view the store's entire shopping assortment. Windows became an invitation for passersby to enter for a closer look. The visual merchandiser's concern changed from "Are our windows dramatic?" to "Are the windows clean?" Store interiors became their new focus.

THE TREND TOWARD CONSUMER INTERACTION WITH THE MERCHANDISE

Consumerism, another trend, meant that customers wanted the opportunity to thoroughly inspect products before making a purchase. In the case of expensive or technical products, they wanted expert demonstrations to determine if all of their requirements were going to be met. Lamps needed electrical power, television screens needed moving images, and stereos needed soundproof demo booths.

The barriers of showcase selling also had to come down if retailers were going to reduce selling costs and stay competitive in a growing market. For economic and competitive reasons, stores began to move in the direction of self service. There are fewer salespeople on the floor now who can remove merchandise from a display case and hand it to a customer or demonstrate an appliance.

Visual merchandisers were challenged to find new ways to put shoppers in touch with merchandise assortments. Improved selling

fixtures were created, and store furnishings became more functional as selling tools. Layouts changed to facilitate customer interactions with merchandise. Signage directed traffic and told customers about merchandise on self-service fixtures. Graphics on the walls set moods and explained lifestyles.

THE VISUAL MERCHANDISER AS TREND FORECASTER

As lifestyles continually changed and new trends accelerated in all areas of shoppers' lives, retailing had to anticipate the changes quickly and provide the latest trend-right merchandise. Competitive retailers added the task of trend forecasting to their merchandise buyers' and visual merchandisers' job descriptions.

Visual merchandisers have had to become experts at anticipating and responding to lifestyle trends. They study how their target customers live their lives. They try to understand what shoppers want in new products and how shoppers use the products they buy. They must interpret the trends within the store's physical setting so that people know what's important today. Stores must be poised to change and then change again. Smart merchandisers are always looking ahead for tomorrow's strategy because they want to be there ahead of the competition. See www .echochamber.com and www.gdruk.com for international retail trends.

THE TREND TOWARD LIFESTYLE CENTERS

A growing retail strategy is the trend of shopping malls transitioning to **lifestyle centers**. In September 2019, "Star Tribune" interviewed Judy Tullius, general manager of Southdale in Minnesota, the first U.S. enclosed shopping mall. Tullius said: "We're reclaiming the whole trailblazing spirit we had when we first opened in 1956. We're striving to be more than a place to shop, a place where the

lifestyle center is a mixed-use commercial development that combines the traditional retail functions of a shopping mall with services like shared workspaces and leisure amenities including table service restaurants, multiplex cinemas and fitness clubs. In addition, other services may be introduced like medical and dental offices and license bureaus.

community enjoys themselves, where people gather to spend time together and come out for special experiences." Life Time Work, a co-working concept with a world-class health club, joined Southdale in 2019. The mall is also considering adding medical and dental offices to address consumers' changing needs.

Another growing trend is open-air lifestyle centers. Beautifully landscaped and located in affluent areas, open-air lifestyle centers include many of the same specialty shops of the enclosed mall but often do not have department store anchors. The Grove in Los Angeles and Bal Harbor in Miami are examples. Ala Moana Center in Honolulu expanded with the addition of a new wing in 2015 and opened a Target store in 2017. It is currently the largest open-air mall in the world.

THE TREND TOWARD INTEGRATED RETAIL AND RESIDENTIAL DEVELOPMENTS

For those who want to live immediately next to their favorite shopping mall, developers are building high-rise condominiums and apartments with walkways directly into the mall. An example is Galleria in Edina, Minnesota, which links to neighboring Galleria Westin Hotel and Condominiums. Residents and hotel guests can shop in over sixty luxury stores or dine in one of seven unique restaurants or cafes. Another integrated retail mall and residence is ION Orchard mall and Orchard Residences in Singapore. Dwellers can shop in a wide variety of luxury fashion stores, dine in the ION Food Hall, and conduct business in OCBC Bank, all without getting into their car (Figure 2.5).

Figure 2.5 ION Orchard, Singapore, an integrated retail and residential development.
Schöning/ullstein bild via Getty Images

THE TREND TOWARD SMALLER STORES

A full decade into this new century, many big-box retailers who previously embraced a supersized philosophy have begun to expand their strategies to include a smaller retail footprint—particularly in densely populated urban areas where new retail space is at a premium. Spurred by retail economics and the fact that America is over-stored, industry leaders like Target are exploring the concept of more neighborhood-oriented stores that can serve niche markets with highly specific merchandise assortments and services. Target's online newsletter, "A Bullseye View," posted this notice March 3, 2020:

> "If you're a small format guest, you're in luck: These stores are on track to pack an even bigger punch in 2020. We've opened more than 100 small-format stores in areas where a traditional Target wouldn't fit. In the year ahead, we're also exploring an idea that's half the size of our current smallest store (think: about 6,000 square feet). The goal? Bringing the joy of Target to new guests and neighborhoods. We'll also be adding Drive Up to dozens more small-format stores, a service guests are already loving at some of our small-formats coast-to-coast."

THE TREND TOWARD NONSTORE SELLING

Nonstore retailing is another trend that is affecting visual merchandising. There are hundreds of home shopping opportunities beamed into your living room 24 hours a day on your television. Infomercials don't have storefronts. They don't need them when merchandise is a phone call away. Specialty shopping by mail-order catalogues is another retail trend that reflects today's lifestyles. People who have less time will take shortcuts, even if they have to spend a little more to have their purchases conveniently delivered to their doorsteps. A new generation of retailers is counting on it. The Internet offers books, movies, music, clothing, medicine, food, business services, electronic products, housewares, automobiles, airline tickets—you name it, it's probably there.

While these trends in retailing present a tremendous challenge to in-store retailers, they also present opportunities for visual merchandisers seeking employment opportunities in a growing field. The merchandise on the electronic shopper's television screen or computer monitor has to be presented well even if it is not in a store. Who arranges the assorted goods for the camera? The goods are arranged by a visual merchandiser whose title may be different but whose duties remain essentially the same. They may be called stylists, but what they do is prepare and present merchandise.

BOX 2.3

DESIGN GALLERY: RALPH LAUREN'S ICONIC POLO SHIRT

Ralph Lauren's flagship store on St. Germain in Paris paid homage to its signature polo shirt in a vibrant window executed with the finest graphic precision. The Ralph Lauren Corporation has been an inspirational leader with its readily recognizable lifestyle brand both in merchandise and in-store environment since its origin in 1967. To Ralph, the importance of an enduring brand is evident in his words, "Style is very personal. It has nothing to do with fashion. Fashion is over quickly. Style is forever." Of the polo shirt, which was introduced in 1972, Ralph said, "On one level, there's an aspirational quality to having a polo player on it. On another level, it's just a great shirt with lots of colors." The Timeline, www.ralphlauren.com.

Today the polo is evolving as a symbol for the corporation's role in "creating an equitable and sustainable future." Ralph Lauren polos now have a purpose in supporting causes varying from climate change to cancer research, human rights, and more. For example, the Earth Polo is fashioned of an average of twelve recycled plastic bottles and dyed in new hues inspired by nature. The corporate goal is to use 170 million recycled plastic bottles in products and packaging by 2025. The Pride Polo contributes 100 percent of the purchase price to Stonewall Community. The Pink Pony collection donates 25 percent of each purchase to Ralph Lauren's fight against cancer.

Clearly the polo shirt still reigns as one of the world's most respected fashion creations, as it stars in the Ralph Lauren window in Paris in 2020, 48 years after its launch. Looking at the window pictured here through the lens of *design:retail*'s three criteria, we can see a winning formula. In category one, *Originality and Creativity*, the window demonstrates how attention to one element of a polo shirt, the collar, can be used to send a message of a timeless, premium, quality product. The arrangement of collars draped in a unique way in the background offers an unexpected twist to the presentation. To contrast, the collars on bust forms stand at attention with crisp wings. The goal of category two, *Captures the Spirit of the Season*, is accomplished with polo

Ralph Lauren on St. Germain in Paris focuses on its iconic polo shirt in this vividly colorful window, which demonstrates outstanding visual merchandising precision in execution. Copyright WindowsWear Inc., http://www .windowswear.com, contact@windowswear.com

shirts in a wide array of summer colors, appropriate for the July season in which it was set. In category three, *Professionalism: Execution and Technical Aspects*, the window wins five stars for the use of the design principles repetition and asymmetrical balance, along with meticulously hung and folded products.

Can you see the triangle that is formed by the position of the mannequin bust forms? This is a technique often used in both windows and interior displays to ensure good composition. Notice how the neutral cube provides a firm base for the folded polo shirts and serves to bounce one's attention back to the focal point of the display, the three forms. Do you think this expertly composed window reflects Ralph Lauren's corporate purpose: "To inspire the dream of a better life through authenticity and timeless style"?

Shoptalk "The Day I Learned What a Brand Really Is" by Aaron Keller Founder & Managing Principal, Capsule, Minneapolis, Co-Author: *The Physics of Brand*

I grew up in an era when a brand was defined as something you bought off a shelf, like Campbell's Soup, Nike, and Apple Computers. Brand managers worked at corporations like General Mills, Levi's, and P&G, defining the discipline and rewards that come with a properly managed brand. Advertising was the powerful creative resource and discipline that connected consumers with the brands they would be encouraged to love. Brands were centered around the promise they made and fulfilled for the consumer. However, the world of advertising was pushing glamour, false hope, and promises that brands could never fulfill.

In time, brands were no longer just on the shelf, they "became" the shelf. Retailers began to look at themselves as brands. At Capsule, we had the opportunity to "rebrand" Byerly's, an internationally known luxury grocery retailer. The Byerly's brand was associated with a quiet, clean, luxurious grocery shopping experience. Yet the Byerly's name was on opening-price-point milk, instamatic cameras, and other less-than-premium products in the Byerly's store. There was a conflict between the premium grocery retailer and the cheap cameras and milk that was breaking an implied promise. My experience on this project helped to craft a definition of brand that my co-authors and I wrote into *The Physics of Brand*: "Brand is a container of all the experiences and meaning a customer associates with the product or company." Therefore, a brand needed to fulfill its "promise" in every element of the store, from products to environment.

When retailers became brands, so did the Kardashians. The definition of a brand expanded rapidly and came all the way back to "people" as brands. And, as my co-author Dan Wallace would say, people were the original brands back in the 1800s when "brands" were the baker, shoemaker, tailor, and grocer. Everyone began to see the importance of managing their own brands. Experiencing the Kardashians was temporary entertainment in comparison to the immersive experience of Apple, Target, or the most coveted Patagonia.

When brands like Patagonia became retailers, it was clear that retailers could indeed be brands. Having the opportunity to work with Patagonia on international research, experience design and packaging was another defining moment for me at Capsule. A brand owner like Patagonia takes responsibility for the role their brand has in society. My new favorite quote was "Patagonia the brand and Patagonia the company are the same thing," by former Patagonia CMO Joy Howard. Few brands achieve this degree of alignment between the internal culture and external perception of what a brand means.

Brands, for me, became a lifelong study. Their purpose and meaning to our culture and humanity is a never-ending curiosity of mine. We've invented these things we call brands and they've gone far beyond the hot metal used to mark the ownership of cattle. Brands become living entities in our lives with enough emotional attachment to cause protests when Marshall Fields was retired by their holding company. Brands become presidents and presidents become brands. People love and hate brands to extreme degrees, but no one can live without brands in their life.

Curiosity is how I define my brand. (www.capsule.us)

Figure 2.6 Patagonia packaging: Capsule conducted global research in retail aisles to find insights and then designed a package to increase interaction, improve shopability and reduce waste in the supply chain. Design by Capsule.

Chapter 2 Review Questions

1. What is a target market? Explain how a target market can impact a retail store's promotional mix.

2. What are atmospherics? Give examples of how atmospherics can theoretically make a customer purchase goods in a retail store.

3. What are the three basic elements of how visual merchandising communicates to customers?

4. How does visual merchandising educate customers and increase sales by using the stages in consumer information processing? Give examples of this and share with the class.

5. Describe how visual merchandising can support or even alter fashion and product trends. Give examples of this for a mass fashion retailer like Gap, a high-end retailer like Nordstrom, and a big box retailer like Target or Walmart.

Outside-the-Box Challenge

Comparison Shopping

LOOK

1. Look at three stores that are selling the same style of jeans in the latest trend wash. Sketch or photograph each presentation as well as make a list of prices, colors, fixtures, and signage details.

COMPARE

2. Compare the three presentations.

INNOVATE

3. Use the ideas to create and sketch a new version of the presentation. Include a sign and new fixture as part of your idea.

4. Scan and/or insert your images into a Word document. Your new, improved idea should be sized larger than the three that you saw in the comparison.

5. Present your idea to the rest of the class.

Critical Thinking

Promotional Mix—True or False?

1. Go online to a retail store's website that targets a specific customer through their promotional mix of marketing.

2. Now, visit that store (write down the time and date you visited) and examine how other parts of their promotional mix are presented to customers, such as in-store marketing, personnel selling the clothes, and visual merchandising.

3. Look at who is shopping and purchasing items in this store. Does the actual shopper match the perceived promotional mix of the retailer? Or is the retailer appealing to a different market?

4. Based upon your observation, is the retailer marketing to the right customer? Or do you think they are aspiring to a target market that is not real or obtainable?

Case Study

Store Brand Image and Visual Merchandising Guidelines

THE SITUATION

Ben is a sales associate who works for the national department store Smith's, which targets the middle-income suburban family. The store's brand image is one of affordable but trend-right fashion for all members of the family. Ben's selling department carries workday casual clothing for men—assorted sweaters, dress pants, casual and dress woven shirts, polo shirts, and accessories such as belts, socks, and hats. The overall brand image is fairly conservative, and the store's presentation style has been detailed in the company's corporate display guidelines. Visual merchandisers implement new wall and selling floor layouts sent from corporate headquarters every ten days.

Ben likes to watch visual merchandisers at work. It looks like an exciting job, with freedom to do different activities throughout the store instead of having to stay in one department. In fact, he hopes to work in the visual department one day. Ben's only current display responsibility is to make sure that a coordinated outfit is shown on the front of every feature fixture in his area. His number one priority is to offer assistance to shoppers.

One evening, when business was slow, Ben noticed that the display forms on the side wall of his selling area featured merchandise that was nearly sold out. Although he needed to complete his own assigned tasks and wall presentation was the responsibility of the visual merchandiser, Ben decided to change the display. Ben reasoned that this would show initiative and would demonstrate to the store manager that he was ready to move into the next available visual merchandising position.

First, he removed the display forms and outfits from the wall. Then, using a visual merchandising technique he had seen once in a store window that he liked, Ben tied monofilament to hangers and began to "fly" the garments high on the wall over the selling fixtures. The project took over two hours, and he did not have time to complete his own assigned tasks.

When he was finished, Ben was pleased with himself. He thought his presentation was much more interesting than anything he had seen set up by the department's visual merchandiser. Besides, Ben told himself, the visual merchandiser seemed to do all of his work with one eye on the guidelines for display section in the company's policy and procedure manual. How creative was that?

The next morning, Ben enthusiastically showed his display to the store manager and the visual merchandiser. To emphasize how challenging the project had been, he described how it required multiple attempts to get the items to fly at pleasing angles. The manager and the visual merchandiser were concerned because the flying technique did not represent the store's conservative brand image. Ben's manager directed the visual merchandiser to replace Ben's display. Then the manager asked Ben to step inside his office. He asked Ben why he chose to work on a wall display rather than complete his own responsibilities. He listened carefully to Ben's justification and acknowledged Ben's enthusiasm. He explained to Ben the importance of maintaining a conservative presentation strategy, which had been carefully developed by the corporate marketing team at headquarters. It was based on demographics, customer preferences, and other factors. Then he asked Ben to complete his responsibilities from the previous night. He closed the meeting by scheduling a meeting with Ben in a few weeks. At that time they would discuss ways that Ben could channel his enthusiasm and energy into a visual merchandising career path. Ben was grateful that his manager took time to listen to him. He apologized for focusing on his own personal goals without considering company guidelines, and not completing his assigned responsibilities. He thanked his manager for helping him to see a bigger picture of all that goes into a store's brand image.

DISCUSSION QUESTIONS

1. Did Ben use good judgment in his decision to forgo his responsibilities in order to further his own personal goals?

2. What's so important about the brand image of the store being communicated by visual merchandising in the department?

3. Is it more important to ensure that every display form features available product than to be concerned about who dresses the form?

4. What has the visual merchandising team failed to do in this case? Have they reacted to sales in the store?

5. Could Ben have communicated his interest in a visual position more appropriately? How?

6. What do you think about the way the store manager handled the situation?

TORY BURCH

3   Core Design Strategies

The Visual Merchandiser Is a Design Strategist

The visual merchandiser must be a strategic thinker. What's that? A strategic thinker assesses a task in relation to available resources (tools) and the goal that's been set. By the end of this chapter, you'll know that it's the visual merchandiser—carrying out design strategies created by the store's management team—who actually brings the store and its merchandise to life.

A **design strategy** is a plan of action to achieve retail store design and displays that effectively utilize basic elements and principles drawn from the art world like: color, balance, rhythm, emphasis, proportion, etc., to create a welcoming place where shoppers will purchase goods and services.

Once the carpenters, electricians, and painters leave and the fixtures and merchandise arrive, the visual merchandiser does the important work that will make the store's blueprinted promise a retail reality. What the visual merchandiser adds to the basic design is a concept known to retail practitioners as *atmospherics*—a strategic tool that, used effectively, gives the retail operation personality and brand image that help it reach its financial goals. It creates a store environment that invites shoppers to enter the selling space and encourages them to stay and browse—and buy.

Atmospherics as a Merchandising Strategy

Basic design strategies used throughout a store create a strong foundation for a successful retail business. Atmospherics—multiple sensory elements for décor and layout that appeal to a shopper's five senses—can be strategically layered into the basic shell of the store to enhance the shopping environment and build the brand image of the store. This layering entails a simultaneous use of sight, sound, touch, taste, and smell that can actually alter

> A **design strategy** is a plan of action to achieve retail goals and create a welcoming place where shoppers will purchase goods and services.

> "I don't consider design a limited activity. Design is intent, intent to communicate something to somebody so they move to action, and that includes practically everything in the world, from making a lunch date to designing an office building."
> *Martin Glaser, graphic designer, famous for his "I heart NY" logo, which he first scribbled on the back of an envelope with a red crayon while sitting in the back of a NYC taxi.*

AFTER COMPLETING THIS CHAPTER, YOU SHOULD BE ABLE TO

- Identify the elements and principles of design used to create a welcoming store environment
- Create harmonious color schemes for effective wall and fixture presentations
- Describe the atmospheric elements and design strategies that enhance store environment and strengthen store brand or image

Figure 3.0 An energy-filled window at Tory Burch illustrates many design principles and elements, most notably line, shape, and contrast. Rodeo Drive, Los Angeles. WindowsWear Photo.

multiple sales are transactions in which two or more items are purchased at one time. For example, a shopper buys a set of bath towels with a matching robe and slippers.

shoppers' perception of time, encouraging them to become so comfortable and pleasantly stimulated in the shopping environment that time becomes less important than it might otherwise be. They may shop longer, see and touch more products, and become more inclined to make purchases.

Atmospherics borrow theories and techniques from the artist's realm. Every feature of a store's makeup—from the display of a single garment to an expansive presentation featuring an entire wall of coordinates—uses some or all of the principles and elements of design. Just as painters choose colors, shapes, lines, and textures to create works of art, visual merchandisers choose colors, shapes, lines, and textures to create store environments. Their use of these creative tools ensures that selling floors will be organized, easy to shop, and filled with eye-catching, merchandise-centered displays that will attract shoppers and encourage **multiple sales**.

If you've shopped in a Victoria's Secret store, you know something about atmospherics. When you enter the store, you see color and texture everywhere—from the silken fabrics of intimate apparel to lavishly printed wallpaper to painted moldings and elegantly carved store fixtures. The soft lighting is easy on your eyes, similar to the type of lighting that is used in your home. You notice a subtle fragrance in the air and hear sweet classical music. How long does it take before you begin to touch the fabric of the merchandise? Was it on the first table as you entered the store? (See Figure 3.1.)

Victoria's Secret does an excellent job of appealing to four of our five senses: sight, smell, hearing, and touch. On occasion, it has done co-branded gift-with-purchase promotions with Godiva chocolates, adding the fifth sense, taste, to create an even more complete sensory experience for shoppers. This strategy also expands the retailer's private-label brand and its value to customers.

Figure 3.1 Victoria's Secret in Soho, New York City, promotes a sensory experience through soft lighting, curved fixtures, and silk and lace textured products. Ericksen / WWD / © Conde Nast.

Figure 3.2 Eataly, an Italian marketplace with an abundance of atmospherics to awaken the five senses. Milan, Italy. *Pier Marco Tacca/Getty Images.*

Another retailer that appeals to all the senses is Eataly, the largest Italian marketplace in the world, with forty locations and growing. The first Eataly opened in 2007 in Torino, Italy, followed by Japan, and then New York in 2010 and Chicago in 2013. The concept was founded and created by Oscar Farinetti, in an effort to merge the best regional ingredients of Italy with the feel of the bazaars of Istanbul. The result is a mecca that compares to none, as this charming and delightful destination serves up pizza, pasta, creamy polenta and braised beef, fish, and so much more at a variety of sit-down restaurants. For those on the go, you can grab an Italian coffee and a sandwich or dessert at one of the many counters. You can also shop their market to take home fresh bread baked in a wood-burning oven, handmade mozzarella, pastries, and beer. A real pleasure for your senses, this is a unique retail environment where atmospherics seem to be as important as the products (Figure 3.2). To learn more, see www.eataly.com.

Art is a personal sensory experience. We are moved by paint on canvas, touched by sculpted shapes, stirred by musical notes, soothed by silken textures. Watch a creative chef prepare a meal that looks enticing, smells wonderful, and tastes sublime, and you know that even food preparation can be elevated to an art form. Your senses tell you so. To begin to understand how design elements are applied to a store environment, this chapter (and photographs throughout the text) shows examples of how they are used in merchandise presentation. Practical applications of design principles are explored in more depth in later chapters.

Core Design Tools and Strategies

The *elements of design*—color, texture, proportion, direction, line, shape, size, sequence, and tension—are helpful tools that you can use to create a selling display.

The *principles of design*—unity, harmony, balance, repetition, rhythm, emphasis, contrast, and surprise—represent strategic rules that govern the way the *design elements* are used in the overall presentation. Using the basic tools strategically, you may select from an array of design principles to create a unique presentation of merchandise that triggers purchases. How will you know which principles and tools to use? It really depends on knowing what each does and what goals you must meet.

Are you trying to show shoppers a new assortment of activewear so that they buy several items from the assortment? Then you might want to set up a display that suggests activity, movement, and excitement. You could apply the tools of direction and color using the rules of rhythm and contrast by alternating a series of light and dark blue running suits along a diagonal.

Are you trying to present a luxurious arrangement of china, crystal, and silver for special occasion dining? Then you might depend on strict principles of formal balance

with place settings identical in the sizes, shapes, and colors of the items to convey stability and elegance to shoppers—whereas a Super Bowl party might call for paper and plastic displayed less formally.

Do you want to create a sweet, cuddly, and irresistible assortment of clothing and accessories appealing to parents and grandparents of newborns? Perhaps pastel colors and soft textures will support your merchandising goal.

The principles of design are the strategic rules that govern merchandise presentation. You may hear those principles also described as important guidelines for using the various tools (elements of design) to select and arrange products for sale to consumers. Rules or guidelines, strictly or loosely interpreted, are part of the visual merchandiser's basic vocabulary.

You may have already had art courses and may have a basic understanding of the elements and principles. Rather than teach them from scratch, this chapter looks at them mostly in terms of workable merchandising strategies—how you, as a practicing visual merchandiser, may utilize the elements and principles to create visual interest and spur sales. They're defined in this chapter in terms of presentation and store design. Your strategy for a display may focus on a particular design element or principle, or a combination of elements and principles.

Never learned the art basics? Take yourself on an electronic excursion to a search engine (such as Google) and key in "principles of art" and/or "elements of design." What constitutes a good website? It is one that interests you enough to follow leads and links from one page to the next. Most sites are visually rich and highly instructional. For instance, a quick trip to www.ask.com for art principles and elements of art leads to http://www .ndoylefineart.com. This is artist Nancy Doyle's website, and it reads like an illustrated treasure trove of things that a visual merchant needs to know. Next, search for "art history." You'll find definitions for every art term you can imagine.

Design Elements—The Tools

In visual merchandising, design is about the way we arrange products, signage, props, and so on, to create a shopping environment that is pleasing to the eye. We work with various design elements—color, for instance—to bring unity, or a sense of wholeness and completeness, to our presentation work. Unity is one of the principles, or rules, governing design. The principles of design will be discussed at length later in this chapter.

▌COLOR AS A MERCHANDISING ▌STRATEGY

The first and most critical of the design elements is color. It is important to realize that color is a private experience. Your earliest caregivers taught you the names of items you saw: "Grass is green, bananas are yellow, and on a sunny day, the lake is blue because its waters reflect the color of the sky." Scientifically, colors are various qualities of light (either reflected onto an item or given off by it) that individuals can perceive with their eyes and describe in terms of lightness, brightness, darkness, richness, purity, and so on. That is, you may tell someone that the sky is blue or the grass is green, but you don't actually know that the shade of blue you see is the same precise shade that the other person with normal color vision sees.

Human physiology and the actual viewing of an environment determine what each of us perceives at any given time and place. Nevertheless, scientists have agreed that the relationships between colors can be shown in the form of a color wheel, using yellow, red, and blue (primary colors), at the 12 o'clock, 4 o'clock, and 8 o'clock positions (Figure 3.3). Moving clockwise around the circle, you'll see that the colors blend and change gradually from one primary color to the next.

Yellow, red, and blue are called **primary colors**, and green, orange, and violet are called **secondary colors** because they are formed by combining the primaries. Red and yellow merge to become orange; yellow and blue become green; blue and red become violet. If you mix the primary colors with the secondary colors, you'll form **tertiary** (third-level) **colors**, combinations like yellow-green and blue-violet.

M. Grumbacher, Inc., a manufacturer of artists' paints, has a very useful product that it calls a Color Computer—a cardboard "color harmony wheel" that illustrates clearly how colors are formed and how they relate to each other. You may want to buy one from an art supply store for your toolbox. Go to www .grumbacherart.com for more information.

You need to know some additional color-related terms because grouping merchandise by color is a common practice, and a particular language is used when discussing color. For example, yellow, red, blue, and green are *chromatic* (highly colored). Black, white, and gray are *achromatic* (the exact opposite of highly colored). **Shades** of a color are made by adding varying amounts of black or gray to darken it. **Tints** are created by adding white to a basic color to make it lighter. **Value** is the amount of lightness or darkness in a color. **Hue** is another word for the name of a color family—red, blue, brown, and so on. In everyday speech, *hue* is used as a synonym for *color*, but technically, the term *color* refers to the combination of hue, value, and **intensity** (brightness or purity of the color).

Color Schemes

There are many ways to coordinate colors in eye-pleasing arrangements or color schemes. Grumbacher's two-sided Color Computer calls these schemes color harmonies. The most basic color schemes or color harmonies are based on six variations of the color wheel. (See Figure 3.3.)

---

primary colors— yellow, red, and blue—are the starting points on the color wheel. Other colors are formed from them.

secondary colors— orange, green, violet—are formed by combining the primaries.

tertiary colors, or third-level colors, are formed by mixing primary colors with secondary colors in combinations like yellow-green and blue-violet.

---

shade is the darkening of a color by the addition of black or gray.

tint is the lightening of a color by adding white.

value is the apparent lightness or darkness in a color.

hue describes a color family—the reds, blues, browns, and so on. It is also used as a synonym to describe color.

intensity is the brightness, purity, and degree of saturation of a color.

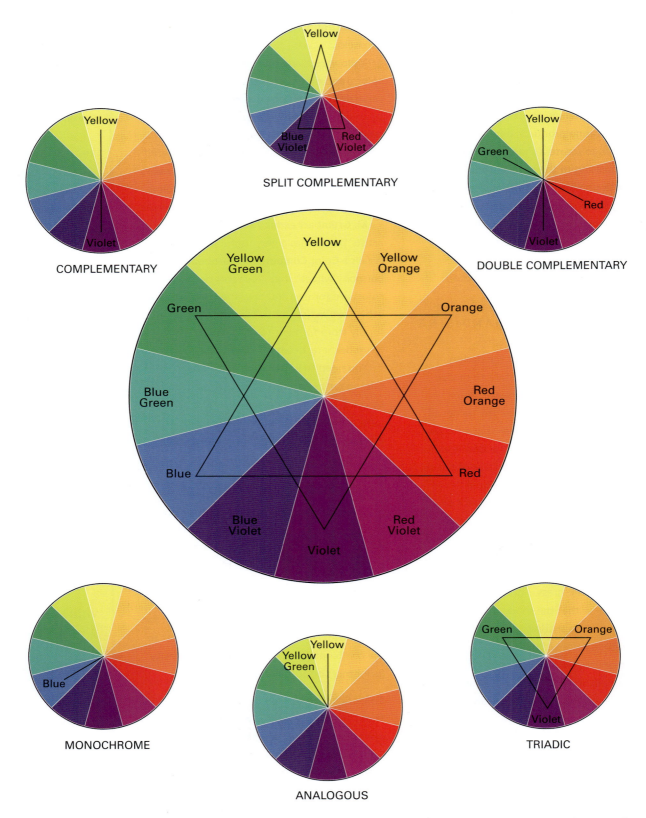

Figure 3.3 The standard color wheel is a convenient reference for planning color schemes. The large wheel in the center shows that the primary hues—yellow, red, and blue—are equidistant from each other. Opposite each primary hue is the secondary hue that is its complement. The secondary hues are also equidistant from each other on the color wheel. Various color schemes are shown on the smaller color wheels. Fairchild Books.

- **Monochromatic schemes** consist of a single color in different values and intensities (more white or gray blended into the basic color). Example: navy blue with medium blue and light blue.
- **Analogous schemes** (color families) consist of two or more colors that are next to each other (adjacent) on the color wheel. Example: yellow with yellow-green.
- **Complementary schemes** consist of two colors that are directly opposite each other on the color wheel. Example: yellow and violet.
- **Split-complementary schemes** consist of three colors—one central color plus the two colors on either side of its complement. Example: yellow with red-violet and blue-violet.
- **Double-complementary schemes** consist of four colors—two colors plus their complements. Example: yellow with violet plus green with red.
- **Triadic schemes** consist of three colors that are equidistant from one another on the color wheel (they form a triangle when you look at the wheel). Example: orange, green, and violet.

These schemes are your color tools in display and presentation. Even if your store is too small to have its own trend merchandising department, you will notice that merchandise is arriving from vendors in colors that are popular for the season. It may be up to you to combine merchandise items on the selling floor, on fixtures, and on walls in ways that make it look attractive to customers.

A lot of common wisdom has evolved from the study of color. Some colors (related to red, yellow, and orange) are said to be warm, while the blues, greens, and some purple shades are spoken of as cool colors. In the language of color, they make a statement. They call up feelings that don't have to be said aloud; they're simply understood because we share common experiences as humans or members of a certain culture.

Warm colors are said to be aggressive, reminding us of fire and sun. They pop out at us to make strong color statements. However, if red is the color of passion, blue speaks to us of cool restraint. Cooler shades like blues and greens are said to be recessive, relaxed, and calm, reminding us of clear skies and grassy meadows at a distance. The idea that warm colors advance and cool colors recede comes from the color theory that makes it possible to create the illusion of depth in a painting.

Color as a Communication Tool

Color has a spoken language of its own. We often use colorful terms to add emphasis and flavor to our thoughts. For example, an expression like "true blue" suggests loyalty; "royal purple" suggests a color once worn only by kings, queens, and members of their courts; "seeing red" denotes angry or passionate feelings; white stands for purity; and black represents depression or mourning. However, you must remember that this is how particular colors signify meaning in Western cultures. Other cultures apply different significance to certain colors. For example, white is worn by brides in Western cultures, but in some Eastern cultures, red is the color for bridal wear because it is a festive color that brings good luck. Certainly, visual merchandisers and store designers working for international chains must be aware of these factors.

Colors may take on names of their own over time. This generally occurs through association with something that people who share a nationality or language recognize as universal. Prussian blue came from dye color used in making that country's national military uniform at one time. Wedgwood blue takes its name from a characteristic gray-blue glaze used to create the famous English pottery with classic white figures and shapes. Chartreuse is both the name of a yellow-green color and the name of a well-known tinted liqueur.

A **monochromatic scheme** consists of a single color in different values and intensities.

An **analogous scheme** consists of two or more colors that are next to each other (adjacent) on the color wheel.

A **complementary scheme** consists of two colors that are directly opposite each other on the color wheel.

A **split-complementary scheme** consists of three colors—one central color plus the two colors on either side of its color wheel complement.

A **double-complementary scheme** consists of four colors—two colors plus their complements.

A **triadic scheme** consists of three colors that are equidistant from one another on the color wheel.

In the late 1960s, a popular maroon color was paired with navy for several seasons in both men's and women's fashion. Each season, that same color was given a new name. One season it was called wild onion, another year it was called burgundy, in another year it was called beet root. This is how copywriters gave a fresh impression to a color that had a remarkably long selling cycle.

Color is a powerful visual element. It can set mood, emphasize features, and highlight a product. In print advertising, research indicates that color increases an ad's attention-getting and recall powers. Certain color combinations have been used for so long that seeing them makes us automatically think of a specific season or occasion—red and green at Christmas; black and orange at Halloween; red and pink for Valentine's Day; or red, white, and blue for Independence Day. However, color can be fickle, too. One fashion season's "in" color can be "out" in the next.

Color in Store Décor

Retailers who build a very current color trend into their store's décor may find themselves looking dated in a very short time—probably before the décor itself is even paid for. Most design practitioners urge caution when selecting storewide color schemes even though the current décor cycle may only be five years in length.

Greg Gorman, store designer and author of *The Visual Merchandising and Store Design Workbook*, suggests that initial store design should use an overall neutral palette that can be "punched up" with colorful accents in key presentation areas within the store or department. For example, colored acrylic bins could be utilized for folded products on white walls to complement the coloration of each seasonal merchandise shift without locking the store into a single overall color presentation (Figure 3.4).

Figure 3.4 Colored display shadow boxes in Marni, Spain, can easily be repainted in the future for a dramatic new look. WWD / © Conde Nast.

Another school of thought on color in store décor emerged in the twenty-first century. Most store environments had been "white boxes" for more than twenty years, but suddenly retailers began to energize their stores with all manner of wall coverings, murals, and bright-colored paint. Issey Miyake featured a colorful, exotic, floor-to-ceiling mural in its Tribeca store. Miu Miu, Swiss Army, Puma, BCBG, and scores of others in New York City painted many of their walls bright red. Paul & Joe on Bond Street in New York City installed black boards and decorated them with colored-chalk illustrations. As fashion apparel and accessories became more neutral in color, retailers infused energy into their selling environments with a wide variety of finishes and textures on their walls, floors, and fixtures.

Color as a Fashion Merchandising Strategy

Retailers promote different color schemes each season. They may introduce new shades of a currently popular color or select an entirely different palette (selection of colors). Standard colors may be combined in unusual ways. These color schemes should be featured in highly visible areas of the store, like store entrances, department entrances, along aisles, in windows, or on interior displays, so that customers can find them easily. If the colors are part of a national trend, or have been aggressively promoted through advertising, customers will be looking for them.

Once customers have entered a store, the next visual merchandising challenge is to draw them through the entire store to the back walls. Experience tells us that, on average, customers pass through only the first third of the store and then exit unless something entices them to stay. If merchandise displays with colorful impact are used throughout the store, it is more likely that the customer will be drawn from one area to the next. The more merchandise customers are able to see and touch, the more likely they are to make purchases—a critical merchandising goal.

It is important to note that color trends are not limited to clothing. Fashion merchandise within a store is generally divided into departments. A store may have a dress department, an accessory department, several sportswear departments, menswear and children's departments, plus gift and housewares departments, among others. Each merchandise category will have its own seasonal differences along with unique fashion and color trends.

In smaller shops, merchandise is often segmented in some way to provide easier shopping. In a gift shop, for example, you might find sections containing candles and candleholders grouped on shelves, or greeting cards, calendars, or small books gathered together in central locations. These are **functional groupings** that pay attention to end use. You might also find a particular brand of gifts grouped in an area. These are **branded groupings**. In other key display areas of the same store, unrelated items might be grouped to create a **color story**. One place where this is particularly effective is in an antique shop where a variety of odds and ends are pulled together to form a merchandise grouping by color. You might see a corner featuring green Depression glass dishes, enameled spatterware pots and pans, hand-painted cloth napkins, silken lampshades, and embroidered bed linens displayed together in a green story. In another corner, you might find items drawn together by their common red, white, and blue accents.

The self-explanatory terms that cover these merchandising techniques are *color-coordinated grouping* and *color-keyed product statement*. Color-keyed groupings provide ease of selection for customers who may not have time to research current color trends and often do not have confidence in their ability to coordinate colors effectively. Look at Figure 3.5 for examples of fashions and housewares grouped by color.

A **functional grouping** of merchandise is segmented according to its end use.

A **branded grouping** is merchandise from a single designer or manufacturer that is displayed together in an area set off on the selling floor.

A **color story** is a color-coordinated or color-keyed product grouping that often shows how to use a season's trend colors.

Figure 3.5a Bright hot pink and bright blue jackets are combined with neutral black and neutral denim blue, delivering an easy-to-shop presentation at H&M, Tokyo. WWD / © Conde Nast.

Figure 3.5b At Crate & Barrel, brightly colored towels are presented together. Notice the towels are arranged by color according to Roy G. Bv: red, orange, yellow, green, blue. Judy Bell.

Bell's How-to of Color Coordination

When author Judy Bell was writing training materials for a chain of specialty stores where she was the visual director, she developed a set of color guidelines that established a uniform merchandising policy for all stores. She organized colors into seven groups according to the intensity of color, like brights, pastels, etc. She had observed that merchants traditionally introduced color groups of merchandise seasonally: pastels in spring, brights and midtones in summer, jewel tones in fall, and muted/dusty colors, earthtones, and neutrals in winter. Next, she arranged the colors within the first six groups according to the rainbow and used the mnemonic device ROY G. BV as a tool to remember the color order.

Why did she choose ROY G. BV rather than ROY G. BIV? Jude Stewart explains the origin of the mnemonic device in his book: "*ROY G. BIV, An Exceedingly Surprising Book About Color*." He explains that Newton, with his Enlightenment-era mind, believed that: "the colors of the rainbow needed to match Descarte's seven-tone musical scale. So while he observed the same rainbow colors that we do— red, orange, yellow, green, blue, and violet— Newton shoehorned "indigo" into the list to bring the number of spectral colors to seven."

Bell held that "indigo" (think blue denim jeans) was in fact a neutral color. Every one of the colors in the six groups she had identified coordinated with blue denim/indigo, so it was a natural fit for the neutral color group. She also thought it was confusing to have both blue and indigo in the same line-up as part of the first six groups, since they are both a form of blue. She pulled indigo from ROY G. BIV and added it to the neutral group, then employed the mnemonic device: ROY G. BV. Newton would probably be proud; at least Bell maintained seven groups of color in her system, even though she scissored the "I" from his Roy G. Biv!

The following step-by-step directions give you Bell's practical guidelines for merchandising by color in today's retail operations

1. Divide the colors of products into groups according to their color intensity. There are seven common color groups (Figure 3.6).
   - **Brights**—the clearest, most vivid primary color intensities
   - **Pastels**—colors with added white to lighten and soften their effect
   - **Midtones**—not bright and not pastel, just in-between values
   - **Jewel tones**—royal colors

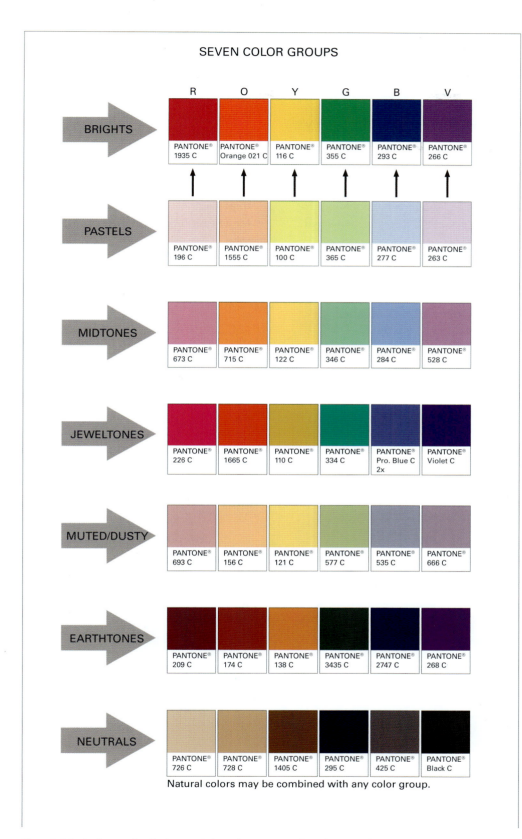

SEVEN COLOR GROUPS

BRIGHTS

R	O	Y	G	B	V
PANTONE® 1935 C	PANTONE® Orange 021 C	PANTONE® 116 C	PANTONE® 355 C	PANTONE® 293 C	PANTONE® 266 C

PASTELS

PANTONE® 196 C	PANTONE® 1555 C	PANTONE® 100 C	PANTONE® 365 C	PANTONE® 277 C	PANTONE® 263 C

MIDTONES

PANTONE® 673 C	PANTONE® 715 C	PANTONE® 122 C	PANTONE® 346 C	PANTONE® 284 C	PANTONE® 528 C

JEWELTONES

PANTONE® 226 C	PANTONE® 1665 C	PANTONE® 110 C	PANTONE® 334 C	PANTONE® Pro. Blue C 2x	PANTONE® Violet C

MUTED/DUSTY

PANTONE® 693 C	PANTONE® 156 C	PANTONE® 121 C	PANTONE® 577 C	PANTONE® 535 C	PANTONE® 666 C

EARTHTONES

PANTONE® 209 C	PANTONE® 174 C	PANTONE® 138 C	PANTONE® 3435 C	PANTONE® 2747 C	PANTONE® 268 C

NEUTRALS

PANTONE® 726 C	PANTONE® 728 C	PANTONE® 1405 C	PANTONE® 295 C	PANTONE® 425 C	PANTONE® Black C

Natural colors may be combined with any color group.

Figure 3.6 Notice how each color in rows 2 through 5 corresponds to the color above it. For example, pink, in the pastel row, corresponds to red in the bright row; pastel peach corresponds to bright orange, and so on. You can easily remember the color order of the rainbow by using the mnemonic device: Roy G. Bv. Elaine Wencl Art.

- **Muted/dusty**—midtones with added gray
- **Earthtones**—the colors of the earth: sand, rust, brown
- **Neutrals**—colors that blend with every color group

2. Combine the colors within each group to create color schemes. Colors of the same intensity blend together harmoniously. For example, look at the flower arrangement in Figure 3.7a. Flowers in several bright colors are combined in a pleasing arrangement.

3. Do not combine colors from the various groups together, except for neutrals.

Neutral colors can be combined with colors from any of the color groups. Look at the floral arrangement in Figure 3.7b. Flowers in bright colors have been combined with a pastel—pink. The colors do not blend harmoniously; they are not of the same intensity. Now look at Figure 3.8 to see one bright color, hot pink, combined with three neutrals—white, gray, and black— for a beautiful presentation that is easy to shop.

Color Systems

There are two color-related professional organizations with websites that you should

Figure 3.7a A floral arrangement with harmonious color is achieved by combining colors from one color group: brights. Judy Bell.

Figure 3.7b The combination of brightly colored flowers in red, orange, and yellow is not harmonious with one pastel pink flower (right). Judy Bell.

know about and visit. The decisions they make will affect your work in many ways. The Color Marketing Group (CMG) is an international association of color designers involved in the use of color applied to the profitable marketing of goods and services. Its members are qualified color designers who interpret, create, forecast, and select colors for manufactured products. Go to www.colormarketing.org, where you will find a valuable glossary of terms and overview of the organization's color forecasting process.

At the website of the organization Pantone LLC you will find useful information about color along with a discussion of the company's role in developing and marketing products for the accurate communication of color for color-conscious industries like textiles, plastics, graphic arts, and film and video technology. The Pantone Matching System (PMS) is an internationally recognized color-coding system of pre-mixed colors, introduced in the 1960s.

Each Pantone color is identified by a specific number, making it much easier for designers and manufacturers to communicate clearly about production details. You will find them at www.pantone.com. A quick trip to their site will give you "must-have" color trend information, such as the introduction of the Autumn/Winter 2020/2021 PANTONE Color Palette, which lists colors like Amberglow, Samba, and Sandstone, colors that will combine well with the 2020 Pantone Color of the Year, Classic Blue, #19-4052.

TEXTURE AS A MERCHANDISING STRATEGY

"Look but don't touch." You probably heard this often as a child because children experience the world through all of their senses—even when it makes their parents nervous. In *Why We Buy*, in the chapter titled "The Sensual Shopper," researcher Paco Underhill says,

Reflecting a "less is more" mindset that is becoming increasingly important to consumers prioritizing value and functionality, our color palette is stripped of excess. Imbued with strength and personality, colors for Autumn/Winter 2020/2021 encourage our ongoing desire for unique self-expression through creative and unusual statements that stand out.
Leatrice Eisman, Executive Director, Pantone Color Institute

Figure 3.8 Three neutral colors—white, gray, black—are combined with bright pink for an easy mix-and-match shopping experience in Victoria's Secret. WWD / © Conde Nast.

BOX 3.2

Designers' Pet Peeves

VM's routinely walk shopping streets and malls together to evaluate their competition. Over the years, text author Judy Bell noted that everyone had their own favorite pet peeves. This is the first in a series of typical "eyebrow raisers" that you will find in many of the chapters that follow. All of the photos were shot "as-is" in well-known retailers.

Let's talk about first impressions—look at the table presentation that greets shoppers as they enter the store. What do you think this table says about the store's brand image? Name a few adjectives that come to mind. What about the way the colors of tops are presented? Are they following ROY G. BV?

Here are five suggestions to turn this one-star presentation into five stars:

1. There are at least seven different styles of tops on this table. The lacy spaghetti strap tops and the cut-out tops are difficult to fold and are not good candidates for a table. They are presented better on hangers. The other styles on the table are sold down. The first table at the store entrance should feature just one style of top that is fully stocked, not an odd assortment as shown in the photo.

   Clear the table except for the jeans, and select new t-shirts for the presentation. Choose just one color group for the table, like all earthtones or all dusty/muted colors, etc.

2. Fold two colors of t-shirts on the short top shelf. Arrange by ROY G. BV. Example: wine, forest green.

3. Present only folded jeans on the second shelf. Arrange from left to right beginning with black and ending with white.

4. Present six vertical rows of t-shirts on the large bottom shelf, using ROY G. BV color order from left to right

like the earthtones: wine, rust, forest green, purple, followed by neutrals black and cream.

5. Dress mannequins in rust and purple shirts in ROY G. BV order from left to right. Hide any tags.

What kind of first impression does this table presentation make?
Photo by Judy Bell

The purest example of human shopping I know of can be seen by watching a child go through life touching absolutely everything.

You're watching that child shop for information, for understanding, for knowledge, for experience, for sensation.

He adds that shopping is "more than what we call the 'grab and go'—you need cornflakes, you go to the cornflakes, you grab the cornflakes, and have a nice day," he

Figure 3.9 The unique variation of materials in this display at Yuta Powell Plaza—smooth, shiny bracelets, soft fabric bags, floral embellishments, and twisted rope drawstrings—evokes textures that beg to be touched. Iannaccone / WWD / © Conde Nast.

explains. "The kind of activity I mean involves experiencing that portion of the world that has been deemed for sale, using our senses—sight, touch, smell, taste, hearing—as the basis for choosing this or rejecting that." (See Figure 3.9.)

Today more than ever, people buy things based on trial and touch. If a product's tactile qualities are its most important feature, shoppers must know for themselves how the product feels. Think about all the plastic-wrapped packages of merchandise you see broken open on store shelves. People want to touch merchandise. And while some **textures** are easy to visualize, some require hands-on experience. In fact, Underhill's research found that some new Americans who hadn't grown up with US–style brand advertising for lotions,

soaps, and shampoos "tore into the boxes or opened the bottles to test the viscosity and scent of the products."

Think of all this in terms of customer response. As Underhill points out,

Touch and trial are more important than ever to the world of shopping because of changes in how stores function. Once upon a time store owners and salespeople were our personal guides to the merchandise they sold. They were knowledgeable enough, and there were enough of them, to act as the shopper's intermediary to the world of things . . . when space was clearly divided between shoppers and staff.

texture is how a surface actually feels to the touch or how it appears that it might feel if touched. For example, roughness and smoothness may be readily visible but softness and hardness may require actual physical contact. Textures are often compared or contrasted in a display of merchandise.

Figure 3.11 An exciting ceiling treatment leads shoppers through Issey Miyake on Madison Avenue in New York City. Ericksen / WWD / © Conde Nast.

line—graphic stripes or arrows—can create a very active rhythm or feeling within a retail space that will guide your eye into and through it. Line is an integral part of rhythm in the composition of a visual presentation. Used effectively, linear elements direct or guide the shopper's visual trip through an entire selling area or stand-alone display.

Vertical lines send a message of dignity, strength, and height. In architecture, a few strategically repeated vertical structural columns hold up entire buildings. People who "walk tall" are society's models for ideal posture. In fact, the taller the fashion model or mannequin, the more refined and elegant the garment shown appears to be.

Diagonal lines speak of action and make us think of rockets launching, jets taking off, and arrows starting their arcs through the air. These could be effective mood-makers in sporting goods, active sportswear, and toy departments. Zigzagging lines are diagonals that are so active that they're almost frenzied. Think of cartoon lightning bolts or the pattern cut into

fabric with pinking shears and you have the idea of zigzag activity.

Horizontal lines are much more restful than verticals and diagonals. They remind us of landscapes and seascapes that seem to go on forever. The status quo (a state of equilibrium) is represented graphically as a flat line. An interior designer who wants to downplay the height of a room to make it feel smaller and more intimate will cut the unwanted vertical impression with horizontal color borders or architectural moldings.

Curved lines—which speak of graceful, relaxed, and carefree movement—can establish a sense of femininity in a department devoted to women's intimate apparel, fine jewelry, cosmetics, a bridal shop, or a maternity wear department. Curves added to checkout counters and fixtures in a department soften the total effect of otherwise masculine, hard-edged construction materials. Study the photographs for displays in Figure 3.12. You will notice that the lines lend a sense of direction and in some cases action to the areas where they're used.

Figure 3.12a Horizontal shelves of shoes become a showstopper when combined with vertical lines of cables that extend from floor to ceiling in Holt Renfrew, Calgary (left). Ericksen / WWD / © Conde Nast.

Figure 3.12b Beautiful architectural curves in the staircase at Mark Shale, Chicago, create a perfect feature area for display of men's products (top right). WWD / © Conde Nast.

Figure 3.12c Vertical, horizontal, and diagonal lines come together at Kate Spade, Manhattan, for an unforgettable shopping environment (bottom). WWD / © Conde Nast.

Figure 3.15 An eye-catching series of similar mannequins in sequence strengthens merchandise theme and brand image. Kasuga / WWD / © Conde Nast.

Figure 3.16 Stretched sheer fabric is used to employ the design element of tension at Harvey Nichols in London. Photo by WindowsWear. Copyright WindowsWear Inc., http://www.windowswear.com, contact@windowswear.com.

There are artists whose goal is to disrupt traditional composition and challenge the viewer to rethink balance and design elements within their works. Artist Salvador Dali, the surrealist painter, used striking and often bizarre images like melting, drooping clocks in his paintings. He purposely created images that appeared to be organized so that viewers saw what he wanted them to see, but he also introduced elements of chaos within the painting so that viewers had to put forth extra effort to explore and fully appreciate it. In many ways, chaos was Dali's artistic trademark.

Simon Doonan was the energetic force behind Barneys' windows in Manhattan for decades. He puts his own personal spin on this important art principle in his book, *Confessions of a Window Dresser*:

> To elicit shock or surprise from a window shopper is not hard at all; people still write and complain about bare midriffs and cigarette-wielding

mannequins. This is where the artists' intuition and feelings about their subjects enter the equation. I have taken advantage of the lowered threshold that attends my métier, and I have toyed with naughtiness in order to increase the impact of my windows. Occasionally my desire to shock has collided problematically with the hyper-offendability of American culture, but has also provided the foundation for my success.

Your displays can do the same with shoppers' minds by creating a certain amount of imbalance, subtle humor, or tension that can make an image more memorable—but it would be prudent to do so with your store's mission and vision always in mind.

Design Principles—The Rules

Once you are familiar with the array of design elements available, you can apply them strategically within the discipline of the various design principles so that shopper attention is directed where you want it to go. That might mean focusing on a single item of merchandise, on an entire product category, a certain selling fixture, a display window, a storefront, or a specific retail department.

▌UNITY AND HARMONY AS A MERCHANDISING STRATEGY

Unity means one-ness. Dictionary definitions often treat *unity* and *harmony* as synonymous terms. As a principle of art, **unity** occurs when all of the elements of a presentation combine to make a balanced, harmonious, complete *whole*. In retail store design and presentation, unity is achieved when a cohesive relationship among fixtures, props, and merchandise is established. Therefore décor elements must be compatible, or in harmony, with the merchandise that is for sale, in order to create a unified whole. (See Figure 3.17.)

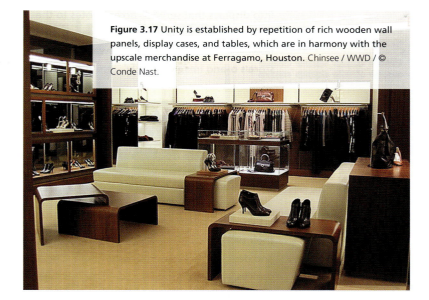

Figure 3.17 Unity is established by repetition of rich wooden wall panels, display cases, and tables, which are in harmony with the upscale merchandise at Ferragamo, Houston. Chinsee / WWD / © Conde Nast.

Harmony is an art element that creates visible unity on many levels. That is a serious challenge to visual merchandisers because it is so easy to forget that the single department they're working in is part of an entire store, or that the single display they're constructing is but one part of an entire department. You must keep the store's overall brand image and merchandising goals in mind the entire time you're working. Resist the temptation to create little islands of blinding brilliance that pay homage to your own cleverness as a visual merchandiser because storewide design and presentation harmony will suffer if you don't.

This doesn't mean that there is no room for creative expression in your work. In fact, the really effective creative person will find ways to insert humorous, surprising, or ironic elements

harmony is an art element that creates visible unity. A careful selection of complementary interwoven elements creates a unified whole in keeping with a store's overall brand image.

unity occurs when all of the elements of a presentation combine to make a balanced, harmonious, complete whole.

Be sure that your creative endeavors are in harmony with your company's visual policies and company brand image before you invest time and resources in anything radically different from what's usual for your store.

retail realities

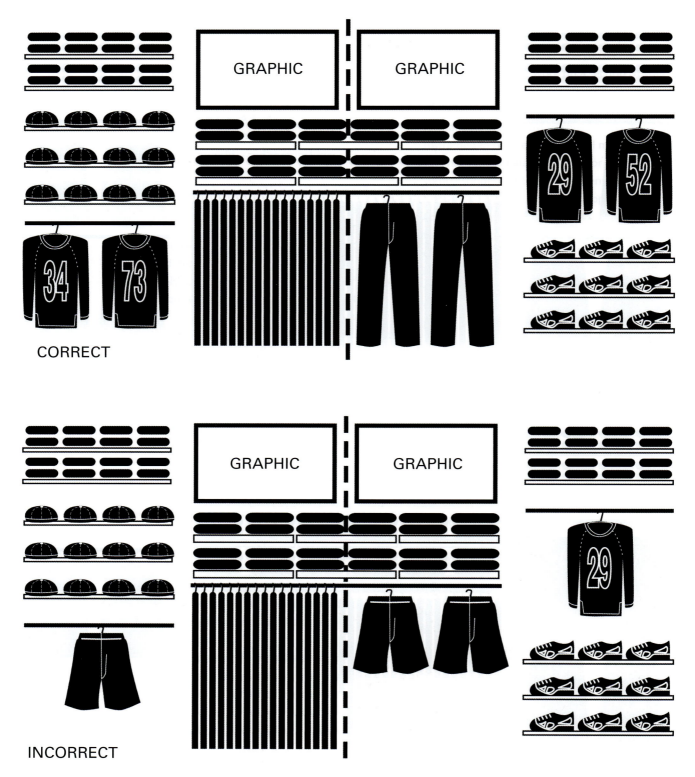

CORRECT

INCORRECT

Figure 3.19 A fashion apparel wall presentation. In the correct example, informal balance is achieved because an equal amount of space is filled on either side of a center line. This does not occur in the incorrect example. Elaine Wencl Art.

REPETITION AS A MERCHANDISING STRATEGY

Repetition has become a familiar display technique in recent presentation trends. Ranks of identical mannequins march in line on selling floors and in windows. Why? Repetition does in display the same thing it does in words and images: it reinforces your message and provides unity and harmony. How? It creates "patterns" of elements that together build a visual unit. You can see in Figure 3.20 how powerful the repeated pattern of identical seated mannequins can be in establishing a sense of order and emphasis. Notice also the way that the crossed legs of the mannequins create "rhythm."

RHYTHM AS A MERCHANDISING STRATEGY

Musicians aren't the only ones who use rhythm in their art. Just as you find yourself tapping your foot to a compelling drumbeat, your displays can impart feelings of movement and rhythm to those who see them. In visual merchandising, **rhythm** can be defined as a sense of visual movement from item to item and element to element in a single display or presentation of an entire department. This movement can come as a result of the effects of lines, shapes, or colors as well as varying heights, lines, and forms used in the overall display's design. Rhythm does not require mechanical animation. Instead, it relies on the viewer's eye following the patterns established by the composition of the design (Figure 3.21).

Rhythm can be understood by taking a panoramic look at a specialty store from the front entrance. If you notice a sea of fixtures of the same height (without any signing to break the horizon), the optical flow of rhythm would be absent. To create visual rhythm, heights of fixtures can be varied. An even stronger sense of rhythm can be created by adding displays

> **repetition** is achieved when recurring design elements like size, color, or shape create a visual pattern that establishes a sense of order and emphasis in a presentation.
>
> **rhythm** is achieved by repetition of design elements that can create a unique sense of visual cadence or emphasis for the viewer. The eye travels along the paths of repeated items and the merchandising message is reinforced.

Figure 3.20 Identical mannequins are repeated to create a show-stopping display at Diane von Furstenberg's flagship in Manhattan. Seckler / WWD / © Conde Nast.

A capstone project is often described as the high point or crowning achievement of a course of study—something that demonstrates that you've mastered the subject matter. Even more important, a well-executed capstone demonstrates that you can *apply* what you've learned. "But wait," you say, "This is just the beginning of the course! Only three chapters so far! Isn't it way too soon to be thinking about the end?" Not necessarily. If you think of this course as a blueprint for a retail career and consider each chapter a career building block, you're going to want a final project to finish it in style.

These first chapters have started you thinking about the creativity involved in designing a one-of-a-kind shopping experience. Now ask yourself, "How great would it be to have a well-developed portfolio piece to show a prospective employer?" It could happen with this project.

Since you've just learned about Judy Bell's *Look, Compare, Innovate* model, you should begin by visiting stores, seeing what's out there in today's retail marketplace, checking out store concepts that are doing well, and picking out appealing features and great ideas that you could later modify for an innovative store concept of your own.

Then, while you are exploring all of the concepts discussed at length in the rest of the text, you'll also be well on your way to creating an innovative retail design—on paper, at least. You will consider retail atmospherics (how stores "feel" when you're in them), the various types of retail stores in today's marketplace, how they're laid out (traffic patterns and merchandise arrangements), how they're furnished and fixtured, and how to make the most of every square foot of selling space. You'll also examine displays of apparel, home furnishing products, sporting goods, and even food products. Something can be learned from every merchandising category out there today—and you may discover something interesting and useful to adapt for use in your dream store, no matter what you're going to sell.

Most of the heavy lifting required for this project comes at its outset—fairly early in the course. Once you have considered the start-up elements for your project store, the remaining assignments correspond to the rest of the text's chapters. You'll find them at the end of each of the first five parts of the text.

Creating and Communicating a Capstone Brand Image

This project concerns a fictional retail opportunity that has many real-world counterparts. In the introductory stage, you're asked to think about a store concept that appeals to you today. Begin to imagine what you might do to bring the concept to life.

Let your imagination take you away. Keep in mind that this capstone challenges you to use information and ideas from all of the chapters in this textbook. Don't be afraid to read ahead. You can always edit your initial imaginings during the first three or four weeks. Most importantly, have fun.

THE SITUATION

Assume that you are an owner, store designer, or visual merchandising executive in a new stand-alone retail store that will be located in a midsized metropolitan area with a well-developed downtown business district. You have a long-term lease on the main floor of a modern-looking brick-front retail building that has 3,500 square feet (50 feet wide × 70 feet deep) on its main floor. It has a pair of (9 × 8-foot) windows set on either side of a generous double-door entry (for a total of four windows). The store's interior is completely open and undecorated—literally a blank page for you to work with in developing a retail concept build-out.

Assume that you will seek financial resources from venture capital investors or from a financial institution. Each of this project's required elements could help you prepare a formal business plan like those required of all start-ups.

Section One

This is the *look* and *compare* (research) stage of the capstone project. It corresponds to Judy Bell's *Look, Compare, Innovate* approach to visual merchandising. Here's a tip: begin to write down your ideas—commit them to print, so that you won't lose any brilliant thoughts about your project store. In the initial phase of the capstone, you will articulate your own merchandising philosophy—describing in some detail what you believe a successful retail entity should be. You will then be able to draw upon these ideas as your project planning progresses.

Innovate based on your reading of Chapters 1 and 2 as well as your prior knowledge of marketing practices. Ask yourself:

- What is happening in the economy (national and local) that could influence any store's success?
- What is happening culturally (national and local) that could influence any store's success?
- What kind of store have I always wanted to own?
- Are there any stores like it in my community today?
- Are they doing well in the competitive marketplace?
- What do I think makes these stores successful?
- Is there a retail business that is *not* in the community but should be?
- Is there a group of potential buyers that is *not* being served but should be?

STEP 1:

Create a unique customer profile for your capstone store. Prepare a fully developed paragraph for each of the following:
- Age, gender, geographic location, family life cycle status (single, married, divorced, etc.), and educational level
- Lifestyle and personal interests (hobbies, leisure activities)
- Occupation and income
- Any other demographic and psychographic factors that you believe will influence your potential customer's buying power and buying decisions

If you have not yet completed a basic marketing course or an advertising and sales promotion course, you may need to do some catch-up reading to handle this section of the project effectively.

Hint: To understand market research that an entrepreneur might use, visit relevant websites, including www.census.gov, before you draw any conclusions about your capstone store's imaginary target customer. Work with your instructor on which websites are best for your course and which ones your library subscribes to in order to find the following market information:

- Who are the targets?
- What are they like?
- Where can I find them?
- How can I reach them?

If you begin your research with www.census .gov, you can find demographic and income information about each local area you want to research.

STEP 2:

Select a merchandise category that you think you'll enjoy researching and working with for this project. Hint: Focusing on a well-defined merchandise category will be easier and more instructive than trying to plan for a general store. Refer to the profile you've just completed. With that potential customer in mind, select your own store idea. Or, instead, look, compare, and innovate using the following list as a starting point:

- A bridal and special occasion shop
- A men's shop for business wear, specialty sport, clothing, and/or sports equipment; or big and tall clothing
- A women's clothing shop specializing in athletic apparel, business wear, or tall, petite, or curvy sizes
- A vintage clothing or home furnishings store
- A tween shop aimed at girls from nine to thirteen years of age
- A specialty bookstore—selling only mysteries, travel books, poetry, or cookbooks
- A specialty tabletop store—featuring merchandise for setting a table and serving food
- A luggage store—with everything needed for travel from carry-on bags and pet carriers to footlockers and wardrobe trunks
- An antiques store specializing in lighting fixtures and lamps
- An ethnic design shop featuring textiles, needlework, art, and handcrafts from another culture
- A plant store or floral design shop
- A greengrocer, artisan bakery, or other food specialty shop
- A restaurant, pub, or fast-food operation

STEP 3:

Now that you have a mental snapshot of your target customers and the store concept you want to develop:

- Compose a mission statement that would explain its purpose to those customers.
- List at least five marketing objectives that your capstone store must achieve and a number of related strategies to meet each objective. Be sure to include the visual merchandising component in one of your objectives.

STEP 4:

- Select a name for your new store.
- Explain how the store's name will help you communicate the brand image ideas you've generated to attract potential customers— for example, what does the name you've chosen communicate about the owner, the business, or the merchandise?

STEP 5:

Describe the store's brand image (how you want potential customers to perceive your store). As you write, think of your store's proposed physical appearance as well as the overall feel you hope to achieve.

Mission statement (no more than one or two sentences), vision statement (what will distinguish your company from others), and brand image should always be compatible and reflect one another.

Section Two

It's time to sample your capstone store's merchandise, using photographs or illustrations from non-textbook sources and including items from *all categories* you intend to stock. For example, if you're doing a food operation, you'll need to develop a fairly comprehensive sample menu; if you're doing a clothing store, you'll need a sampling of a fashion inventory in all applicable merchandise categories.

If you prepare a comprehensive cut-and-paste scrapbook to house your merchandise choices, you'll have a useful reference for the remaining assignments.

STEP 1:

- Describe store merchandise. Select key items that will fully illustrate your merchandising intentions.
- Name each department or merchandise category.

STEP 2:

- List and show examples of items that will be stocked in *each category* (department) you intend to offer. One or two example garments per category will give viewers a minimal feel for your store.
- As you build your inventory on paper, you should see a harmonious overall theme emerging that reflects your potential customer's taste as well as your stated mission and brand image. Be prepared to justify your merchandise choices with those factors in mind.

Part Two   PRACTICES AND STRATEGIES FOR THE SELLING FLOOR

Creating Retail Atmosphere

Think of a retail store as a box that's enclosed by ceiling, walls, windows, and floor. The strategic design of the store involves its exterior aspect (storefront and surroundings) and its interior (walls, floors, windows, doors, signage, lighting, furniture, and fixtures) as well as the arrangement of merchandise, fixtures, and displays on the selling floor. The total effect of these elements creates a statement about what shoppers will find in the box—retail atmosphere.

Effective store designs link store atmospherics with management's merchandising philosophies to offer a pleasant, productive shopping experience. The retail store should always be more than a place for a shopper to exchange money for products. It should also be the best place to inspect and interact with products—trying before buying. Nothing about a store's design or layout should interfere with that process. When shoppers leave retail stores with products they have purchased, they may not realize that they have bought the entire retail experience as well, but that's really what has happened.

Gian Luigi Longinotti-Buitoni, author of *Selling Dreams: How to Make Any Product Irresistible*, believes that successful dream sellers should create products and services that convey intense emotions. They should also do everything possible to enhance customers' perceptions of added value. For example, if customers believe there is more to a store than just a building and merchandise, they will happily shop there and pay whatever prices are asked. Buitoni's term for the marketing of dreams is "dreamketing." He says, "The

"Visual excitement is truly achieved once the key focal areas of the 'box' are determined and then occupied with stimulating and attractive fixtures. They become the merchandising tools and partners with products and signage . . . for a successful design that increases sales and word-of-mouth marketing." *Greg M. Gorman, vice president, new business development, Triad*

AFTER COMPLETING THIS CHAPTER, YOU SHOULD BE ABLE TO

- Identify the different types of retail stores
- Demonstrate how and why floor department layouts are planned
- Categorize a wide variety of floor and wall fixtures
- Present garments and accessories on fixtures

Figure 4.0ab These two gallery-like minimal floor layouts present product as though it were fine art. Sonia Rykiel, 5th Avenue, New York. WindowsWear Photo. Copyright WindowsWear Inc., http://windowswear.com, contact@windowswear.com.

dreamketer should ensure that the company's communication, distribution, special events, and any type of customer relations consistently support the brand's mission to build that dream in the customer's mind."

Fixturing (furnishing) stores is an aesthetic and financial challenge for successful retailers. They want their stores to be attractive and effectively communicate their unique messages about their stores' brand image and merchandise to shoppers, yet they want to do it economically. An expensive store design does not guarantee an effective store environment.

Effective store design places merchandise and customer service at the heart of the effort. At the same time, it presents the store in a way that differentiates it from competing stores. The store's visual message must fit in with everything else the store does to communicate its brand image to the shopping public. For example, if the retail store employs a warm, friendly approach in its print marketing copy, then the shopper will expect the physical store to feel warm and friendly, too. This consistency implies that store owners and managers have a plan—a retail brand strategy.

Types of Retail Stores

There are twelve retail store categories describing the way stores may be designed, organized, or operated: department, specialty, boutique, discount, dollar stores, hypermarkets, warehouses, outlets, thrift stores, consignment stores, pop-ups, and fashion trucks.

■ DEPARTMENT STORES
Department stores consist of many departments, each devoted to a specific category (product classification). In terms of square footage, department stores are large retail operations that offer a broad variety of products and cater to an equally wide range of customers. To merchandise this expansive selection of goods and services, the department store retailer uses many styles of specialty and custom fixtures designed to showcase each merchandise category. The size of the typical department store—Bloomingdale's and Macy's, for instance—depends on the size of its basic floor plan (also called its footprint). In order to calculate basic floor plan needs, the retailer must multiply length by width for the main floor selling space footage and then multiply again by the number of similar-sized selling floors above the main floor.

■ SPECIALTY STORES
Specialty stores have a limited number of departments or merchandise categories, with a wide range of footprints. Forever 21 stores range from 900 to 162,000 square feet, but their average stores are around 38,000 square feet. Uniqlo's Soho location is 36,000 square feet, while its 5th Avenue store is over 89,000 square feet.

The specialty store's product selection is, as the term implies, more specialized or limited than that of a department store. It usually caters to a narrower range of customers, as well. The specialty retailer often uses unique fixtures and seeks to project a more exclusive store image based on appearance, price, and status.

■ BOUTIQUES
Boutiques are small specialty shops featuring assorted items that fit specific merchandising themes or appeal to a specialized clientele. You'll find entire blocks of boutiques in areas like Manhattan's Greenwich Village or on Castro Street in San Francisco. The term *boutique* may also be used to describe cross-merchandising within a department store, when retailers bring items from several departments together for a special promotion (a tropical cruisewear shop, for example, which features swimsuits, sandals, beach towels, and suntan lotion).

■ DISCOUNT STORES

Discount stores have many departments that appeal to a wide variety of customers with a wide range of products at discounted prices. They utilize mostly no-frills metal gondola fixtures (long racks of shelving or pegboard) that hold a great deal of merchandise. Discount stores may also utilize custom-made fixtures or vendor-supplied fixtures in a few departments.

Walmart discount stores come in three formats: supercenters at about 182,000 square feet, discount stores average 106,00 square feet, and neighborhood markets at around 38,000 square feet.(www.corporate.walmart.com.)

■ DOLLAR STORES

Dollar stores generally vary in size from 7,000 to 16,000 square feet. Dollar Tree prices everything at $1 while other stores' items fit into a specific range of prices. Five Below, for example, prices everything under $5, except for a selection of items priced as high as $10. In Dollar General and Dollar Tree Plus the price range is broader. Dollar stores tend to be located in communities that are too small for mass market discount retailers.

■ HYPERMARKETS

Hypermarkets (hybrid supermarkets and department stores) are concepts borrowed from European retailing. These stores are also sometimes called SuperCenters or Superstores as in Walmart Supercenter and Real Canadian Superstore. Carrefour, which originated in France more than thirty years ago, is one of the first and most famous examples of this mega-merchandising concept. Several merchandising categories are housed under one very large roof—softlines (apparel and health and beauty aids) and hardlines (home, gardening, automotive, sporting goods)—along with a grocery store. These one-stop shopping destinations can be as large as 260,000 square feet.

■ WAREHOUSE STORES

Warehouse stores—built to house massive quantities of goods on grids of industrial shelving and pallets—offer no-frills shopping at reduced prices (Sam's Club, Costco). Fashion goods may or may not be part of the stores' offerings. These stores are large, plain, fluorescent lit, and have a decidedly industrial ambiance. Fitting rooms, if they have them at all, may be utilitarian, separated only by gender. Shopping carts are oversized and, in some instances, are not really carts at all but rather low, flat hand-trucks large enough to handle furniture items or heavy cases of goods. Some warehouse stores don't even furnish bags to carry smaller purchases, assuming shoppers will make case-lot purchases rather than buy single items.

■ OUTLET STORES

Outlet stores are either stand-alone stores or small stores located in outlet malls. They use fixtures similar to those found in specialty stores, but merchandise presentation sometimes has less visual impact because stock quantities may be sold down with incomplete color, style, and size assortments. Most of the newest outlet stores, however, have presentations and fixtures that rival mainstream specialty stores. The largest outlet stores are filled with capacity fixtures for massive clearance presentations. Outlet stores may sell catalogue overstocks; manufacturers' irregulars or overstocks; or a combination of out-of-season items, special purchases, and stock consolidations from retailers who are reducing postseason inventory or from those who are going out of business. Marshalls, T.J. Maxx, Coach, Converse, Calvin Klein, Ralph Lauren, and a multitude of other retailers operate outlet stores.

■ THRIFT STORES

Thrift stores are often operated by nonprofit organizations such as Goodwill and the Salvation Army as fundraising and employment

"Target stores average about 130,000 square feet. And we're also continuing to open small-format stores, which are generally about ¼ the size of a full store (roughly 40,000 square feet), with some featuring as little as 12,000 square feet. These small-but-mighty stores allow us to serve new guests in urban and dense suburban areas and near college campuses where a traditional Target simply doesn't fit."
www.corporate.target .com.

training ventures. They often resemble garage sales with wildly assorted merchandise categories—from clothing in all sizes to small appliances to furniture and books. Their products are all donated by private citizens or business organizations. Some operations are more sophisticated than others. You may see traditional fixtures, décor, traffic patterns, and standard checkout arrangements, with displays of seasonal categories in some. In other stores, you'll see a blend of makeshift shelving and traditional fixtures. Thrift stores are generally categorized as no-frills merchandising.

■ CONSIGNMENT STORES

Consignment stores accept used items for sale from individual owners, price them and agree to pay the consignors a percentage earned if the items sell. In upscale consignment stores only the most desirable items are accepted: gently worn, dry cleaned, current season and style, and generally no older than two years. The merchandise is placed to sell for a limited time period, for example 90 days, and any unsold items may be picked up or donated to charity as the consignor desires. The average square footage of consignment stores is 3,000 square feet.

■ POP-UP STORES

Pop-up stores are temporary store concepts that blend retail with event marketing. Frequently, pop-ups are temporarily located in vacant store spaces. They may be used to launch new product lines or explore new retail approaches for existing stores. For example, Meow Mix opened a café for kitties in Manhattan for two weeks and Target docked a huge boat at a pier in the New York harbor filled with products during one holiday selling season. In many instances, pop-ups can be in and out of a site in a few days or a few weeks. However, a Limited pop-up in Soho was so successful it remained open permanently. The concept of pop-up stores has quickly become a mainstream idea because it is an effective tool for creating storytelling experiences and will undoubtedly continue to evolve in new ways.

Melissa Gonzalez, the founder of Lionesque Group in Manhattan, has launched over 150 retail pop-up experiences across the US. In her book, *The Pop Up Paradigm: How Brands Build Human Connections in a Digital Age,* she writes, "On the consumer end, pop-ups allow customers a unique experience in a lifestyle-branded environment. From the business perspective, pop-ups allow companies the chance to gather invaluable information that can be used to further grow and better the brand. Your pop-up will give you information that impacts production, pricing strategy, merchandising presentation, homepage design, email marketing, and more."

■ FASHION TRUCKS

Fashion trucks have taken a cue from the trend in food trucks, as they drive their business on wheels from one location to another. Most offer fitting rooms and even air conditioning. An obvious advantage is their ability to reach shoppers during prime selling hours, wherever they are, at a local art show, a music festival, or a farmers market. Loft Girls is a mobile fashion truck operating in Ontario Canada. www .theloftgirls.com.

Store Layouts

Over time, retailers have evolved several basic floor plans to move shoppers past fixtures of merchandise in their stores. Early on, their aim was to efficiently expose the maximum number of shoppers to the maximum amount of merchandise in the minimum amount of space and time. Today, selling space, traffic control, and sales productivity still matter, but an increasing number of retailers are paying attention to shopper comfort and store aesthetics as well.

The **grid layout**, as the name implies, is a linear design with fixtures arranged on parallel

A **grid layout** is a linear design for a selling floor in which fixtures are arranged to form vertical and horizontal aisles throughout the store.

aisles. Fixtures are positioned in a checkerboard pattern, with vertical and horizontal aisles that run throughout the store. There may also be one primary aisle and several secondary aisles, depending on the total square footage of the store. This layout is efficient in terms of space use, allows orderly stocking, helps shoppers see (and reach) a great number of items easily, is simple and predictable to navigate, and is efficient to maintain. The grid layout creates natural **sight lines**, which lead to focal points at the ends of aisles. The customers' attention naturally focuses on these areas, so visual merchandisers can take advantage of this by creating displays that act as "interior windows" (Figure 4.1).

The **free-flow layout**, shown in Figure 4.2, is the opposite of the grid pattern. In this kind of layout, merchandise fixtures are arranged in a number of interesting formations to encourage browsing. There may be several round racks grouped loosely around a central

cash wrap desk, as well as merchandise tables interspersed with four-way fixtures along a department's exposure to an aisle. The critical factor is providing enough room between fixtures to allow traffic to flow smoothly. Shoppers will not linger at a fixture if another shopper is nudging past them or trying to maneuver a baby stroller between tightly packed tables. The free-flow layout also encourages shoppers to easily move from one department into another, increasing exposure to other categories of merchandise.

Every square foot of a store must be profitable. Often retail space is leased, and rent is based on sales per square foot. When total sales ($) are divided by leased square footage (store length × store width), the merchant is able to determine productivity or sales per square foot.

This figure can be broken down to measure earnings by classification or department as well.

In store presentation, **sight line** refers to the area a person can see from a particular vantage point—the view at the end of an aisle or at the top or bottom of an escalator, for example.

The **free-flow layout** has selling fixtures arranged in loosely grouped, informal, nonlinear formations to encourage browsing.

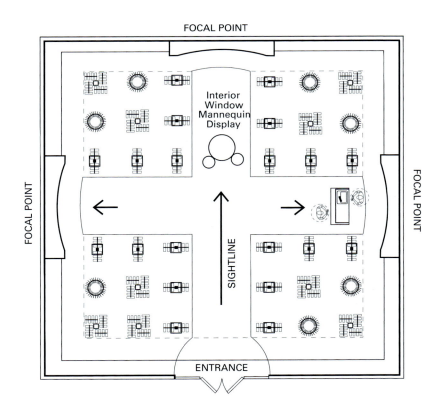

FOCAL POINT

FOCAL POINT

FOCAL POINT

Interior Window Mannequin Display

SIGHTLINE

ENTRANCE

Figure 4.1 A grid floor layout with sight lines, focal points, and an interior window. Fairchild Books/ Rendered by Craig Gustafson Art.

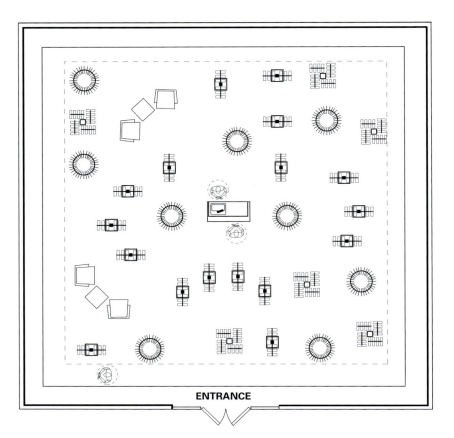

Figure 4.2 A free-flow floor layout. Fairchild Books/ Rendered by Craig Gustafson Art.

ENTRANCE

A **racetrack layout** features a traffic aisle that loops around the store's perimeter (Figure 4.3). There are departments on the right and left of the circular, square, rectangular, or oval track. This type of layout exposes shoppers to a great deal of merchandise. You often see this layout employed in a discount or department store (Figure 4.4). Overhead directional signage and departmental graphics provide visual cues to the location of other departments, helping shoppers to plan their shopping trip throughout the store.

In the **soft aisle layout**, fixtures are arranged into groups, sometimes with a 5-foot aisle along merchandised wall sections (Figure 4.5). This technique encourages customers to shop the walls and to move easily around the entire store. Walls are considered to be the most important sales-generating locations in the store utilizing this layout strategy.

The **minimal floor layout**, as the name implies, is almost like an art gallery in its simplicity. In fact, the merchandise may sometimes be wearable art—handcrafted, designer-made, in one-of-a-kind fabrications. More often, however, this layout is used in very high-end retail stores with designer merchandise. Borrowing from the artistic school of aesthetic minimalism, products are presented dramatically on the walls of the store—much like art objects—with a minimal use of selling fixtures on the floor. This allows for wide-open spaces in the center of the store, where customers may stand and survey the entire offering of the collection before they approach the merchandise for a closer look. The minimal layout option requires dramatic merchandise, simple display strategies, and effective sales associates (Figure 4.6).

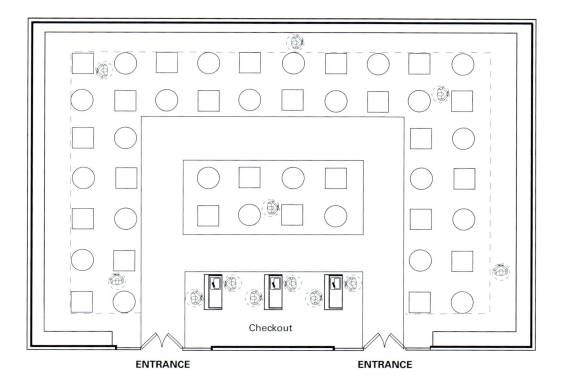

Checkout

ENTRANCE   ENTRANCE

Figure 4.3 A racetrack layout. Fairchild Books/ Rendered by Craig Gustafson Art.

Figure 4.4 Target's racetrack runs along Cat & Jack kids shop. Judy Bell.

Figure 4.7 A combination floor layout (racetrack and free-flow) in Nordstrom, Pacific Centre, Vancouver BC, Canada. Courtesy of Nordstrom, photo by Connie Zho

benefits people of all ages and abilities. To learn more, visit www.universaldesign.ie

Many of the seven principles of universal design speak to selling floor spaces: Principle one, for example, relates to "equitable use" and says that a design should be "useful and marketable to people with diverse abilities." Principle seven calls for an appropriate size and space for approach, reach, manipulation, and use regardless of the user's body size, posture, or mobility. Its guidelines include:

- Providing a clear line of sight to important elements for any seated or standing user
- Making reach to all components comfortable for any seated or standing user
- Accommodating variations in hand and grip size
- Providing adequate space for the use of assistive devices or personal assistance

LAYOUTS WITHIN SELLING DEPARTMENTS

All of the store layouts discussed can be either permanent or nonpermanent. Permanent layouts indicate that the location of departmental selling areas within a store seldom changes. Since department stores are large, often with three or more floors, it is costly to move entire departments. Even more important, customers can become confused if their favorite shopping areas constantly shift from floor to floor.

Discount stores do not usually change department locations, but they may expand or contract categories according to sales trends. A 24-foot gondola fixture with skiing gear and apparel could expand to two 24-foot gondola runs during ski season. There are usually two or three traditional "swing spaces" in discount stores, and customers soon adapt to the seasonal shift when this week's lawn and garden section becomes next month's back-to-school department. Effective directional and informational signage helps orient customers to the location of seasonal merchandise.

Several types of specialty stores maintain permanent floor layouts:

- Designer stores cater to customers who visit regularly to purchase specific brands or designer fashions. In stores featuring just one designer or brand, there are often shoes, handbags, accessories, fragrances, and cosmetics, in addition to fashion apparel. "Home bases" for these accessory departments are often designed into the architecture of the store and not easily shifted to other locations.
- Career stores for men, women, or both, are stores where suits, career separates, and shoes are the most important items featured. This merchandise is always positioned at the entrance and front of the store. Accessories, casual wear, and coats are located toward the middle and rear of the store. Ann Taylor is an example of such a store.
- Specialty stores with merchandise for both men and women rely on permanent layouts. Shoppers would become confused if these departments shifted location without notice. Examples are Banana Republic, Club Monaco, COS, Express, Gap, H&M, J. Crew, Uniqlo, and Zara.

Nonpermanent layouts imply that changes do occur. Some small-to medium-sized specialty stores and outlet stores change the locations of departments according to trends and seasonal changes. These retailers consider the front third of the store to be the prime selling space, and they take advantage of the stores' manageable size to rotate their product offerings routinely.

Seasonal rotation of stock allows stores to present:

- A fresh face to shoppers, implying that the store is very responsive to new and exciting fashion developments
- Current season or trend merchandise in cutting edge merchandising schemes that inform and invite
- Preseason merchandise at special prices in prime store locations, allowing store buyers to take an early reading on which items to buy in depth for the rest of the season

PRESENTING CURRENT SEASON MERCHANDISE

In the specialty store merchandising example that follows, the first third of the store features products that customers are currently seeking. In the floor layout shown in Figure 4.8, for March and April, the career department is positioned on the right side of the store at the entrance. This is prime selling space, and since shoppers are looking for new wear-to-work options in March and April, it seems wise to present career wear at the front of the store. There's a bonus to this move—passersby may see the presentation from outside as they approach the store and come into shop.

In Figure 4.8, you see dresses located next to the career department. Here's the strategy—if a customer is unable to make a selection in the career department, she may notice an appealing dress in the neighboring area and be drawn further into the store's selling space. This explains why selling areas must be laid out in a logical progression, often referred to as **adjacencies**.

Look at Figure 4.8 again. Casual spring sweaters, shirts, and pants are also important during March and April, so they are placed at the front of the store. For this merchant, presenting both casual and career categories at the front of the store may appeal to a wider range of shoppers. It's a workable plan because the merchant has a broad storefront. However, a store with a narrow front would present just

adjacencies are thoughtfully planned layouts that position same end-use products next to each other. A logical adjacency, for example, would be shoes and hosiery positioned side by side.

Clearance Merchandise

Clearance merchandise consists of products that have been permanently marked down for quick sale. These items may be handled in several ways:

- Clearance items may be pulled together at the rear of each department. For example, clearance suits may be positioned on one or more fixtures at the rear of the career department.
- Clearance merchandise from all departments may be pulled into one area of the store to form a permanent clearance department. This catch-all clearance department should be positioned in the rear of the store.
- Clearance merchandise in specialty stores may be pulled to the front of the store for traditional major clearance events in January or early July.
- Some chain retailers consolidate clearance merchandise into a few larger stores (with high traffic or ideal bargain shopper demographics), send it to a company-owned outlet store, or remove their own tags and sell the lot to an outlet store.

▌ CLEARANCE PRESENTATION ▌ GUIDELINES

While clearance merchandise no longer merits major promotional effort, it remains a company asset until sold. The visual merchandiser's role is to present clearance goods effectively enough to sell them at their highest possible clearance price so that the company can reinvest the dollars in newer, more appealing merchandise. The following guidelines will ensure that optimum presentation is achieved:

- Present clearance merchandise on floor fixtures only. Clearance product with **broken** styles and color assortment cannot result in a fresh, exciting wall presentation; wall space is best used for new stock. The exception is when clearance merchandise is presented on

an entirely separate clearance floor. There, you may utilize the entire space—walls and floor.

- Never feature clearance merchandise on mannequins or in displays. These are your premium silent selling tools and must be reserved for only the newest products. In addition, clearance merchandise must be immediately available to shoppers, never out of reach on display.
- Present clearance goods on large fixtures, such as round racks, superquads (extra-large four-way racks with arms that may be extended) or rolling rack fixtures. Overcrowding these fixtures is never a good strategy. If shoppers cannot easily inspect items on hangers, they will quickly abandon the bargain hunt. Clearance tables for foldable goods are very effective because there is a general perception among shoppers that clearance tables hold the best bargains.
- Sort clearance garments by size (with sizing rings or hangers with built-in size tabs) and then by color within each size range so that shoppers can readily see what is available. Example: Size 5 (red shirts, yellow shirts, and blue shirts) followed by size 7 (red shirts, yellow shirts, green shirts, and blue shirts).
- Always clearly sign clearance merchandise with **price points**, percentages-off, or at least a clearance sign.
- Make selling-floor maintenance a routine aspect of any clearance presentation. Clearance merchandise gets handled (and mishandled) continuously as shoppers look for bargains. Store staff must check clearance areas frequently, straightening sale racks, refolding table goods, checking for damaged goods and lost tickets and so on. These are aesthetic as well as security issues that tell customers how your company feels about its image, its merchandise, and its atmosphere. Customers should see clearance merchandise as an added benefit to doing business with your store. Even

---

The **price point** is the actual number (for example, $12.99) used on signs to inform shoppers of prices.

broken merchandise refers to assortments with missing sizes, styles, and colors after sell-down.

when merchandise is marked down, you should be adding value to it through your presentation.

Store Fixtures

A wide variety of fixtures is available for the presentation of products. Like the furniture in your home, each fixture type has a useful purpose (holding quantities of merchandise) and a decorative purpose (reinforcing retail décor decisions). Store fixtures include:

- Conventional metal fixtures
- Furniture fixtures
- Found objects
- Vendor fixtures
- Custom fixtures

Purchasing the store's fixtures is a fairly long-term and expensive investment—much like furnishing a home. Just as you wouldn't

retail realities

Display signs must be accurate and correspond to what's being presented, or customers will be confused about what seem to be careless or deceptive sale policies. Stores generally honor mistaken prices or sale terms—an unnecessary embarrassment and financial loss. Customer service is a visual merchandising responsibility, too.

BOX 4.2

🪢 Neuroscience Pop-Up!

Imagine you are striding past retail stores in your favorite shopping mall. Suddenly something catches your eye: Express is boasting up to 80 percent off clearance merchandise. Four mannequins dressed in vivid red t-shirts stand at attention in front of a striking red and black sale sign. Would you stop to take a closer look? Would you enter the store? If your answer is yes, there may be something more at work than meets the eye.

In his book, *RETAIL (r)EVOLUTION,* David Kepron writes about "The Pleasure Rush of Getting a Good Deal: Ideally, shopping feels good. We love the excitement of a great bargain. One thing is for sure: something very powerful is taking place during the shopping process. Within the limbic region of the brain are structures regarded as the 'reward center.' And the chemical that stimulates the pleasure that we feel: Dopamine." Kepron goes on to talk about a study by Brian Knutson and George Loewenstein at Stanford University where researchers "tried to look at the macroeconomic theory of buying decisions from the point of view of the brain." One of the results they found was that increased desire and excitement went up when price points were dropped!

Express calls out their Clearance Event with savings up to 80 percent.
Judy Bell

buy a new sofa simply because you're bored
with the one you have, visual merchandisers
expect the store fixtures they select to
perform effectively and efficiently for as
long as possible. They must choose carefully,
taking purpose, function, and durability into
consideration along with style and fabrication.

CAPACITY, FEATURE, AND SIGNATURE FIXTURES

In addition to the various types of fixtures
retailers may choose from, each fixture
category can be further differentiated by its
end use.

- **Capacity fixtures** hold large quantities—
  usually showing one style of a product
  bought in depth, like several dozen
  sweatshirts in assorted sizes from S to XXL,
  trimmed with a variety of colorful cartoon
  characters. Because capacity fixtures are
  the largest floor fixtures in the store, they
  should be positioned primarily in the rear of
  a department or store layout.

- **Feature fixtures** are designed to hold fewer
  items and are used to highlight category
  groupings or smaller coordinate groups. You
  might see a four-way fixture with a dozen
  cotton sweaters in bright yarns paired with
  matching polo shirts and walking shorts.
  Feature fixtures bring together coordinated
  outfits to make shopping easier. They are
  best used as lead-in fixtures to any fashion
  department but may also be interspersed
  throughout that department to add interest
  and variation to the layout.

- **Signature fixtures** are one-of-a-kind units
  that are positioned at the entrance to a
  store or department. Their unusual, unique
  design is created specifically to attract
  shoppers' attention. The signature fixture's
  design must reflect the brand image of the
  store, both in fabrication and style (Figures
  4.13 and 4.14).

"Ask leading retailers
about purchasing
store fixtures and they
invariably point to three
important criteria: cost,
quality, and service.
Although price of
the fixture is always
of concern, the real
priority seems to be cost
effectiveness. Retailers
want to spend the
least amount of money
possible but still meet
project expectations."
*Karen Doodeman
Callahan, former
Executive Leadership,
Shop! Association*

Figure 4.13 A signature fixture leads into an
Esprit shop. WWD / © Conde Nast.

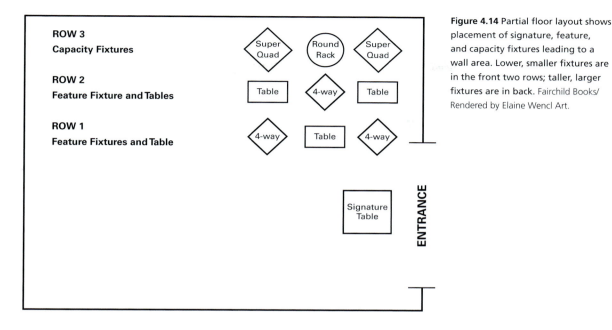

ROW 3
Capacity Fixtures

ROW 2
Feature Fixture and Tables

ROW 1
Feature Fixtures and Table

Super Quad

Round Rack

Super Quad

Table

4-way

Table

4-way

Table

4-way

Signature Table

ENTRANCE

Figure 4.14 Partial floor layout shows placement of signature, feature, and capacity fixtures leading to a wall area. Lower, smaller fixtures are in the front two rows; taller, larger fixtures are in back. Fairchild Books/ Rendered by Elaine Wencl Art.

CONVENTIONAL METAL FLOOR FIXTURES

Simple metal fixtures like round racks and T-stands have been used in retail stores throughout the twentieth century. Their design forms the basis from which custom fixtures are created, so it is important to have a solid understanding of their function. Early fixtures were fabricated in chrome, and they are still widely used today. In the 1980s and 1990s, some retailers used brushed bright black, brushed satin black, and even white finishes. Today, brushed stainless steel and buffed satin are often preferred for their softer, less reflective look, which is easier to maintain because fingerprints are less visible.

Round Racks

A **round rack (rounder)** is a capacity fixture. Its chief function is stocking basic items that have been purchased in depth. Round racks are also used to stock broken assortments and clearance merchandise. This fixture is available in several diameters and adjustable heights so that dresses and pants can be presented with their hems an adequate distance from the floor (Figure 4.15).

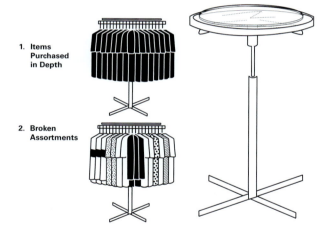

1. **Items Purchased in Depth**

2. **Broken Assortments**

Figure 4.15 A round rack with two common functions. Fairchild Books/Rendered by Elaine Wencl Art.

You can easily determine fixture fill for a round rack by measuring the circumference. A 36-inch diameter round rack is 118 inches in circumference. It can comfortably hold 118 tops or bottoms. A 42-inch diameter round rack is 136 inches in circumference, and it could hold 136 tops or bottoms. If garments are thinner, like T-shirts, the quantities increase; if they are thicker, like winter coats, the capacity will decrease.

A **round rack** (or rounder) is a capacity fixture fabricated in several diameters and adjustable heights for stocking basic apparel items.

Presentation Guidelines for Round Racks

- Round racks should not be positioned at the store entrance or along aisles except during special promotional and clearance events. At those times it may be effective to line them up along the aisles or down the center of the store.

- Sleeve lengths and hem lengths should be the same on the entire fixture, unless the rack is being used for clearance merchandise.

- For the best presentation, a single rack should hold products from just one of the seven color groups. Neutrals may be combined with any group.

- Arrange colors in a sequence that follows the natural color order of the rainbow—red, orange, yellow, green, blue, violet. Begin the

color sequence at the nine o'clock position as you stand in front of a round rack and work counterclockwise. If there are neutral colors, they should follow the rainbow assortment. When working with brights, midtones, jewel tones, and earthtones, it is more appealing to arrange neutrals from dark to light. Example: bright red, bright yellow, bright blue, neutral black, neutral white. When working with pastels and muted/dusty colors, it is more appealing to follow the sequence with neutrals arranged from light to dark. Example: pastel pink, pastel yellow, pastel green, neutral white, neutral grey, neutral black.

An easy way to remember the rainbow sequence is with the mnemonic device Roy G. Bv (the Bv can be pronounced "Biv"), which stands for red, orange, yellow, green, blue, violet. The mnemonic may be used as a training tool to ensure that there is continuity in the color arrangement of merchandise on fixtures in any size retail organization. Roy functions as an "invisible visual merchandiser," in charge of all color decisions (Figure 4.16).

All color schemes are based on relationships to the basic rainbow colors described by Roy G. Bv, except for neutrals (see Figure 3.6). In the pastel color group, pastel pink relates to bright red, peach relates to bright orange, pastel yellow relates to bright yellow, and so on. Even looking at the earth tones, you'll see that wine relates to red, rust relates to orange, gold relates to yellow, and so on.

Some retail presentation guides advise arranging colors from light to dark. However, perception and interpretation of color values is an individual thing, so a light-to-dark guideline offers no guarantee of storewide color continuity. One of the biggest drawbacks to a light-to-dark color sequence is that it allows bright schemes, jewel tones, midtones, and pastels to be mixed on a rack—at the expense of strong color impact. If the store you work

Fixtures should never be so overstocked that shoppers have difficulty previewing items. A simple way to determine fixture fill (the quantity of merchandise a fixture will hold) is to measure the length of the fixture arm or garment rod. You can hang one item per inch of its length—a 12-inch arm holds twelve garments. If items are thinner, like T-shirts, you may be able to add more pieces. If the items are thicker, the arm may hold fewer pieces.

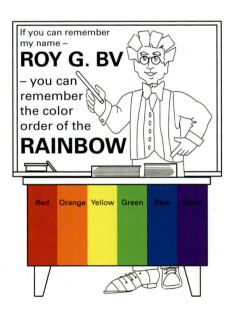

If you can remember my name – **ROY G. BV** – you can remember the color order of the **RAINBOW**

Red Orange Yellow Green Blue Violet

Figure 4.16 An easy way to remember color flow with the mnemonic device *Roy G. Bv*. Fairchild Books/ Rendered by Yelena Safronova.

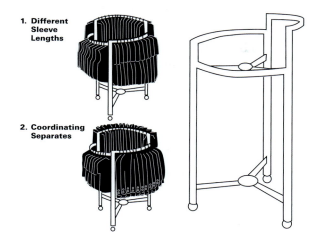

1. Different Sleeve Lengths

2. Coordinating Separates

Figure 4.17 A tri-level round rack with two common functions. Fairchild Books/Rendered by Elaine Wencl Art.

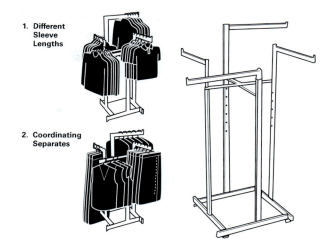

1. Different Sleeve Lengths

2. Coordinating Separates

Figure 4.18 A superquad with two common functions. Fairchild Books/Rendered by Elaine Wencl Art.

in recommends the light-to-dark coloration format, you will need to use it; but if you have a choice, we believe that rainbow colorization is easier to remember and will provide more impact in your fashion presentations.

If the round rack is used for clearance merchandise, first size the items, then colorize within each size. Example: size 5—red, yellow, blue; size 7—red, yellow, blue; size 9—red, yellow, blue. The smallest sizes should be positioned on the side of the fixture that faces the front of the department and then sized from there, working to your right (counterclockwise).

The round rack has one variation—the trilevel round rack (Figure 4.17). This fixture has three levels that are all height-adjustable. It's an ideal fixture to separate garments with differing sleeve lengths or show a group of top and bottom coordinates. Each of the three sections provides 39 inches of hanging capacity, so the trilevel could hold 117 garments (1 inch per garment). The lowest level of the tri-level round rack should always face the front of the department or an aisle. Like the round rack, this capacity fixture should be positioned primarily toward the rear of any department.

Superquads

The **superquad** is a four-armed capacity fixture designed to hold basic items that have been purchased in depth (Figure 4.18). This fixture allows display of items with different sleeve or hem lengths and works extremely well to feature coordinate groupings composed of pants, skirts, blouses, and sweaters or jackets. The superquad is useful to show broken or unrelated assortments and can be used for a collection of clearance merchandise, as well.

The arms of a superquad can be set at a variety of heights. One technique is to start low in the front of the fixture, setting each level a few inches higher as you move around the fixture, from left to right. Another method is to set the arms with tops higher than the arms with bottoms. This creates a natural look that mimics the way tops and bottoms are worn. The arms of a superquad should be colorized from left to right. Begin with the arm that is in the 9 o'clock position and move counterclockwise around the fixture (Figure 4.19).

A **superquad** is a four-armed capacity fixture with an adjustable height feature for showing items purchased in depth or coordinate groupings of pants, skirts, blouses, and sweaters or jackets.

Figure 4.19 Directional color flow with a superquad fixture. Notice the color flow begins at the 9 o'clock position. This technique may be used with any floor fixture. Fairchild Books/Rendered by Elaine Wencl Art.

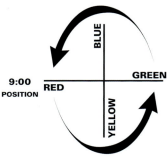

Gondolas

The length of a **gondola** can range from as short as 48 inches in a small specialty store to 60 feet or more in a superstore (Figure 4.20).

The ends of the gondola are called **endcaps**. Approachable from all four sides, these versatile capacity fixtures are used by discount stores to house basic merchandise like socks and intimate apparel—usually faced-out on pegs. Foldable and boxed merchandise like shoes can be stacked on gondola shelves. Large gondolas must be disassembled in order to be moved. Consequently, floor layouts seldom change. Specialty stores use shorter gondolas that often have locking wheels or casters so that they're easy to move when resetting the selling floor. Gondolas can be colorized from left to right, using Roy G. Bv. Product should be arranged with smaller items on the top shelves, moving to larger items on the bottom shelves.

Bins and Cubes

Bins and **cubes** are interchangeable terms, although many retailers define cubes as containers that are open on their sides and define bins as containers that are open from their tops. You might see tilted bins used for bulk items like candy or filled with nuts and bolts in a hardware store, while cubes are reserved for use in fashion stores as wall treatments or in stand-alone floor fixtures.

When used as selling-floor fixtures holding folded fashion merchandise, cubes are permanently stacked on gondola bases ranked in pairs so that they are shoppable from both sides. It isn't unusual to find entire walls of folded basics arrayed in banks of cubes. The visual impact of a cubed wall with a rainbow array of goods stacked from ceiling to floor is tremendous. It tells shoppers that the store has a wide selection of merchandise.

Basic fashion items that come in several colors and straightforward sizing sell well from cube fixtures. A floor fixture with basic turtlenecks in four colors and three sizes is shown in Figure 4.21. This is an extremely adaptable fixture from a merchandising point of view—systematic and uniform. The cubes you see in the denim presentation (Figure 4.22) can be merchandised by fabric finishes, colors (stone-washed to deep blue), waist and inseam sizes, and leg styles. The shirts in Figure 4.23 are presented in individual bins for a very dramatic, upscale shopping experience.

Figure 4.20 Gondola fixtures merchandised with boots and shoes packaged in bold orange boxes at Merrell Outlet, Byron Center, MI. Fixtures by Econoco Corp. Sellutions by Econoco. Courtesy of Sellutions by Econoco

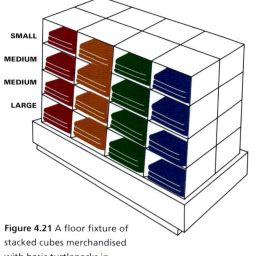

SMALL
MEDIUM
MEDIUM
LARGE

Figure 4.21 A floor fixture of stacked cubes merchandised with basic turtlenecks in three sizes and four colors. Fairchild Books/Rendered by Elaine Wencl Art

ACID WASH	STONE WASH	VINTAGE DARK WASH	DEEP INDIGO WASH
29x30	29x30	29x30	29x30
29x30	29x30	29x30	29x30
29x30	29x30	29x30	29x30
Straight Leg	Straight Leg	Boot Cut	Boot Cut
30x30	30x30	30x30	30x30
30x32	30x32	30x32	30x32
31x30	31x30	31x30	31x30
32x32	32x32	32x32	32x32
33x32	33x32	33x32	33x32
33x30	33x30	33x30	33x30
34x32	34x32	34x32	34x32
34x34	34x34	34x34	34x34
35x30	35x30	35x30	35x30

Figure 4.22 A floor fixture with jeans in cubes, arranged by fabric finishes, color, size, and leg style. Fairchild Books/Rendered by Elaine Wencl Art.

Figure 4.23 An upscale presentation of men's shirts in individual bins is easy for the store to maintain and easy for customers to shop. Bloomingdale's, Manhattan, New York City. Centano / WWD / © Conde Nast.

Furniture fixtures may be used exclusively as display props, creating focal points and highlighting special products. Or they may serve a dual purpose and actually be a part of the store's merchandise inventory. For example, an antique armoire filled with ancient bed linens, lace doilies, and pillows may be for sale as well. The cupboard sells the linens and the linens sell the cupboard. Finally, it's also possible that furniture pieces may be used as non-merchandising atmospheric elements to add to the store's overall ambiance.

■ TABLES

The single most important fixture in the retail industry is the table. Tables of some type greet shoppers at the entrances to most stores or departments. Such display tables may be permanent fixtures or temporary installations with a mission. They can be circular and skirted to the floor, rectangular and as substantial as any fine wooden furniture, or combined, as in a multilevel grouping of nested serving tables.

A table is an ideal introductory fixture because it has a low profile. It shows merchandise effectively at the front of a department while providing clear sight lines into the rest of the area—where more merchandise is presented. Figure 4.33 shows a low table that is enhanced with a riser and several mannequins.

Tables set out in mid-aisle also offer a great way to test or feature new items or offer regular products at special prices, enticing passersby to stop and shop on impulse. Sale tables are effective during clearance periods because customers are conditioned to finding bargains on temporary tables. However, do not overuse the bargain table device. If you do, your bargain table strategy will lose impact and credibility with shoppers.

Special sale table tops that look like shallow boxes on legs are called jumble or dump tables

Figure 4.32 Furniture is used as fixtures in Milkmade, Los Angeles. Boye / WWD / © Conde Nast.

Figure 4.33 This table features every item needed to complete an outfit: shirts, vests, pants, shoes, and handbags. H&M, Moscow, Russia. Centano / WWD / © Conde Nast.

because they will hold all types of sale items that might normally slide in all directions when shoppers sort through them. Stores that have tracked sales results for products presented on tables versus round racks have often found that tables are more productive. Perhaps it's the possibility of discovering a treasure that draws shoppers to them. Tables that look jumbled and shopped must be sorted, inspected for lost tickets or damage from rough handling, and rearranged periodically to keep the area attractive-looking and to assist shoppers in their search for legitimate values.

Found Objects as Fixtures

There is another source of store fixtures that bears mention in this section—*found objects*, such as wooden packing crates, antique trunks, wooden barrels, buckets, washtubs, 1950s kitchen tables and chairs, even sections of car or truck bodies. Large and substantial, these items may fit very well into certain stores' atmospheric or thematic plans.

Found object fixtures are not for everybody—and probably not for an entire store. Used strictly as accent pieces, they can add that magical element of whimsy or surprise that every designer delights in using—a signature statement. However, fixtures like these must fit the store's atmospheric intent, and overuse may limit their appeal. The principal benefits of found objects as fixtures are their novelty, price, and disposability. Since they're not as expensive as conventional store furnishings, found objects are easy to discard when they are no longer effective as merchandising tools.

Vendor Fixtures and Shops

Merchandise manufacturers sometimes supply retailers with fixtures that are designed specifically for their company's products. They may even offer to provide the store with décor elements, signage, and fixtures to create an entire shop for their brand. By doing this, manufacturers hope to control how their products are presented and thereby strengthen their own brand image.

This business arrangement may look like a bargain to retailers because they do not

5 Fashion Apparel Wall Setups

Walls as Retail Selling Tools

Walls are the largest selling tool and one of the most important fixtures in any retailer's overall selling strategy. Effective use of store walls as selling tools meets several visual merchandising objectives. Well-designed walls capture shoppers' attention as they enter the retail space. Wall displays draw shoppers farther into the store, exposing them to as much merchandise as possible. Wall presentations communicate fashion information, and they encourage multiple purchases. Clearly, the more attractive merchandise shoppers see, the higher the probability they will buy.

Store walls act as **way-finding** tools, guiding shoppers to products they have come to see and buy. Walls serve as merchandise locators, reflecting product categories featured on adjacent selling floors. To reinforce these important merchandising messages, retailers often use appealing lifestyle graphics that offer both product category and trend direction—even when viewed from a distance.

Graphic elements must be large enough and be placed high enough on walls to be visible from store entrances and aisles. If the arrangement of selling floor fixtures provides clear sight lines leading up to the walls, effective wall signage will inform shoppers about the categories of merchandise featured on the walls below and in areas nearby. Wall signage is particularly useful to call out brand, size, gender, or a category of merchandise.

In addition to attracting shopper attention and moving people through the store, walls form the retail background. Walls reinforce store brand image through the strategic choice of interesting textured surfaces, paint colors, and wall coverings.

way-finding is a term used by architects to describe any tools that help customers to "find their way" through a store. Signs positioned in highly visible areas—on walls or hanging from the ceiling— are examples of way-finding strategies.

AFTER COMPLETING THIS CHAPTER, YOU SHOULD BE ABLE TO

- Explain the importance of wall presentations as selling tools
- Analyze the impact of walls on customer traffic patterns and sales
- Create dramatic wall presentations using a variety of fixtures, signs, visual props, and mannequin alternatives

"Walls create different experiences in retail spaces and help communicate what you want your consumers to see."
Tony Mancini, Chief Executive Officer, ThinkTank Retail Hospitality Group

Figure 5.0 Red-framed, lighted walls filled with products in a variety of textures. El Palacio de Hierro Polanco, **Mexico.** *Design Firm: TPG Architecture / Photographer: Alec Zaballero.*

Architecturally, *perimeter walls* (outer walls) define the store's overall shape and support its basic construction. Perimeter walls are commonly divided and then merchandised by sections, generally ranging in size from 4 to 20 feet (depending on the type of store). Inside the store space, strategically placed *interior walls* guide traffic, separate merchandising departments, and increase the merchandiser's ability to present products. These interior structures (sometimes called *T-walls* or *divider walls*) are also useful in defining and separating specific selling spaces and enclosing fitting rooms, restrooms, offices, and storage areas. Because they can be merchandised on both sides, interior walls are very important in department stores. They may be built to meet the ceiling or may rise only part way. Because of their large size, whatever their construction or location, walls generally provide visual merchandisers with opportunities to create some of the most dramatic presentations in the store.

Walls as Destinations

If merchandise is presented effectively on the walls of a store, the walls will become destinations. Store planners can design traffic patterns that move shoppers toward the store's side and back walls—as opposed to leading them directly down an aisle (traffic lane) or stopping them in the front third of the selling space. Dispersing traffic into selling departments and drawing shoppers toward merchandised walls offers several strategic advantages that will have a positive impact on sales:

- Shoppers will be exposed to and inspect more merchandise.
- Once out of main traffic patterns, shoppers are more likely to spend time browsing through the store's entire merchandise assortment.
- Once they've made their way to see the merchandise on the walls, customers will return to the main aisles through the departments they have already visited. On that return trip, they will see merchandise housed on the back side of floor fixtures.

Walls as Store Fixtures

Since walls are the tallest store fixtures, visual merchandisers should be concerned with the height of the topmost shelves and displays. While they want shoppers to see merchandise on the walls, they should not encourage them to reach above their heads to pull down products. Safety and service must always be the prime considerations.

Stocking shelves several tiers high and then signing them with directions to seek help can provide opportunities for sales associates to work with shoppers and develop additional sales. Of course, that tactic implies that sales assistance is going to be readily available. If that is not the case, visual merchandisers must be certain that shelved merchandise is accessible to most customers.

You may prefer that a shelf of sweater styles on bust forms is not accessible to shoppers. Perhaps you've placed them there strictly for display. You will need to ask these questions:

retail realities

As a profit-minded retailer, your goal is to make the most effective use of every square foot of your store. Using store walls—from floor to ceiling—to communicate with shoppers will make profitable use of every cubic foot (length × width × height).

Merchandisers frequently overlook back-to-front merchandising opportunities. Stand with your back to a selling department's wall and develop merchandising strategies for shoppers who are returning to the main aisles after visiting merchandise arrayed on the walls.

Anything that frustrates shoppers risks sending them away disappointed and empty-handed. If your store must shelve duplicate products overhead on the selling floor, every size and style must be readily accessible on the fixtures below.

"Is there adequate selling stock of the displayed sweaters shelved below the display? Are those sweaters easy to reach? Are they sized?" If not, adjust the shelves to a height that the average customer can reach and add sizing to channels on shelf edges, or apply sizing stickers directly to the front folds of the sweaters.

Some retailers claim to be self-service stores, but they routinely place products out of reach, undermining their intent. Other store chains place waterfall face-outs on walls featuring selling stock of sweaters and tops well over 10 feet from the floor. Rather than providing the service of sales associates to assist shoppers, they place 5-foot extension poles in a few locations around the store. Typically the poles are difficult to locate because they quickly become hidden among the merchandise on garment rods or face-outs after shoppers have used them. Think twice before employing this selling technique—it is not without its drawbacks.

The Visual Merchandising Tool Kit

Visual merchandisers have a multitude of tools to work with as they create exciting wall presentations. Like most craftspeople, they may not use every tool at their disposal for each task they do. Carpenters may use hammers and measuring tapes all the time, but they carry other tools just in case they're needed. Visual merchandisers will use their basic tools—themes, art principles, and elements of design—for every wall they set up. Other tools, like wall fixtures, mannequin alternatives, props, and lighting techniques will be used on an as-needed basis. What follows is a discussion of the way each of these tools contributes to the development of wall presentations that sell.

■ WALL DIVIDERS

The primary function of wall dividers is separating a long wall into shorter, clearly defined sections. Dividers may be permanent, like architectural columns, or semipermanent like painted walls or textured wall coverings. Nonpermanent dividers, like outriggers and detachable panels for displaying coordinated outfits, may be repositioned as merchandise categories expand and contract. Whatever the style, these sections can effectively create departments or shops within a store, and combined with directional signage, make it easy for customers to quickly locate the products they want to see.

Look at Figure 5.1. The yellow-gold painted back wall creates a focal point in an expansive wall. In this example, the retailer has merchandised one color story—yellow, black, and white—across the entire back wall. As an alternative, the divided wall makes it possible to create three separate color and fashion statements if desired.

The materials used for dividers and wall surfaces can shape the store's atmospherics and enhance its physical image. For example, galvanized metal **outrigger** panels could be very appropriate wall enhancements for the sports apparel store—clean and spare. Polished oak panels with ornate moldings would add elegance to an upscale specialty store's image and create a more intimate mood.

Many times stores that were not initially designed with dividers will be **retrofitted** with these elements to break up wall space. Whenever dividers are installed, it is important to select materials that fit both store brand image and merchandise. If the materials are not compatible, the designer sends a confusing message to shoppers.

Architectural **soffit** treatments—long ledges, permanent arches, or shadow boxes reaching down from a store's ceiling to its top shelves or usable wall space—can limit merchandising flexibility. If the soffit treatment is an arch stretching out over several wall sections in a store, the best practice is to treat the entire area under it as one section. Even though an

outriggers are decorative or functional elements mounted to a wall at right angles in order to define, separate, and frame categories of merchandise presented on shelves or display fixtures.

To **retrofit** is to add architectural features, fixtures, or other elements after the original structure is completed.

A **soffit** is a long ledge, permanent arch, or box reaching down from a store's ceiling to its top shelves or usable wall space. It is often used to mask non-decorative (functional) lighting fixtures that serve to illuminate merchandise displayed on store walls.

Figure 5.1 The center section of this wall is painted yellow, which is an effective way to divide a long wall. SoCa, Costa Mesa, California. Boye / WWD / © Conde Nast.

arch doesn't reach the floor, it communicates a shop-like feeling to that area.

Compare the two wall presentations in Figure 5.2. Which presentation do you think is stronger? In the correct example, three sections of casual merchandise presented under a single architectural band make a dramatic fashion statement. In the incorrect example, the combination of casual and formal wear shown under the same architectural band results in a wall presentation that would be confusing to a shopper.

DECORATIVE LIGHTING FIXTURES

Decorative lighting fixtures are an excellent way to add warmth, interest, and personality to wall treatments. Basically atmospheric in nature, decorative lighting should not be the only method of lighting used. There are decorative fixtures to fit any store's image. They can add warmth to the cooler tones of general lighting in large retail spaces and highlight fashion colors without distortion.

They may range from small-scale feminine fixtures, with beaded or fabric lamp shades, to industrial photography fixtures and high-tech theater lights.

LIGHTING TECHNIQUES FOR WALLS

Merchandised walls are lit separately from the store's overall illumination. An ideal store design will set track lighting into the ceiling 5 or 6 feet away from a merchandised wall. The goal is accent lighting that highlights merchandise on a department's perimeter walls. A combination of general (floodlight) and specific (spotlight) lamps gives merchandisers flexibility to vary visual presentations. When the store's initial construction does not include track lighting for perimeter walls, accent lighting fixtures can augment the general lighting plan.

Accent lighting is, by definition, more dramatic than general store illumination. It is meant to set displayed merchandise apart in visual "hot spots," according to Greg

Gorman's *Visual Merchandising and Store Design Workbook*. He says that accent lighting provides focus, orientation, and visual impact supporting merchandise presentation: "Accent lighting allows specific areas on the walls and sales floor to stand out from the rest of the general illumination. When used properly, it can control traffic flow through a space."

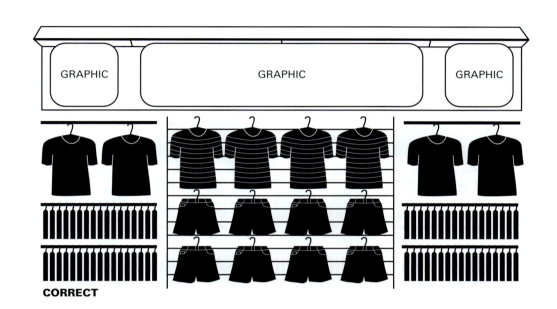

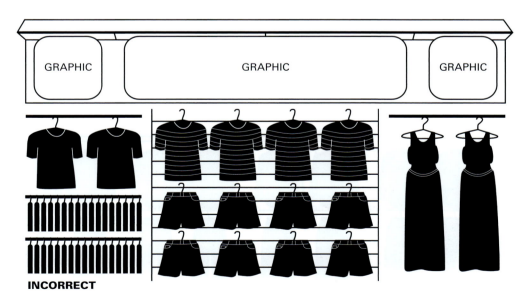

Figure 5.2 Wall presentations under a single soffit. In the correct example, only casual merchandise is presented, which makes one fashion statement. In the incorrect example, the combination of formal wear with casual merchandise results in a confusing message. Fairchild Books/Rendered by Elaine Wencl Art.

Figure 5.6 Formal balance creates a dynamic presentation in this 2016 Shop! Store of the Year Award winner: Under Armour Brand House, Chicago, designed by Big Red Rooster and A+I. Photo Magda Biernat, Design Big Red Rooster and A+I.

Figure 5.7 A wall presentation of men's shoes using formal balance; Adora, Phillipines. Lam / WWD / © Conde Nast.

Figure 5.8 Informal balance is employed throughout wall areas to feature a variety of shirts, ties, belts, and jackets; El Palacio de Hierro Polanco, Mexico City. Design Firm: Gensler / Photographer: Paúl Rivera.

Figure 5.9 A wall presentation of handbags and boots demonstrating informal balance in Tommy Hilfiger, Rue St. Honoré, Paris. Chomel / WWD / © Conde Nast.

6 Fashion Apparel and Accessory Coordination

Fashion customers depend on their favorite retailers to have the newest merchandise—in the right colors, fabrics, sizes, and prices. They also expect merchandise to be grouped together by the activity for which it will be worn. When the selling floor is set and the fixtures are filled with trend-right apparel, you may think that the only thing missing is a store filled with shoppers—but there is some very important unfinished business.

How will shoppers begin to visualize themselves wearing the garments they find on the department's racks and hangers? Who will help them pull entire outfits together before they enter fitting rooms? Who will advise them about accessories? Visual merchandisers!

Shoppers rely on visual merchandisers to bring garments and accessories together in ready-to-buy fashion looks. With that in mind, what is the final step to preparing the store for business? Silent selling, of course! Displays showing distinctive fashion looks accessorized with taste and style enable the merchandise to practically sell itself—in multiple units. This retail tactic offers value-added and highly visual services that shoppers really appreciate— fashion know-how, wardrobing guidance, time-saving tips, and simplified shopping.

Fashion coordination takes place in every fashion department—on mannequins, forms, and display hangers—wherever there are opportunities to bring apparel and accessories together for shoppers' benefit. Some visual merchandisers call these coordinated presentations outfits, some call them capsules or costumes, some use the term *display coordinates*, some call them trend looks. The terminology isn't nearly as important as the

> **"Style is a way to say who you are without having to speak."**
> *Rachel Zoe,*
> *American designer,*
> *businesswoman, and*
> *writer*

AFTER COMPLETING THIS CHAPTER, YOU SHOULD BE ABLE TO

- Coordinate fashions by end use, fabrication, style, and color
- Dress a display hanger with a coordinated outfit
- Identify resources to expand your knowledge of current fashion trends

Figure 6.0 Beautifully coordinated accessories take center stage in this lavish and intricately patterned window setting. Dolce & Gabbana, Hong Kong. WindowsWear Photo. Copyright WindowsWear PRO http://pro .windowswear.com contact@windowswear.com 1.646.827.2288.

7 Home Fashion Presentation

Home Fashion Stores

There was a time when home fashion referred only to wall coverings, paints, window treatments, and furniture. Today the steady influx of well-designed home products involves everything from pots, pans, and pepper mills for the kitchen to bedding and blankets for the bedroom. Even the books placed on the coffee table in the living room have beautiful, artfully designed covers. Shoppers care passionately about all the trappings of their lives, not merely what they wear. Their home environment is another means of self-expression. Williams Sonoma says it very well: "We believe that home is at the heart of everything. A place where curiosity lives and generosity is served. Where lives are nourished and every day inspires."

As you begin this chapter, take a look at www.williams-sonoma.com to open your mind to their stunning and colorful world.

Today, fashion touches even traditionally unglamorous housekeeping items like rubber gloves, brooms, and buckets. Visit any home store or discount store and you'll see hundreds of housekeeping basics in trend colors and updated, ergonomic designs. Furthermore, it's not unusual to find commonplace household items in specialty gift stores—complete with coordinated themes and current trend colorways. Turn on cable television and you'll find multiple networks devoted to homes, gardens, and lifestyles. Retailers like IKEA are advocates of affordable, democratic design, as posted on their website, ikea.com: "We believe everyone deserves to feel at home, wherever and however

> "Home. Going there, staying there, and entertaining there. Designers, and then soon everyone else in the world, will discover self-expression, not just in what they wear, but suddenly—and most likely from now on—in where they wear it, and what they do when they get there."
> *Peter Glen in* 10 Years of Peter Glen

> "A room should never allow the eye to settle in one place. It should smile at you and create fantasy."
> *Juan Montoya, interior designer*

AFTER COMPLETING THIS CHAPTER, YOU SHOULD BE ABLE TO
- Identify the different types of home fashion stores
- Recognize several styles of home store entrances
- Coordinate home fashions by end use, fabrication, style, and color
- Create tabletop and wall presentations
- Identify resources to expand knowledge of current home fashion trends

Figure 7.0 RH, The Gallery at the Historic Museum of Natural History. The RH Boston flagship features elegant showrooms in a stately 1863 structure that was originally home to the New England Museum of Natural History. Kathryn Barnard.

they live. Our research has revealed five core emotional needs connected to life at home: privacy, security, comfort, ownership and belonging. When we have all these needs met, we are more likely to feel at home."

People are interested in making all aspects of their daily lives—especially precious free time—more enjoyable. And that includes surrounding themselves with useful, pleasant-looking, functional household products and home furnishings. As a result, the number and variety of home products sold has expanded, and the number of specialty stores dedicated to home fashion products continues to grow. A sampling of well-known retailers that specialize in fashionable home décor products today includes:

- **Department Stores**—Bloomingdales, Macy's, Nordstrom, Liberty, Harrods, Printemps, Galeries Lafayette, Rinascente

- **Specialty Stores**—Crate&Barrel, Muji, Pottery Barn, Room & Board, RH (Restoration Hardware), West Elm, Williams Sonoma
- **Discount Stores**—IKEA, Bed Bath and Beyond, Target, Walmart
- **Outlet Stores**—Pottery Barn Outlet, RH Outlet

Store Entrances

From the list of competitors entering the field, you can see that differentiation is a major factor in positioning home fashion stores as branded entities. In brick-and-mortar retailing, differentiation begins at the front door. The entrance to the store or department offers home fashion retailers their first opportunity for creativity.

In the past, the home specialty store entrance was approximately 16 feet wide with a standard plate-glass display window on both sides of the door. In Figure 7.1, the Apple

Figure 7.1. A 30-foot square glass cube forms the most memorable and unique home technology store entrance in history. Apple Store, 5th Avenue, New York. Tim Clayton/ Corbis via Getty Images.

Figure 7.2 An abundance of space and artfully cut-out trees invite shoppers to experience a nature-like setting; Andrei Duman Gallery, Westfield Village at Topanga Mall, Los Angeles. Tima Bell.

Store features a show-stopping 30-foot square glass cube entrance, a true original in retail architectural design. The transparent entrance invites curiosity and welcomes shoppers inside. Before they are exposed to merchandise in the underground store, the open space builds visual anticipation for the products to come. In a store like the Andrei Duman Gallery, an even greater abundance of space is necessary to allow dramatic photographs room to breathe and to be viewed from a distance. Notice the benefit of the white cut-out trees in creating an appropriate natural setting for the nature-themed art (Figure 7.2).

Visual designers who position a signature fixture immediately inside the store entrance believe that the first item shoppers see will be imprinted on their memory for later retrieval. In addition to selling merchandise, they also want to make a brand image statement. The unique fixture is designed to draw shoppers in for closer inspection of product that the retailer believes will be a best seller. Shoppers may not make their product selections right away, but they will file the information away for comparison to other items in the featured categories as they travel farther into the store. See Figure 7.3 for a grouping of signature fixtures at the store entrance.

Figure 7.3. A grouping of sleek metal signature risers lead the way into a fantasy world of art prints, books, and gifts; The Broad Retail Shop, Los Angeles. © Ryan Gobuty/Gensler.

Part Three   COMMUNICATING RETAIL ATMOSPHERICS

8   Signage

Communication through Signage

Retail stores begin to communicate with potential shoppers before they ever enter the store. From the minute shoppers read the store's name or see its logo on the storefront, they are getting a message. An effective sign attracts attention and conveys brand identity, giving shoppers their first impression of what they will find inside the store. Marciano's graphic banner in Figure 8.1 is an excellent example. One glance at the image in the window and the message is clear: Marciano sells glamorous fashion.

■ COMMUNICATING BRAND IMAGE

A retail store's brand image should be carried through on every sign in the entire store environment, from operational signs to merchandise signs. The most successful signs have an identity that is so clear that if they were taken out of the store environment, the name of the store would be evident. An exercise to compare signs from four home stores is included later in this chapter.

Some stores repeat their brand names inside their stores. William Rast calls out its brand on architectural design elements in a way that suggests the company stands for more than just fashion. Unfinished wooden boxes and tables bring to mind an image of hand-crafted quality for this high-end denim retailer (Figure 8.2). Also see Figure 8.3 to see how Under Armour calls out their brand name behind the cashwrap.

■ COMMUNICATING THROUGH OPERATIONAL SIGNAGE

Information on **operational signs**, such as the location of departments, checkouts, and restrooms, can be communicated in a variety of ways. One-level stores often use ceiling

> "Excite the mind, and the hand will reach for the pocket."
> *Harry Gordon Selfridge*

operational signs relate to the day-to-day business of a store—listing store hours, return policies, emergency exits, locations of help phones, department locations, and fitting-room policies.

AFTER COMPLETING THIS CHAPTER, YOU SHOULD BE ABLE TO
- Identify various signing functions
- Compare the expanding variety of signing media
- Decide when to sign merchandise
- Explain the guidelines for setting up signs in the store environment
- Write sign copy using a variety of techniques
- Design your own sign layout

Figure 8.0ab Chicago shoppers are welcomed with a bold message at Under Armour Brand House. The store exterior dominates the Chicago retail scene. Photo by Magda Biernat, Design and Project Mgmt. by Big Red Rooster and A+I.

or wall-mounted signs, while multilevel stores post department and restroom locations near elevators and escalators. Some stores have interactive monitors that pinpoint the exact location of the particular item you're looking for on a map.

Under Armour Brand House in Figure 8.3 makes selection easy by employing both graphics and bold type in its operational signage to help shoppers locate departments. Basketball product is called out and the checkout is clearly labeled and beautifully lighted with the Under Armour brand. As you can see, operational signage can enhance both store environment and brand identity—and never seem as mundane as the term *operational* implies!

COMMUNICATING THROUGH SIGNING MEDIA

A store's ability to communicate is enhanced by the use of the following graphic elements:

- Dimensional letters are effective in creating a strong focal point, as in Figure 8.4 Macy's Arcade. These letters are available in colored acrylics, woods, and metals. Foam letters in

Figure 8.1 A billboard-size banner in the window of Marciano in Manhattan clearly conveys the message of the style of product you will find inside the store. Antonov / WWD / © Conde Nast.

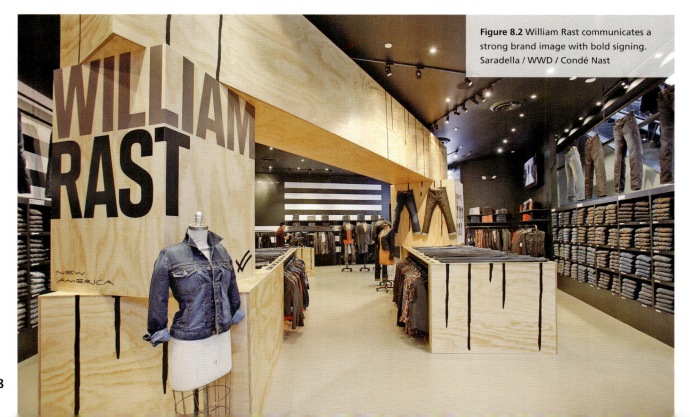

Figure 8.2 William Rast communicates a strong brand image with bold signing. Saradella / WWD / Condé Nast

Figure 8.3 Operational signage is employed to help shoppers locate the basketball department and to call out the checkout in rear of store; Under Armour Brand House, Chicago. Photo Magda Biernat, Design & Project Mgmt. Big Red Rooster and A+I.

Figure 8.4 Macy's department signage features dimensional letters lit in a traditional arcade style. Macy's Herald Square, One Below shop, New York. Mark Steele Photography.

many fonts and sizes may be covered with metallic papers to create upscale looks at a modest price.

- Static-cling decals may be applied to glass doors or windows for an artful, hand-painted look. They are easily removed and may be reused if carefully stored.

- Fabric scrims (hanging panels) made of sheer fabrics like silk and polyester may be printed with images or sign copy.

- Floor graphics add unexpected emphasis and sometimes are used to set a playful mood. Floor graphics may be permanently cut into the floor tile or applied in a nonpermanent version that adheres to the floor. A manufacturer-sponsored hopscotch game on the floor of a grocer's cereal aisle practically guarantees that a shopping parent and child will spend 15 to 20 extra seconds in front of that specific brand. See Figure 8.5 to see how Macy's incorporated a lighted floor graphic for a delightful effect under a central mannequin grouping in its One Below department.

- Light source signage systems include neon, fiber optics, projected images, and lightboxes that hold Duratran images. Look again at Figure 8.5, Macy's One Below department, to see how overhead lights accent a colorful banner in front of a column as a lead-in to the department, and how neon lettering is employed to draw shoppers further into the department.

■ COMMUNICATING TONE

Have you ever thought about a sign's tone of voice? Look at the difference between, "TAKE A NUMBER BEFORE ENTERING FITTING ROOM!" and "Please take a number before entering fitting room." Subtle details like type font, case, and copy style make a dramatic difference in the tone of communication. A sign in uppercase type shouts, while lowercase copy is friendlier and easier to read. In some London stores, signs are very polite. You might find one that says: "We would appreciate it if you would kindly take a number on your way into the fitting room."

Signs rarely have a playful tone, which is a missed opportunity for many retailers to connect with shoppers in a more emotional way. The best examples are found in one-of-a-kind boutiques, like a Chicago shop that

Figure 8.5 Ceiling spots effectively light up a colorful banner graphic, and neon lighting headlines a digital media wall to draw shoppers further into the department. Macy's Herald Square, One Below shop, New York. Mark Steele Photography.

Figure 8.6 Bebe's former younger concept store, 2b, in San Francisco played with different type fonts and sizes for a show-stopping back wall. Antonov / WWD / © Conde Nast.

painted "You look beautiful!" over its fitting room mirrors. Imagine what the rest of the store might look like from the tone of that single sign. A sign that engages emotions adds to the feeling or tone of the store and strengthens the brand image for the retailer. Look at Figure 8.6. Bebe's 2b (www.bebe.com) former concept store used a variety of type fonts and sizes in its signage to create a playful back wall. The tone was young and fun and beckoned shoppers to come all the way into the store.

Signing Merchandise

Merchandise may be signed with price points or copy to communicate that it is:

- Advertised with sale pricing
- An unadvertised in-store promotion with sale pricing
- Value-priced merchandise
- Brand-name merchandise
- Trend merchandise
- A new product with special features
- Clearance merchandise

Clearly, these are all excellent reasons to sign a fixture. However, you need to take your store's routine pricing strategy into consideration as you decide how many fixtures will be signed. Retail stores with moderate or discount pricing often sign every fixture in the store, which sends a strong savings message to bargain shoppers. Shoppers expect to see signs announcing great values every time they visit the store. Some truly committed bargain hunters won't even look at merchandise unless there is a sale sign on the fixture.

When a store employing a strong regular-price strategy has limited sales events, it has to be more selective about signing its fixtures. If every fixture in the store were signed routinely, it would be difficult to emphasize particular items because they would not stand out. A major sale might lose impact because shoppers wouldn't notice much visual contrast between special sale days and business as usual.

Too many price point signs can have a negative effect on a store's brand identity. Imagine a high-end Madison Avenue fashion store filled with pricing signs. Incongruous?

BOX 8.1

🪢 Neuroscience Pop-Up!

If you were walking down the sidewalk in Southampton and saw "Best Sandwich in the Hamptons" topped off with five stars, would you be intrigued? Would it tempt you to enter the store to learn more, even if it wasn't lunch time? Now look at the window adjacent to the door that calls out "The Finest Coffee and Emily's Chocolate Chip Cookies," and a whole host of other items, listed in an eye-catching variety of type fonts. Does the boldness inspire trust in an establishment so self-confident? What kind of tone of voice is the proprietor using? Check out www.seansplacehamptons.com to see mouth-watering photos of Sean's offerings.

This savvy café owner is using "curation" to draw in diners. Who doesn't want to taste the best sandwich and the finest coffee? In the book *Think Tank: Forty Neuroscientists Explore the Biological Roots of Human Experience*, an essay by Paul A. S. Breslin states: "The sense of taste has two fundamental roles in relation to our eating: to help us identify and recognize foods to establish their palatability—and to prime digestive and metabolic activities that will optimize the efficiency of how nutrients from food are processed and used by the body." In addition, our brains have a tendency to reach for rewards, and calling out the best and the finest in an act of curation invites passersby in to test the claims for themselves.

Allbirds shoes' tagline is: "The Most Comfortable Shoes in the World." www.allbirds.com. What other businesses claim to offer the best? How do you respond when you hear claims like these? Do you think it's a good marketing tool? When might it have an adverse effect?

Best Sandwich in the Hamptons at Sean's Place. Judy Bell

Bargain store strategies simply don't fit an exclusive store's image.

Retail consultant Peter Glen once wrote that the proliferation of signs in retail stores was management's apology for not having enough salespeople on the floor. Somewhere between too many and none at all is the right number of signs for a store's image. Too many signs cause shoppers to ignore them all; too many words and shoppers won't read any; too few signs or words and customers won't get enough information.

Merchandise may also be signed with lifestyle graphics—signs that show apparel or home fashions in use—alone or in combination with price points. Some lifestyle graphics show only a portion of the actual product and focus more on models' faces. That's a soft-sell strategy. It tells shoppers that the retailer cares as much about the enjoyment of their product as it cares about making a sale. Photos that show expression or set moods that shoppers can relate to communicate brand image successfully. For example, Celine's store in Milan features a lifestyle graphic that sets a definite tone for the store—the epitome of sophistication (Figure 8.7).

Some retailers have experimented by portraying everyday people for lifestyle photography. French Connection—a New York and European junior and young men's fashion store—once featured large close-up images of young women wearing glasses, even though they did not sell eyewear. These graphic images grabbed shopper attention because they were unexpected and also incorporated the design principle of repetition. They showed real people like you, doing real things, wearing real clothes, and using real products. As a visual merchandiser you must always be on the lookout for the next fresh idea for images that capture shopper interest.

Signage Presentation

The accuracy, clarity, and appearance of signs communicate something about a store's brand image. Inaccurate or unclear signs set up negative reactions because shoppers resent the time it takes to locate sales associates for correct prices or other information. If signs are damaged, torn, or curled, shoppers may feel the store does not care about its customers or its image. Shoppers may respond by becoming careless about rehanging garments or about refolding merchandise properly after they have handled it.

Here are five guidelines for effective signing presentation:

- Be certain that a sign is necessary.
- Display every sign in a holder. Signs should never be tacked to walls or taped to fixtures.

Figure 8.7 Celine's Milan store promotes sophisticated style in this column-mounted graphic. Miranda / WWD / © Conde Nast.

- Do not write on preprinted signs. Do not cross out old prices or tape new prices on top of the old. If a price changes, the sign must be replaced.
- Do not mix the type of signs used. If your store uses commercially printed signs, extra handmade signs are not appropriate.
- Replace any signs that become soiled or damaged.

9   Lighting

Lighting Defines Store Brand Image

Lighting plays a major role in defining and strengthening a store's brand image. It contributes to the overall atmosphere and mood of the entire store environment. Think about the lighting in a Victoria's Secret store. It may remind you of the lighting in your own home, soft and warm with highlights and shadows. Compare that mental image to the lighting in a Walmart—bright, cool, and shadow free. Now imagine Victoria's Secret with Walmart's lighting and vice versa. Aside from the fact that such a thing is highly unlikely to happen, think about what this kind of change would do to either store's brand image. Victoria's Secret's intimate environment would be entirely altered. Walmart's value message would not be clear if it were lighted like a residence. This example demonstrates the degree to which lighting affects a store's brand image.

Ed Pettersen, Pettersen Retail Consulting, described how lighting in the retail environment has changed over the years:

> Lighting has become far more than the utilitarian device that it once was. It should be used to set an overall tone for the space, while accentuating specific product. Through various ranges of color and temperature, lighting can either illuminate the space in a generalized way, or it may be distinctly focused so as to elevate the perceived value of a particular product, particularly where soft goods are concerned.

> "Lighting significantly affects how comfortable a customer feels while they're in your store. The more comfortable they feel, the longer they tend to stay."
> Brad Stewart, executive vice president sales, hera lighting

AFTER COMPLETING THIS CHAPTER, YOU SHOULD BE ABLE TO

- Describe how lighting helps to define store brand image
- Identify the four functions of lighting
- Explain why a lighting expert must always be consulted when a lighting system is purchased
- Recognize various lighting systems
- Establish lighting priorities
- Discuss current best practices for lighting

Figure 9.0 Page restaurant's flowering light sculpture. Terminal A, Ronald Reagan Washington National Airport, Washington, DC. ICRAVE, Designer and Eventscape, Fabricator.

Figure 9.1 Nordstrom's award-winning light weave LED fixture is ceiling hung over an open area for a dazzling, decorative effect; Pacific Centre, Vancouver, BC, Canada. Courtesy of Nordstrom, photo by Connie Zhou.

Light fixture styling contributes to brand image, too, as you see when you look at Figure 9.1. Nordstrom's award winning LED light weave display demonstrates that lighting fixtures are more than functional. They add interesting atmospheric dimensions to store designs, helping to draw shoppers through the entire environment. This airy, sparkling starlike lighting inspires a feeling of nature against the cloud-white ceiling and columns.

In Figure 9.2, Whole Foods Market, in their 40,100-square-foot store in Pompano Beach, FL, designed their environment around a vintage nautical theme. Their rope lighting fixture carries through that relaxed beach feeling in a unique, eye-catching manner. Imagine this seating area without any decorative lamp fixtures. Would the brand lose impact? How important is lighting to the overall image and feel of the environment?

Lighting Functions

Lighting systems actually perform four functions in a store environment: ambient, accent, task, and decorative lighting.

Figure 9.2 Whole Foods Market's award-winning decorative rope lighting fixture in Pompano Beach, FL. ID & Design International.

Figure 9.3 Varying levels of ambient lighting combined with accent lighting produces a dramatic store interior at Louis Vuitton Rodeo Drive, Beverly Hills, CA. © Louis Vuitton Galleries/Stephane Muratet.

■ AMBIENT LIGHTING

The general, overall lighting that determines color rendition is called **ambient lighting**. If you've ever had to ask a salesperson to take two garments out of the store into daylight to compare or match colors, you were shopping in a store environment that didn't provide adequate lighting. With continual developments in the lighting industry, it is an advantage to retailers to explore new systems that give merchandise the best **color rendition** possible.

Just as colors appear brighter on a sunny day and duller under cloudy conditions, merchandise colors appear to change under different lamps within a store. Color rendition will vary from one store to the next, just as lamps vary from store to store. Even if two stores used identical lighting systems, other factors like ceiling, wall, and floor coverings all influence the lighting levels in any environment. Dark-colored carpeting, for example, will absorb more light than a light carpet, resulting in a lower level of ambient lighting in a store. Ambient lighting can also be intentionally varied to create a mood in a luxury shopping environment like Louis Vuitton (Figure 9.3).

■ ACCENT LIGHTING

Accent lighting is a supplemental light fixture that adds sparkle or punch to displays and creates special focal points in areas that already have general light sources. The type of lamp used in accent lighting determines the scope of the defined area. Flood lamps light a wide area; spot lamps cover a narrower area. Once you understand the range and capabilities of individual spot and flood lamps, it's simply a matter of choosing the correct one for the desired result and fitting it into an adjustable receptacle on a track system.

Look at Figure 9.4 and notice how reduced ambient lighting adds to the impact of accent lighting focused on the mannequins. Accent lighting also adds eye-catching interest to the back wall where cords and light fixtures are arranged in an artful graphic design.

ambient lighting
describes general, overall lighting.

color rendition
is the degree to which lighting allows colors to be viewed under conditions that are closest to those offered by natural light. The lighting industry uses the term Color Rendering Index (CRI) when listing specifications on each lamp.

accent lighting
describes lighting effects designed to emphasize certain wall areas, merchandise displays, or architectural features in a retail setting.

One of the most visual trends in retail and commercial lighting is the balance between ambient and accent lighting. More and more retailers are reducing ambient lighting levels and increasing accent lighting. Employing new LED technologies, retailers are reducing costs and increasing light levels. The net result? Customers are more drawn to various products and sales rise.

retail realities

part three communicating retail atmospherics

It is time to decide about your plans for signage and lighting—important means of communicating retail atmospherics to shoppers—as discussed in Chapters 8 and 9. Build on the work you've already done for Parts One (Chapters 1, 2, and 3) and Two (Chapters 4, 5, 6, and 7).

Section One

How will your capstone store announce its presence to passersby and potential customers? How will they know what's for sale? How will this store's signage greet them?

- Design (illustrate and/or describe) your capstone store's exterior appearance and its exterior signage. Refer to the storefront description from Part One.
- Prepare a rationale statement that explains how your exterior design strategies support your brand image as well as the interior atmospheric choices you've already made in Part Two.

Section Two

- Do lifestyle graphics enter into your communication strategies? Explain why they would or would not be appropriate for your store.
- Explain what you hope to accomplish with the language and tone you've chosen for your store's interior signage.
- Would handwritten signs ever be appropriate for your capstone store? Why or why not?
- Explain why the age of your target customer might or might not influence your store's signage strategies.
- Write sign copy that enhances your store's brand image and demonstrates the tone of voice that you will use to communicate with your customers. Choose fonts, type size, and layout orientation (vertical or horizontal).
- Render examples of each on 8½ x 11-inch paper or cardstock. Prepare examples for each of the following categories:
    - Directional sign—for example, location of service desk, restroom, or fitting room—one sign
    - Policy statement—for example, returns or store hours—one sign
    - Special promotion or special event—one sign
    - Regular-price merchandise—sign(s) for three items
    - Sale-price merchandise—sign(s) for three items

Section Three

In Part Two, Section Two, you made several generalized choices relating to the store's overall atmospheric elements—sounds, lighting and lighting levels, displays, and traffic patterns. In this section, you'll be making more specific plans for lighting.

- Describe and then prepare a rationale statement for your store's:
    - Ambient lighting scheme
    - Accent lighting scheme
    - Task lighting scheme
    - Decorative lighting scheme
- Explain why the average age of your target customer might influence your lighting fixture/lamp selections.
- Refer to the lighting plan example in this chapter as you develop and render a comprehensive lighting plan for your capstone store. Consider creating an acetate or tracing paper overlay for your existing merchandise and fixturing layout drawings. Devise a key to identify the types of lights you plan to use. Pay special attention to fitting and display areas.
- Using photographs or catalogue illustrations from any source(s), show the selection of lighting fixtures that you believe will accomplish your goals for lighting your store attractively and effectively.

Part Four   VISUAL PRACTICES FOR NONTRADITIONAL VENUES

10 Grocery and Food Service Stores

Food as Fashion

Just as fashion has touched every item in the home, from trend-colored vegetable brushes to Zen-style woven place mats, fashion has reached out to food. Minneapolis-based Lunds & Byerlys once launched the opening of one of its stores with an unusual promotional show. It featured fashion models dressed in outfits fabricated or trimmed in food products such as cinnamon sticks, chocolate pieces, and Coca-Cola cans. See Figure 10.1 for an example of a model in a stunning dress made of chocolate.

Minneapolis *Star Tribune* staff writer Terry Collins reported as follows:

> *Denishia Simmonds had a case of the chills Thursday. No, the Minneapolis model wasn't nervous before taking the runway at a benefit fashion show at a soon-to-open upscale grocery store in Maple Grove. She had to spend three 2-minute intervals in a 36-degree freezer to keep her dress, made mostly of milk chocolate, from melting. Later, model Dawn King shook, rattled and rolled onstage in a dress made of aluminum Coca-Cola cans, much to the delight of the diverse audience.*

Taking the "food as fashion" promotional theme a step further, Lunds & Byerly's placed full-sheet posters in the store entrance featuring a woman wearing a red beret—feathered with a croissant! With this creative campaign, this grocer proved not only that food can be fashion, but that food can be fun.

How is the "food as fashion" trend reflected inside today's grocery stores? This trend is visible from floor-to-ceiling—in store design, signage, packaging, and even the product inside the package. Good design and effective retail strategies are not limited to apparel

> "Food is always at the height of fashion—whether it's the newest, most chic restaurant in New York City or a local farmers' market in your hometown. Visual presentation is a key ingredient for any food strategy. Color, texture, shape, and style all combine to create a visual harmony that will appeal to all of the senses."
>
> *Cindy McCracken, independent retail professional*

AFTER COMPLETING THIS CHAPTER, YOU SHOULD BE ABLE TO

- Recognize important trends and fashions that drive grocery retailing
- Identify different types of grocery and food stores
- Recognize common layouts and fixtures
- Describe key locations for product displays
- Utilize techniques to create mass displays and focal areas
- Locate resources for creative inspiration

Figure 10.0 Clever conversational signage and appetizing open-sell display invites shoppers into this award-winning SuperValu flagship. Blackrock Shopping Centre, Dublin, Ireland. Client: SuperValu, Agency: Household, Photographer: Malcolm Menzies.

Figure 10.1 An example of a model wearing a dress made of chocolate during the 5th Salon du Chocolat in Moscow, Russia. Sefa Karacan/ Anadolu Agency/Getty Images.

retailing. They can bring new excitement to gourmet chocolates as well as to basic cans of green beans. And grocery stores, with their tremendously varied product assortments, have thousands of opportunities to be fashionable!

In 1968, Byerly's was billed as the first premier grocery store in the country. Reviewed like a theatrical debut in Twin City newspapers, the store opened with top-of-the-line gourmet and private-label products, an upscale deli, wide carpeted aisles in its dry grocery departments, an elegant gift shop with a crystal chandelier, and service shops located at the store entrance. Years later the store was rebranded Lunds & Byerlys (both grocery concepts long owned and operated by Lund Food Holdings Inc.). Locating its 51,000 sq. ft. flagship Edina, MN store near multiple apartment complexes proved to be a perfect marriage. Apartment dwellers can easily stop in for a quick meal at Lunds & Byerlys' "Creations Café," which is filled with tasty ready-to-eat

offerings. It features rotisserie meats, artisan sandwiches, pizza, and pasta plus hot cases for breakfast, lunch, and dinner. Lunds & Byerlys mission: "Extraordinary Food, Exceptional Service, Passionate Expertise," embodies the company's long-standing desire to be a best-in-class grocer. See lundsandbyerlys.com and click on How We're Different to learn more about how this innovative grocer differentiates their brand from other grocers.

Grocery Brand Image

How do grocery retailers develop visual merchandising techniques that fit their brand image? Some, like SuperValu in Ireland, employ creative and clever signing with an open marketplace presentation to invite and engage shoppers. SuperValu operates 222 stores, all part of the Musgrave Group based in Ireland. Look at Figures 10.2a and b for two outstanding examples of brand image. Architectural design elements like curved aisles set the stage for visual merchandising. Notice how lemons and veggies line the fish counters in bins as a reminder to shoppers to pick up that important seafood enhancer. Along the cheese aisle, a galvanized bucket filled with loaves of French bread is next to a table with plates, crackers, and pears. Everything shoppers need to provide appetizers for their next party are all within reach. Now take a closer look at the wide variety of signage: overhead illustrations, lifestyle photography, chalkboards, banners; truly a rich assortment that all ties together to build a distinctive SuperValu brand image. It is evident that visual merchandising expertise has played a role in creating an exceptional shopping environment

Consumer-Driven Changes

Grocery retailing is truly consumer driven. For years grocery consumers have wanted to shop where, when, and how they want to. For the most part, that would be near home, any time of day or night, and quickly. Consumers have

🕸 Neuroscience Pop-Up!

Did you know that using our noses to smell is actually a myth? In his book *Smell, A Very Short Introduction*, Mathew Cobb, who has been studying the sense of smell for over thirty years, writes: "Although we can indeed smell by inhaling through our nostrils, we detect odors using neurons that are directly connected to the brain. . . . Really, you are smelling with your brain."

Taking this idea further, Cobb writes about how memories are easily triggered with our sense of smell. "One of the most famous stories about smell is that told by Marcel Proust in *A La Recherché Du Temps Perdu*: "The narrator describes how as a grown man, his mother makes him some tea; child-like, he takes a small piece of madeleine cake and soaks it in a teaspoon of the hot beverage. As he places the soggy cake in his mouth he is suddenly overwhelmed by a sense of the extraordinary, an exquisite feeling of happiness, the source of which he cannot immediately identify. Then he remembers—when he was a boy, his Aunt Leonie would give him madeleine dunked in tea: this in turn unlocks a whole series of complex memories of his childhood. As Proust puts it, these unfold in is mind like Japanese paper flowers in a porcelain bowl full of water."

Grocery shoppers in Lunds & Byerlys in Minneapolis follow the scent of warm chocolate cookies wafting from the bakery every day from 11 a.m. to 7 p.m. The thick, melt-in-your–mouth signature recipe has some shoppers beginning to fulfill their grocery lists *only* after they take a coffee and cookie break. Descriptive signage and large, warm, baking sheets filled with plump cookies create a

presentation that is irresistible! Do you think that the scent of warm cookies might evoke enjoyable childhood memories in shoppers? Did you ever find your own pleasant memories awakened with the scent of different foods? What sensory food service experiences have nudged you to return to a favorite destination?

Lunds & Byerly's continues to lead with innovative ideas that speak to shoppers without words. Judy Bell.

asked grocers to provide a pleasant ambience, easy-to-understand floor plans and shelf layouts, and accurate and informative pricing and signing, along with innovative and value-added products or services.

Over time, the average consumer's waking day became increasingly busier and longer. Evening meals and their preparation sometimes felt like unaffordable luxuries—largely based on the time necessary to shop, prepare, and eat—when consumers were pulled in ten directions to meet family schedules. Food marketers responded by developing ready-to-eat offerings known as HMRs, or home meal replacements. Customers could choose from a wide variety of meals to please every family

Figures 10.2a and b A clear brand image is communicated through friendly tone in signage, easy-to-approach grocers, and appetizing presentation; SuperValu Flagship, Blackrock Shopping Centre, Dublin, Ireland. Client: SuperValu, Agency: Household, Photographer: Malcolm Menzies.

member. A quick warm-up in the oven or on the range, and a meal close to home-cooked was served. As HMR increased, authentic home-cooked meals decreased, but with the pandemic of 2020, consumers' lifestyle and shopping habits abruptly changed.

In 2020, Harvard Business Review writer Eddie Yoon wrote a column titled *3 Behavioral Trends That Will Reshape Our Post-Covid World*.

"Typically, consumers' supermarket shopping habits are stable and slow to change. When people do dramatically change their behavior around food and beverages, it's usually driven by a major life event such as having a baby, moving to a new town, or changing jobs. As millions of people shelter in place, that appears to be changing. A study done by Hunter, a food and beverage firm, noted that 54 percent of Americans are cooking more than they were before the pandemic, and 35 percent say 'they enjoy cooking more now than ever.'"

Yoon goes on to discuss how changes like the vast increase of people working from home, single-person households continuing to rise, and the new trend to live away from densely populated areas will all play a role in consumers' demands in shopping environments of the future. As a visual merchandiser it will be vitally important to watch how these changes unfold and consider how you can effectively respond to consumers' evolving needs.

■ HOME-COOKED MEALS

Home-cooked meals are on the rise. Faced with less frequent trips to the grocery store to ensure personal safety during the 2020 pandemic, plus a deep reduction in dining out, many consumers turned to preparing authentic home-cooked meals. Healthy eating became even more top of mind for many, and shoppers began to purchase more fresh fruits and vegetables. When changes like these

are continued over an extended period of time, new habits are formed. Home cooking, canning, and baking and the pleasures therein are likely to continue well into the future. For those who want a break from menu planning, grocers have developed Meal Kits that serve two adults with premeasured ingredients. Aspiring home cooks only need to add a few ingredients from their own pantries—like olive oil, salt, and pepper—to prepare an almost effortless meal. Consider how this trending "return to the kitchen" opens the door for visual merchandisers to enhance the appeal of home cooking through marketing and in-store presentation.

■ HOME MEAL REPLACEMENT

Many grocery stores have positioned an actual convenience food department near their front doors. These "specialty shops" feature ready-to-warm-up **home meal replacements** in addition to soups, salads, wine, breads, and desserts. Looped near the store entrance, it is the ultimate convenience for one-stop shoppers looking for HMR foods on the way home from work. In a way, this floor plan creates a food boutique featuring higher-end, higher-margin (profit) convenience food that deserves the prime location on the larger store's floor plan. In terms of atmospherics, this approach immediately displays the megastore's most attractive sights (garden fresh produce) and scents (freshly baked breads and roasted chickens) to shoppers entering the building— presenting atmospheric elements that promise a pleasant shopping experience. Checkouts are often just a few steps away, or right at the deli counter, with quick in-and-out service for time-starved shoppers. See Figure 10.3.

■ IMPULSE SHOPPING

Consumers' time crunch continues to influence impulse shopping, but the increase in shoppers' search for healthy options has broadened the range of impulse products. Centra Hi-C,

home meal replacement (HMR) foods are take-home, ready-to-warm-up and ready-to-eat meals like nutritious salads, hearty pasta dishes, and protein and veggie combinations.

Figure 10.3 Fruits on ice and bins of fresh veggies offer shoppers a healthy pick-me-up; SuperValu Flagship, Blackrock Shopping Centre, Dublin, Ireland. Client: SuperValu, Agency: Household, Photographer: Malcolm Menzies.

a convenience store in Ireland, calls out their "Good on the Run" message to shoppers, offering healthy food choices in clearly labeled 4-foot wall sections: QUENCH, LUNCH. PACKED, and LIGHT.BITE. (Figure 10.4). Notice how colorful yellow bins on the floor feature fixture are filled with tempting apples, peaches, and oranges. The colored bins grab attention in an otherwise neutral store environment.

ONLINE CONVENIENCE SHOPPING

Online grocery shopping was steadily on the rise for years, but instantly catapulted with the pandemic in 2020. Russell Redman at Supermarket News reported these findings from Coresight Research: "Almost half of shoppers reported that they are buying more groceries online or have started making

online purchases because of COVID-19." In his summary however, Redmond noted: "Despite sharp growth in e-grocery sales, a relatively small proportion of food shopping in the U.S. is done online." He noted that even though the landscape is shifting, online is still considered to complement, not substitute for in-store shopping. Among retailers Amazon continues to lead in the online grocery category with Walmart, Target, Costco Wholesale, and Kroger following.

This boost forward for online shopping will obviously influence the future of grocery stores, opening the doors to opportunities for visual merchandisers to make in-store shopping more compelling. It is in times of change that businesses of all sizes are more open to innovative thinking on how to invite shoppers in, engage them, and keep them coming back.

labeled organic usually have seals of approval. This affects presentation adjacencies, as these products must be clearly separated. With the growing demand for organics today, visual merchandisers should ensure that signage used to call out organic products is readily visible to shoppers as they walk down grocery aisles.

Types of Grocery and Food Service Stores

There are nine types of stores in this category: traditional or conventional grocery stores, specialty food stores, hypermarket/superstores, warehouse stores, wholesale clubs, public markets, pharmacy/food, convenience stores, and co-ops.

■ TRADITIONAL SUPERMARKETS

The traditional supermarket is a full-line, self-service grocery store with annual sales of $2 million or more. The median size for these stores is around 42,000 square feet, and in addition to food they carry a variety of household gadgets, paper products, health and beauty aids, and sometimes books, gifts, greeting cards, and apparel. They may even provide one-stop-shopping amenities like a pharmacy, banking, post office, coffee shops, and other services. Some focus on specialty foods like organic/natural and international products. Examples in the United States include Albertsons, Central Market, Kroger, Harris Teeter, Lunds & Byerlys, Meijer, Publix, and Wegmans. London examples include Tesco, Sainsbury's, and Marks & Spencer.

■ SPECIALTY GROCERS

Smaller than most conventional supermarkets, specialty grocers generally range from about 5,000 to 40,000 square feet and focus on a particular grocery category. In the United States, EatZi's Market & Bakery stores range from 5000 to 10,000 square feet and feature gourmet foods and desserts, freshly baked breads, and hot meal delis with daily specials.

Figure 10.4 This cleverly signed convenience store addresses both the desire for healthy foods and the time-crunch facing consumers today; Centra Hi-C, Ireland. Client: SuperValu. Agency: Household Photographer: Malcolm Menzies.

■ ORGANICALLY GROWN FOODS

The consumer movement worldwide toward healthier foods—particularly organics—is booming. The US Department of Agriculture (USDA) has developed a system for certifying producers and manufacturers to ensure that food items on store shelves labeled as organic are produced according to acceptable organic standards. As part of that system, the USDA has provided guidelines for food companies that are marketing their organic products as *organic*.

Visual merchandisers who are involved with signing and presenting organic foods as well as foods labeled "natural" need to pay close attention to definitions. Natural products are usually not organic, and those

Figures 10.6a and b The Landmark Supermarket in Makati, Philippines, features beautifully curved, custom floor fixtures. (Above) Landmark's wine department. (Below) Landmark's fresh produce area. Hugh A. Boyd Architects, photo by Toto Labrador.

GRAPHICS

Graphics are a beneficial element in grocery environments because they serve multiple purposes. They can effectively emphasize new and best-selling products, provide serving suggestions with appetizing lifestyle photos, suggest nonfood products that facilitate meal preparation, act as wayfinding devices, and function as silent salespeople. Two excellent examples of signing that serves multiple purposes can be seen at Whole Foods Market in Honolulu (Figures 10.7a and b). Conversational signing is used in billboard-style department headers above the wine department, encouraging shoppers to engage in a journey of discovery. To facilitate this mission, a sign topping a floor fixture highlights twenty-one varieties of wine personally selected by the Whole Foods Master Sommelier. In the produce department, conscientious product cultivation is called out on the billboard, and beneath it signs posted on the walls read: "We have 200+ organic items," and "We have 90+ local items." Look at all of the signs in the two photos and think about how many purposes they are fulfilling.

The Visual Merchandiser's Role

It's easy to assume that visual merchandising in the grocery category is the shelf stocker's responsibility, but it couldn't be further from the truth. The proliferation of products, as well as an increase in consumer sophistication due to the growth of food and lifestyle programming on cable television, has raised expectations for food presentation in the retail setting.

PROFESSIONAL DEVELOPMENT

Continuing professional development should be at the top of your to-do list, no matter what aspect of the retail industry you work in—fashion, food, hardware, or home store. There are three strategies—looking, comparing, and

Figure 10.7ab Whole Foods Market in Honolulu calls out "Grow it LIKE YOU MEAN IT" and "Discover Your Next Favorite Thing" in fresh produce and wine departments. Judy Bell.

innovating—that will always help you grow professionally. You can use them in virtually any segment of the retail industry. Moreover, you can apply them in this chapter to discover and even forecast grocery retailing trends by:

- Reading trade magazines that specialize in foods and learning from valuable statistics on consumers' eating and shopping habits

Figure 10.8 Fresh produce on stage at Whole Foods Market in downtown Denver. Blaine Harrington III/The Image Bank Unreleased via Getty Images.

as fashion. Tables are portable stages, giving grocers great flexibility to stimulate appetites for store products. A simple tabletop displayed with a basket of lemons, a pitcher, glasses, a stirrer, and a bag of sugar for making lemonade could sell crates of lemons in a produce section by the power of suggestion alone. And if that display were to include a tablecloth, napkins, and a serving basket filled with lemon-iced cookies, an attractive platter with a lemon-frosted cake, or a lemon

meringue pie in addition to the lemons, you would have devised a cross-merchandising opportunity for multiple sales.

You can apply all of the principles you've learned from other chapters to build displays like the hypothetical lemon-themed tabletop. In fact, the list of considerations for a fashion apparel display is exactly the same as the one used to merchandise grocery displays. If you were setting up a planogram for a grocery chain, you'd probably devise a form that would resemble a list of considerations for a fashion apparel display.

Today, food really is fashion—or at least one aspect of it. How we view food and other elements related to our home lives is our expression of the things we value, how and with whom we spend our leisure time, and where we live our lives away from work.

retail realities

Cross-merchandising influences many grocery shopping decisions. Shoppers are pleased when salad fixings like croutons and dressings are conveniently merchandised with main salad ingredients in the produce department. Smart grocers were selling one-stop salad "kits" long before suppliers started packaging them in plastic bags.

Virtual Reality Technology

Virtual Reality (VR) has been used for the past 15 years in the retail industry to help companies innovate new retail concepts and make decisions in virtual retail stores. VR saves time and expense allowing retailers to instantly change product layouts without handling products.

One of the leading suppliers of VR for the retail industry is Kantar Retail Virtual Reality. Its client list includes retailers such as Tesco and M&S in the UK and Target in the US. As Cedric Guyot, chief executive officer of Kantar explains:

Not so long ago, when retailers and suppliers went into a range review, either (or even both!) would build a physical model of the new proposed planogram. They would then invite the other party to discuss, they'd make changes and iterate until they found a mutually acceptable model. These could run in the 100,000s of dollars for large suppliers. Kantar Retail Virtual Reality turns this into a much more efficient and cheaper

process: we use a virtual environment in which the supplier and the retailer can jointly design the planogram in a live mode, and then navigate the store like they would in a first-person game. They can iterate as many times as they want, they can invite shopper feedback at all stages in the process, and they can do this as many times as they want—for each new product, for each new packaging concept, for each new campaign, for each range review!

For retailers, VR becomes an incredibly powerful tool for continuous innovation. As the pace of retail change accelerates, with traditional channel definitions blurring, omni-channel growing, shoppers becoming more vocal and influential in driving the experience they want, and margins shrinking, retailers and suppliers need a better, nimbler tool to design the store and the shopper experience of the future. Virtual Reality helps provide that workbench, from the store concept five years in the future to the new product hitting the shelf next week (Figure 10.9).

Figure 10.9 An image of a grocery store gondola created with Virtual Reality technology from Kantar Retail, headquartered in the UK, serving retailers worldwide. Red Dot Square Solution (a/k/a Kantar Retail Virtual Reality UK Ltd.).

BOX 10.2

DESIGN GALLERY: SUPERVALU, BLACKROCK SHOPPING CENTRE, DUBLIN IRELAND

SuperValu is part of the Musgrave Group, Ireland's largest grocery and food distributor. With over 223 stores in Ireland, they have been in service for over thirty years. Their Dublin store was a gold award winner in the Shop! Design Awards. Matthew Brown, of echochamber.com, describes the Dublin store here:

> *Innovation is being driven by value brands. This has to be one of the most profound trends in retail; transforming old notions of value and quality and bringing democratic luxury to the mass market. Irish supermarket SuperValu's new Blackrock flagship store is a perfect example and a radical departure for the brand. With its handcrafted, artisanal design notes, the new concept store has a new identity that emphasizes richness, quality and freshness, with storytelling and expertise at its heart.*

Look at the role signage plays in communicating this store's values. Local expertise is called out with the image of a confident baker, and passion is portrayed by an oversized tray of mouth-watering chocolate treats topped with whipped frosting and drizzled caramel. A banner boasts: "Freshly made right here by us, every day." To add an element of fun, conversational signage chimes in with "Anyone for CAKE?" and "FLIPPIN' BEAUTIES, Delicious and Fresh Pancakes all day." This engaging bakery even offers ideas on pairing up favorites like high-fiber bread with ginger jam in their "Food Friendship: Tastes-Good-Together" signage.

The product itself takes center stage with an open marketplace approach—the bread is so fresh and ready to grab and go, who can resist? Textured and flour-dusted loaves, in a variety of toasted colors, rest on tables and pullout carts that add dimension to a stage set for an entertaining shopping experience.

Shop! Design Awards: Household Design, London.

Resources

As with apparel and home fashion fixtures, a wide variety of feature and capacity fixtures for floor and walls are available from grocery fixture manufacturers.

■ FIXTURE TRADE SHOWS

Euroshop is held in Düsseldorf, Germany, every three years. Its website describes Euroshop as the "very first trade fair to cater for the entire needs of the shopfitting industry." This international show features more than a dozen warehouses filled with exhibits from hundreds of international manufacturers with every type of fixture needed in any retail store. Products relating to grocery and food stores include checkouts, shopping carts, deli and meat showcases, dairy cases, and specialty bakery fixtures. Manufacturers that specialize in lighting for food products also exhibit at the show. For more information, see www.euroshop.de.

■ MAGAZINES, BOOKS, AND TELEVISION

Browse magazine stands regularly to stay on top of food trends. Some of the current best include *The Art of Eating, Bon Appetit, Cooks Illustrated, Eating Well, Food & Wine,* and *Real Simple.* The complimentary catalogues at the entrances to major traditional and specialty grocers are packed with colorful food photography, recipes, and party ideas. The Food Network cable channel is another abundant resource for cooking techniques from top chefs, healthy eating advice, and newest food trends and recipe books.

Shoptalk "Fresh Ideas Fast!" by Greg Duppler, Former Senior Vice President, Grocery Merchandising Manager, Target

Creativity and innovation are essential elements in the success of any retailer in today's ultracompetitive world. There is an overabundance of "sameness" as you walk through shopping centers and malls. People who take risks, break the molds, and innovate will have the most fun and become the most successful.

Before coming to the grocery industry, I was in the toy business, which is as exhilarating as work can be. Creativity, trend, and innovation are ways to bring life to toys. Meanwhile, food was viewed as a mundane category. However, in the past couple of years, there have been quantum-leap improvements in merchandising, packaging, and visual presentation of food.

Today's business world is a sprint. If you stand still, you'll be passed! Great ideas are quickly copied so you need to relentlessly pursue differentiation. You always need to listen, look, be open-minded—really open-minded—to generate new ideas and then implement them quickly to stay ahead of the competition.

The bottom line is . . . have fun, think outside the box, and make things happen—fast!

11 Nontraditional Retailing

Specialized Marketing

Changing shopping preferences, emerging technology, and life-changing events like the pandemic of 2020 have encouraged retailers to alter some of their customary methods of communicating about their stores and the products they sell. In some cases, retailers have even changed where and how their goods are sold. These new retailing strategies may affect your career path because they are opening up new opportunities for visual merchandisers. You'll never be able to say that visual merchandising is static. There are several developing trends discussed in this chapter that will influence the work you'll do—and where you'll do it. In this chapter, we will consider six types of specialized marketing in which visual merchandisers may apply their competencies: augmented reality and artificial intelligence, robots, online retailing, kiosks, pop-up shops, and special events.

Augmented Reality and Artificial Intelligence

Augmented reality, commonly called AR, and **artificial intelligence**, AI, are advantageous ways for retailers to personalize their shoppers' experience and differentiate their business offerings from others. Sephora has been a trailblazer by creating two engaging experiences for their shoppers. Their "Virtual Artist" AR tool allows shoppers to try on different shades of lipstick, shadow, eyeliner, and cheek and lash products both in-store and with the Sephora mobile app. It offers a safe and easy way to try on dozens of colors in an instant. See Figure 11.1.

augmented reality is the real-time use of text, graphics, and other virtual elements to integrate with real-world objects.

artificial intelligence refers to computer systems' ability to perform tasks that normally require human intelligence.

AFTER COMPLETING THIS CHAPTER, YOU SHOULD BE ABLE TO

- Define augmented reality and artificial intelligence
- Explain ways in which robots can connect with shoppers
- Explore the career potential for visual merchandisers in online retailing
- Identify the various types of retail kiosks
- Present merchandise on a cart
- Evaluate the visual merchandiser's role in fashion show and special event production
- Develop a special event or fashion show concept

Figure 11.0ab ShopWithMe, a traveling pop-up that debuted at Pioneer Court in Chicago, offers the ultimate in non-traditional retailing as it integrates online with a physical retail store.
Benny Chan/Fotoworks.

flower arrangements, and adding accent lighting to the trunk area.

- Tearoom/restaurant shows are mostly informal with models working a predetermined pattern through the dining area. This is generally done with appropriate music and no commentary.
- Informal department shows are likely to involve models and clothes, but little else. If there is to be commentary by a sales representative or retail fashion director, things may become more formal. Perhaps a low stage will be erected, at which point you'll be required to create a small on-stage vignette or a simple backdrop and perhaps provide special accent lighting. Seating is generally provided if there is a stage.
- Themed expositions (a women's fitness expo, or a bridal fair, for example) take place in auditorium settings with retailers often participating in sponsoring roles. If your store hosts a fashion show, it's frequently done on a main stage at the venue. You might be required to supply a special stage setting for that show or as your store's contribution to the event overall. In addition, your store may have a large booth space to decorate—related to merchandise that fits the expo theme or to the corporate image and brand image of the store.
- Special event shows in the community frequently team retailers with other businesses in co-sponsorship roles. For example, a major fashion store may partner with a newspaper or magazine to present a spring and a fall fashion show at a theater or concert hall, auditorium, arena, or other public venue. The events may be part of a downtown retailers' initiative to bring shoppers into the city or, with charitable tie-ins, be positioned as fundraisers. These tend to be rather elaborate shows with large budgets and tremendous production value. They often have the excitement of a Broadway stage show and offer a

challenging but satisfying medium for the visual merchandiser.

Location

Fashion shows take place in many types of **venues**. A show's location is important only if you're the one who must select the site and make the rest of the arrangements. Otherwise you and your visual team simply handle whatever the venue offers in the way of staging challenges.

Themes

All shows have themes, stated or implied. Sometimes they reflect the fashion seasons; sometimes they name or honor notable fashion designers; sometimes they link retailers with nonprofit causes or civic or social organizations; sometimes they tie in with major community events. Themes often dictate the mood and the pace of the production. Themes also assist show planners in creating effective advertising and publicity campaigns necessary to bring a targeted audience to the fashion show. Retail sponsors often schedule and coordinate fashion windows to be part of the overall publicity and advertising campaign. Themes also give visual merchandisers their basic window and set design cues.

Equipment

Most of the places where you'll be asked to stage fashion shows won't have appropriate lighting or sound equipment for your purposes. That means specifying and renting equipment and arranging for lighting and sound professionals to set the equipment up and run it during the show. Be aware that most nonretail venues have contractual requirements to provide union labor for any stage lighting or sound production required.

Store departments generally have adequate accent lighting for perimeter and aisle displays but haven't been fixtured for stage lighting. In-store sound systems don't have to be elaborate.

venues are locations where a special event or entertainment takes place. The word comes from the Latin verb venire, which means "to come."

example of an event

To see how all of this works, let's envision a large-scale fictional charity fashion show to launch a spring pop concert series in an orchestra hall. It will be a joint venture for several sponsors.

Theme
Spring on the Seine

Beneficiary
The USO—an organization with sites in major airports—offers hospitality and assistance to traveling military personnel and their families. The nonprofit organization needs to upgrade its airport facility. All proceeds (after expenses) from this event will go to this project.

Specifics
The following details represent the kinds of considerations that would occur in the planning of a fashion show:

- The orchestra plays as part of its spring concert series and donates the cost of added catwalk staging sections plus lighting and sound technicians. Since the event is planned for a scheduled concert, there is no hall rental fee.
- The airline donates round-trip tickets for two to Paris (or any destination on its normal routes) plus catered food and soft beverages for show attendees during the concert. The trip will be the event's major door prize.
- The florist donates fresh-cut spring blossoms for patron tables and set pieces. Table pieces will be arranged in vases; cart flowers will arrive in galvanized containers scaled to fit the carts.
- The newspaper donates three full-page ads, plus a feature story about the USO's good works, its current needs, and the benefit show. It guarantees advance publicity in prime space right up to show time. It also furnishes the event signing and programs.
- The retailer supplies all garments; arranges for a well-known fashion designer to do commentary; books and pays models for fitting rehearsal and show; pays the fashion coordinator's salary; furnishes a professional choreographer; and donates set design, execution, props, and services of the visual merchandising department.
- The USO handles ticket sales and all related expenses.

For this hypothetical show, set design will be influenced by structural changes made to the concert hall. Venue managers plan to install a false floor to cover their normal main floor theater-style seating. Ranked in tiers that follow the floor's natural slope, the new decking will hold tables and chairs where patrons may eat and drink during the concert and fashion show. Table-high decorative white fencing and shrublike greenery provide safety and add to a parklike atmosphere.

The visual merchandising team sits down with the fashion coordinator and decides to

- Design their set pieces to tie in with the hall's existing parklike décor.
- Install two catwalks leading from the stage to the first deck aisles so that models can walk into the crowd and exit into the side halls leading backstage. As a safety measure, potted summer flowers will edge the catwalks.
- Build twelve white flower carts as stage set pieces and fill them with fresh-cut flowers. Models will gather flowers from one of the carts and present them to patrons at tables as they come off the catwalks.
- Project light-effect silhouettes of Parisian images on hanging screens in colors matching each segment's fashion statement.

Although the planning must take place months ahead of the event, this project will be executed in a few hours, since the flower carts, platform riser unit, and catwalks will be completed well in advance of deadline and delivered to the hall by rehearsal time. The rest of the visual merchandisers' chores will depend on the arrival of the flowers and the amount of time needed to set them in place.

◀ B O X   1 1 . 2 ━━━━

part four visual practices for nontraditional venues

Unless your capstone store is actually related to the grocery or food service industry, you may believe that the contents of this chapter do not apply to your store. However, given that bookstores now commonly host coffee bars and small lunch counters, and grocery stores also sell cards, books, and gifts, you might reconsider. Many current practices by grocers and restaurateurs might be ahead of the trend and worth your consideration—cross-merchandising, for example.

Section One

- Create two separate lists of cross-merchandising options for your capstone store based on your previous selection of merchandise categories in Part One, Section Two, of the capstone project.
- Explain how cross-merchandising could positively impact sales totals in any department where you employ a cross-merchandising strategy.

Section Two

- Design an appropriate retail mobile unit (RMU) for one area in your capstone store.

Sketch at least one elevation and include a list of materials and colors you'd employ.
- Explain its purpose (this could be your cross-merchandising opportunity) and the strategic manner in which you plan to use it (as a demonstration table, perhaps, or a way to introduce a new product or vendor to the store, or as a seasonal presentation, for example). Will this be a selling unit with assigned personnel? Why or why not?

Section Three

Describe in detail an in-store special event that's appropriate to your capstone store's merchandise and its clientele. Include enough detail that someone could actually begin production planning (for example, what, where, when, who, and why, at a minimum).

Part Five   TOOLS AND TECHNIQUES FOR MERCHANDISE DISPLAY

12 The Magic of the Display Window

Store window displays have the potential to cast an almost magical spell on passersby. Look at the spectacular effect of a single mannequin dressed in a gown that is in itself, a work of art (Figure 12.0). Window displays can entertain, educate, and engage shoppers in a wide variety of ways, from an animated holiday scene to merchandise imaginatively displayed in lively **vignettes**. Strategic window designs draw traffic into the store from the street and actively support sales.

Retail Theater

From a creative point of view, presenting merchandise in the confines of a traditional store display window can be likened to a theatrical production. Retail theater, like conventional theater, is a vehicle for communication. It has the potential to carry merchandising messages. The traditional enclosed window offers an advantage because nothing happening inside the store can distract attention from the window's presentation of fashionable, desirable merchandise.

Window designers can isolate and emphasize merchandise to create moods, project attitudes, teach lessons, make announcements, or present fashion statements. By controlling every vehicle they use—like lighting, props, color, texture, scale, mannequins, forms, signing, and theme—visual merchandisers also control communication. They believe that windows help shoppers project themselves into the displayed merchandise and prompt them to step inside the store.

vignettes are a condensed version of a larger scene. For example, a home furnishings vignette might establish the mood and the scene of a larger room with only a few elements—a chair, an end table, and a lamp.

"Now don't forget that nice wrist movement we've been practicing!" squeaked Professor Flitwick, perched on top of his pile of books as usual. "Swish and flick, remember, swish and flick. And saying the magic words properly is very important, too . . . ."
Professor Flitwick
Harry Potter and the Sorcerer's Stone

AFTER COMPLETING THIS CHAPTER, YOU SHOULD BE ABLE TO
- Recognize a variety of architectural window formats
- Explain how windows function as vehicles for communication
- Apply basic window display theory to meet retail goals
- Plan effective window merchandising themes
- Identify appropriate props and signs to carry out specific display themes
- Adjust lighting for windows and editorial displays

Figure 12.0 An artful ball gown filled with floating floral appliques is the star in this magical window. Harrods, Knightsbridge, London. Copyright WindowsWear Inc., http://www.windowswear.com, contact@windowswear.com.

Window designers also believe that memorable windows are an integral part of both store brand image and reputation for fashion leadership—that windows say something tangible and important that differentiates the store and its products from competitors.

Architectural Window Styles

There are two dominant styles of windows in retail stores today, enclosed and open-back.

■ ENCLOSED WINDOWS

A fully enclosed display window has a solid back wall, two side walls, and a glass front that faces the street (or indoor mall lease line). It is essentially a box. Visual merchandisers generally enter these windows via hidden doors leading from stockrooms or fitting rooms. A bank of three or four windows may share a common access door.

Most enclosed windows borrow elements from theatrical production to create ambiance—like painted backdrops, scrims,

and lighting grids. (See Figure 12.1.) Windows can also be "masked" to reduce the size to create a focal point for smaller items, like the Gucci shoes in Figure 12.1. Jewelry stores in particular feature closed shadow box windows that are situated several feet above the sidewalk for eye-level viewing of smaller-scaled merchandise. In New York City, some of the display windows at BVLGARI, Cartier and Tiffany & Co., feature elegant shadow boxes.

A few retailers employ freestanding island windows that have glass on all four sides, rendering them viewable from any direction. You might find this type of window as a stand-alone display feature to mark the entrance to a department or in a courtyard or indoor mall setting.

■ OPEN-BACK WINDOWS

Open-back windows sometimes have little formal display; merchandise shown on the store's interior fixturing becomes the display. However, some retailers place a display platform in front of the window glass and

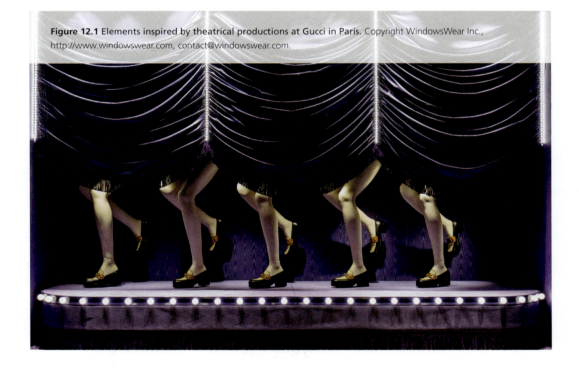

Figure 12.1 Elements inspired by theatrical productions at Gucci in Paris. Copyright WindowsWear Inc., http://www.windowswear.com, contact@windowswear.com.

create a formal display there. The platform differentiates the display area from the selling floor, and the presentation is viewable from both inside and outside the store. People who are on the street will see not only the merchandise display, but also other merchandise and any activities taking place on the store's main floor. Open-back window displays must be propped simply and focused carefully or viewers will miss the fashion message in the competing visual clutter. For these reasons, it is important to develop strong focal points, color schemes, or merchandise themes for window displays and any feature fixtures in the window's immediate vicinity.

Occasionally visual merchandisers will drop swags of fabric or no-seam paper panels from the store's ceiling to the floor behind the open-backed window displays. More often, a large graphic poster is suspended from ceiling to floor, providing a visual anchor for the merchandise being presented. Either strategy provides the impression of a backdrop for the display without limiting too much of the view to the store's interior. Another unusual open-backed window treatment might involve painting or applying colorful seasonal scenery or graphic messages directly onto the window glass.

Window Display in Practice

Open or enclosed, windows play a critical role in a store's merchandising strategy; they are communication tools that reach out to current customers and potential customers. When store management commits marketing and promotional dollars to an item of merchandise, a chain of retail communication activities begins.

As soon as department store and specialty chain-store buyers return from market trips where they have purchased goods, they communicate with the sales support departments in order to launch promotional campaigns featuring some of the more important fashion items. This retail support team—composed of buyers, merchandise managers, the marketing group, and visual merchandisers—discusses ad timing, theme development, and relevant trends. Support team members decide what the intent of the window display should be—promotional, institutional, fashion, or sale-oriented.

Merchandise managers make plans for receiving the merchandise and placing it on the selling floor. The marketing department prepares, schedules, and places ads in selected media. Visual merchandisers schedule display windows and plan in-store editorial displays and department presentations, selecting props and mannequins and ordering signs that tie directly to the ad copy or theme.

When the merchandise arrives in the store's receiving department, it is unpacked, hung, steamed, ticketed, and moved to the selling floor where it will be strategically placed on wall or feature fixtures. Visual merchandisers visit the selling department and select agreed-upon merchandise and accessories for windows, platforms, and displays in the selling department. Then they do their magic. The artfully presented merchandise sells out, and the cycle is repeated with new merchandise. If the store is a smaller mom-and-pop operation, there may be fewer specialists involved, but the process is essentially the same.

▌WINDOW MERCHANDISING ▌ FUNCTIONS

Fashion apparel windows advertise the store's fashion leadership position by presenting the store's newest trend merchandise. They also educate shoppers by showing mannequins that exemplify how current trend garments may be coordinated with accessories and shoes.

Home fashion windows may feature the latest dining trend, complete with the utensils needed to cook and serve a meal. They may also feature candles, dinnerware, and table linens that relate to the dinner theme, encouraging shoppers to create all of the ambiance they might find in a restaurant in their own homes.

Promotional windows feature products that are part of a marketing strategy promoting an entire line of goods, a single item, or a special storewide event. Holidays like Mother's Day and Valentine's Day also provide opportunities to stage exciting window productions.

Sale and Clearance windows announce the store's major sale events and may not feature any merchandise at all—implying that the store is stripped down and ready to sell out to the bare walls at low, low prices.

Drive-by windows are exterior store windows viewed by people driving on city streets or passing through shopping mall parking lots. As you might imagine, these window treatments must be larger in scale to be seen and understood from a distance. Large items—if they are repeated—can say a great deal about the store and its products. Visual impact can also be achieved by using masses of merchandise, larger-than-life graphics, backdrops, and intense, well-lit color schemes.

Live or demo windows are one of the more effective ways to capture shoppers' attention. Live models in windows have caused many shoppers to stop and notice when the model subtly moves or winks at an unsuspecting passersby. It never takes long for a crowd to gather in front of a window that has activity and movement.

Imagine a kitchen product shop with crisp white café curtains hung on a brass rod across the lower third of its display window. Inside, raised up on a black-and-white tiled platform, stands a butcher-block demonstration table. The window's sign—a hand-chalked menu board—asks: "What's Cooking?" In smaller letters, you see the response: "Pasta al Pomodoro! At 3 p.m. and 5 p.m."

What will be on display in this hypothetical window? According to the sign, one special element would be the store's resident chef—

demonstrating how to use many of the kitchen utensils and equipment the store sells. During non-demonstration hours, there could be dozens of display possibilities for the butcher-block table: stacks of cookbooks, small appliances, cooking pots and utensils, spice racks, kitchen linens, and packaged food products.

The final touch could be to send cooking aromas wafting out into the street through strategically located ventilation fans which would entice window shoppers to enter the store.

Interactive windows, once featured in a Stores of the Future exhibit at a national retail conference, were created by retail architect/ designer David Kepron. The store windows in Kepron's "dot com" shop could literally communicate with shoppers day and night. Electronic components, connected to oversized screens set up in the window's interior, invited passersby to interact with window displays by touching sensitive panels on the exterior glass. Viewers could virtually design their own window displays by calling up brands and images that interested them from a programmed menu.

According to Kepron:

> The "dot com" experience demonstrates that we no longer need to consider e-commerce and traditional bricks-and-mortar retailing as separate approaches to selling goods or services. Indeed, technology and retail design can exist together, where the root of retailing— the social experience—is enhanced, **leveraging** your brand to create lasting customers.

Kepron points to the practical opportunities that interactivity offers for retailers whose shopping mall stores close by 10 p.m. nightly:

leveraging, used as a verb, means gaining a mechanical advantage, or adding impact, power, or effectiveness; for example, adding impact to a store's brand identity by using an interactive display window.

Look at the number of malls whose tenants include entertainment [movies, restaurants, nightclubs] venues that operate beyond the mall's normal shopping hours. Why shouldn't retail stores continue to interact with shoppers after hours? Imagine the possibilities if shoppers could still look at and order merchandise after the store's doors closed for the evening.

An artist, retail architect, and store designer, David Kepron adds, "Technology does not have to be an either/or proposition for a retailer. Stores of the future can blend real and virtual boundaries into truly three-dimensional catalogs that function twenty-four hours a day, seven days a week."

NON-MERCHANDISING WINDOW FUNCTIONS

Window displays serve purposes other than showing tangible items of merchandise. Non-merchandising displays—devoted to intangible ideas and causes—are described as **institutional windows**.

Institutional display windows are often donated by civic-minded retailers to publicize and support special events that benefit nonprofit charitable organizations in their communities. Examples are the Special Olympics and The Easter Seal Society, local museums, orchestras, and zoological gardens. These institutional windows can also be used to publicize social issues.

Retail store windows respond to national and local news events, too. Cities with championship sports teams may do congratulatory windows. There have been special windows during local, national, and international crises—racial unrest, weather disasters, etc.—showing support for the people and issues involved. It all revolves around retail management's desire to project an image

of community involvement, humanitarian concern, or support for the topic. Retailers do these special windows to enhance corporate image and build goodwill for their companies. In addition, they may choose to celebrate milestones in their stores' histories, publicize their own activities, or simply promote their own community leadership positions in windows that exhibit no merchandise at all.

Window Display Theory

Many retailers believe that exciting fashion displays in store windows are miniature theatrical productions that turn passersby into window shoppers. A display window's fashion image must be strong enough to stop traffic—foot traffic, that is. The fashion message must be strong enough to compel window shoppers to enter the store and locate the item in the department. Effective fashion windows mark the first step in a planned progression that leads shoppers from viewing to purchasing.

Fantasy-to-Reality Theory

Window theatrics may be retail fantasies, romances, dramas, comedies, or adventure stories, but they are always designed to engage imagination and make shoppers think about what it would be like to own or wear the merchandise on display. The fantasy-to-reality theory guides shoppers from their first look at merchandise in windows and editorial displays to the selling floor and into the fitting room in three steps:

Step 1 The window's larger-than-life version of fashion—merchandise that is propped or posed to amaze, amuse, and enthuse—draws window shoppers into the store. This is the fantasy stage.
Step 2 The retailer presents the window merchandise inside the store and less theatrically, using editorial space in prime interior locations. These are stepped-down presentations. That is, they echo the theme of the window display, but are now

institutional windows are devoted to intangible ideas and causes and promote an image for the store as an institution rather than featuring merchandise.

presented in the context of the store. If the window display is fantasy, the platform presentation is more realistic. Merchandise here looks more true to life than it does in the window, and lighting and props (if any) seem less dramatic. Shoppers now have a chance to personally inspect the merchandise—touch the fabrics, examine garments and accessories, and look at price tags. Editorial signing directs them to appropriate selling departments.

Step 3 In the selling department— on feature fixtures or walls, shown on mannequins or not—the window merchandise is ready for purchase. Here is reality, where shoppers can actually handle the items they've admired and try them on. Departmental signing gives information about price or product use and care, or it may describe occasions where shoppers might wear the featured fashions or use the displayed products appropriately.

Alternatively, fantastic window displays featuring out-of-this world themes may function as mood setters. A lush setting with butterflies and garden fairies may urge winter-weary window shoppers to enter the store to enjoy the store's spring flower show. A holiday-themed window may invite shoppers to bring their little ones to the store's toy department or auditorium Santa Land presentation (Figure 12.2). The general strategy here is retail "soft-sell"—entertaining and encouraging a shopping mindset rather than pushing sale of specific products. Repeated annually, productions like these become "must-go-must-see" traditions that draw shopper traffic and build goodwill.

Figure 12.2 Bergdorf Goodman's holiday windows are designed to delight both children and adults with a candy cane fantasy theme. Copyright WindowsWear Inc., http://www.windowswear.com, contact@windowswear.com.

Window Display Themes and Inspiration

The prime source of thematic inspiration for window displays is always the merchandise itself. Visual merchandisers take their creative cues from the store's merchandise, looking at each product's end use, fabrication, style, and color as they begin to develop display themes. The window's motif (dominant theme idea) is only a supporting device. When theme choice is the visual department's responsibility, the window designer seeks ways to support the selected merchandise with ideas that will bring focus and direction to the presentation. Because the store window is a powerful communication tool, it is crucial that themes speak directly to targeted customers and focus attention on the merchandise. In this case, communicating requires a common language—

fantasy-to-reality theory

Step 1: Window display features fashion in a theatrical presentation.
Step 2: Interior platform features fashion in the context of the store.
Step 3: Department features fashion on hangers, to try and buy.

◀ B O X **1 2 . 1**

theme—that the store's target audience will relate to and understand (Figure 12.3).

Sometimes window themes are set by the corporate advertisers who also use merchandise to drive theme. When the advertising department composes a theme, the visual merchandiser's task is to find a creative way to reinforce the retail ad's message. Tying in with the ad can double the impact of the fashion message. Shoppers who see both

Figure 12.3 An Elton John theme at John Lewis in London featuring a musical light show that was projected from the Oxford Street windows every 30 minutes starting at 4 p.m. Copyright WindowsWear Inc., http://www.windowswear.com, contact@windowswear.com

- Use gels to create theatrical effects and make colored merchandise pop, or to mute the color somewhat. Light-blue gels, for example, can make black look richer.
- Position window track fixtures carefully, in front of merchandise displays and as close to the window line as possible. If the track is placed in the center of the window you will be lighting the top of the merchandise rather than the face.
- Incorporate [open] window displays into the interior architecture of the store. Because most mall stores have no dividing walls behind their window display areas, dramatic lighting using high color gels is usually not feasible, but floods and spots will suffice.
- To optimize lighting's effectiveness, visual merchandisers need to pay close attention to maintenance issues—not only changing burned-out lights but refocusing lights as merchandise changes seasonally so that luminaries don't wind up shining onto blank walls or walkways.

You can even find professional window lighting tips online. One particularly good website is www.fashionwindows.com, where visual merchandisers can read articles excerpted from trade publications, view window photographs from all over the world, chat with others in the field, search for new and used props and mannequins, or look for employment.

TECHNIQUES FOR LEDGES AND DISPLAY CASES

Ledges and display cases may be thought of as small windows, especially when it comes to composition and propping. These atmospheric presentations add visual interest to store areas that primarily stock packaged goods in secured showcases (cosmetics, small leather goods, jewelry, watches, etc.). They may be used to create focal points in select areas throughout a department, including perimeter walls. Choose

locations carefully and edit the number of ledge and countertop displays, or they will add clutter instead of emphasis.

The same is true for the interiors of display cases. If a department has a center island display case for stock surrounded by a perimeter counter over glass-front stock cases, select one space per side for decorative displays that incorporate stock, props, and graphics. From a distance, these small displays can break the visual monotony of row upon row of packaged merchandise and highlight certain important products. They focus shoppers' attention and are very useful reminders about advertised items. Display case interiors should be reset when advertising changes or when new products arrive.

Look at Figure 12.9, where a multitude of display windows are stacked to feature high-end sunglasses and handbags. Each case is individually lit and displays only one or two items. The resulting museum-like quality is very appropriate for the Versace line.

■ HOUSEKEEPING

Begin any display in windows, on ledges, and in showcases with a thorough dusting and glass cleaning. As you complete a display, seek out and remove any loose threads, staples, wire trimmings, and so on. Check to ensure that fashion items have no tags or threads showing. Step outside store windows and inspect displays for minor details.

Daily, before the store opens, revisit displays that are accessible to shoppers and reposition merchandise that has been handled. Walk through all of your areas; dust and clean as you go. A display, even in an enclosed showcase, gathers dust. Remember that shoppers' first impressions are lasting impressions. They reflect the store's image and your professional reputation.

Don't forget the safety and security aspects of this housekeeping tour. Be sure that mannequins aren't tipped precariously,

⧉ Designers' Pet Peeves

Imagine that you are the merchant who went to market and carefully selected the coats and jackets and apparel that you see on the two mannequins in this window. Or if you were the accessories merchant who chose the colorful cross-body handbag and fluffy mittens and shoes to outfit shoppers. If you were either of the two merchants who decided to purchase these playful fashions to sell to and delight their customers, what would your first impression be when looking at the window?

Is it possible that you might ask, "Are we selling the lighted backdrop or the fashions on the mannequins?" And if you were the visual merchandiser who designed this window, how would you answer them? And what would you do to light the window so that the lively colors of the garments take center stage?

It's easy to see that even an imaginative and brilliantly lighted graphic as a backdrop can miss the point of a store window: to engage shoppers' interest and invite them into the store to try and buy the fashions. To attract their attention, proper lighting is obviously vital. When a visual merchandiser completes setting a window behind the glass, there is one final step. They must journey outside the store and look at the window with new eyes, from the point of view of the merchants who purchased the products for the business, and from the point of view of the shoppers who are passing by.

What's for sale? The backdrop or the fashions on the mannequins? Judy Bell.

Figure 12.9 A series of sleek black display cases offset by a clean white display wall and floor cubes creates a glamorous setting for Versace merchandise; Versace, Northpark Center, Dallas, Texas. Coulter / WWD / © Conde Nast.

Chapter 12 Review Questions

1. Describe the difference between enclosed windows and open-back windows. Give examples of retailers who utilize each and how they do so.
2. Give two examples of how retail store windows communicate to the customer using the theoretical foundations in this chapter.
3. Where can theme inspirations for a window come from? Explain at least two of these.
4. What are the seven mechanics of window magic?
5. What does striking a mannequin mean?
6. Give examples of how lighting is used in store windows.
7. How are ledges and display cases used as small windows?

Outside-the-Box Challenge

Window Review

LOOK

Visit three stores with enclosed windows and evaluate each window. Take notes on the categories of merchandise, color scheme, theme, props, mannequins (if any), product accessories, and housekeeping, using the form in Figure 12.11. You may make as many copies of the form as you need.

COMPARE

Compare the presentations.

INNOVATE

What would you do to improve each of the presentations? Be prepared to discuss and justify your critique in a class discussion.

Critical Thinking

Theme Development and Critique of Store Windows

Visit three different retail stores. Photograph or sketch their store windows. Next, identify whether they are using:

1. Current directions in fashion design or popular color palettes
2. Recent or upcoming local events
3. Influential cultural directions
4. Historical perspectives
5. Retail image decisions
6. New developments in props or decorative items available from the display industry

Once you have identified how the themes are developed and executed, explain how these particular concepts target various demographics of retail consumers and consider their level of effectiveness. Discuss whether you feel these windows will be successful in selling the merchandise they are displaying and why. Back up your answers with facts and figures if necessary from various sources.

Case Study

Design Challenge

THE SITUATION

You have applied for a position as the visual merchandising director of a local department store. Until this time, you've worked exclusively as an independent contractor in the menswear area. One of your pre-employment challenges is to prepare window presentation concepts to be executed by the staff. The interview committee asks you and the other two finalists to complete an impromptu design challenge that you will present during your second interview.

YOUR CHALLENGE

The bulleted items that follow are your tasks. The numbered items represent four specific challenges—with specific design requirements.

*   Identify a theme for the window that could also be used as a sign copy headline.
*   Write sign copy (or specify a lifestyle graphic to be placed in the display as a means of communicating the window's theme).
*   Specify colors, props, and style of mannequin (if used).

- Sketch a front view of your window concept.
- Label any figures or items necessary for the interview committee members to understand the concept.
- Be prepared to present all four concepts, although time may permit you to discuss only one of them with the committee.

The four concepts are:

1. Design a fashion window display concept for the fall season that does not rely on traditional autumn leaves or pumpkins for its props.

2. Design an institutional window concept that celebrates the opening of a new exhibit at a local art museum.

3. Design a white sale window concept for a department store using large banners announcing the sale. Assume that you have state-of-the-art display props and materials.

4. Design a tween trend window to appeal to a back-to-school audience in August.

STORE WINDOW REVIEW

Window Function

1. Function is fashion, promotional, institutional, sale, or other?

_____

Merchandise

2. Merchandise theme is seasonal, fashion, trend, dressy, casual, or other?

_____

3. Merchandise category is:_____

4. Merchandise included accessory items.	Y	N	NA

5. Merchandise color scheme is bright, pastel, or other?

_____

6. Merchandise is wrinkle free.	Y	N	NA

Mannequins (if used)

7. Mannequin use is appropriate for merchandise.	Y	N	NA
8. Mannequin pose is natural.	Y	N	NA
9. Mannequins appear to relate to each other.	Y	N	NA

Props

10. Props selected for the window relate to theme.	Y	N	NA
11. Props do not dominate the window display.	Y	N	NA

Signing

12. Identifies trend, designer, brand, or item features.	Y	N	NA
13. Directs shopper to selling area in store.	Y	N	NA
14. Signing type is large enough for easy reading.	Y	N	NA

Housekeeping

15. Window glass is clean (inside and outside).	Y	N	NA
16. Window floor is clean, lint-free, dust-free.	Y	N	NA
17. Fixtures, buildups, mannequin bases are clean, dust-free.	Y	N	NA

Figure 12.11 Fairchild Books/rendered by Elaine Wencl Art.

13 Mannequins and Mannequin Alternatives

Communicating Self-Image and Fashion Image

The mannequin is regarded as one of the fashion retailer's most powerful communication tools. Used strategically, it speaks volumes about fashion trends and a store's brand identity. We know that in order to communicate effectively, a store mannequin must relate to a shopper's self-image. When shoppers follow current fashion—read about it, talk about it, look at it, buy it, and wear it—they are defining self and describing who they are through the clothing they wear. In fact, more than one industry writer has suggested that visual merchandisers would gain valuable insights into shopper self-image by observing and studying shoppers in stores.

You could easily practice this technique on your own. Station yourself outside or inside of a store where you can observe shoppers. Are they hurrying by or are they stepping closer to examine the items on display? What conclusions can you draw from your observations? How could you relate your findings to merchandise presentation?

■ MANNEQUIN EVOLUTION

To trace the history of the mannequin as a medium for communicating fashionability, you may also want to consider the evolution of the human body. A discovery made in preparation for a 1997 Christian Dior retrospective show at New York's Metropolitan Museum of Art shows just what kinds of changes have taken place.

As the Metropolitan's Costume Institute designers prepared to dress mannequins in costumes spanning Dior's haute couture career, they found that many of his garments didn't fit their standard exhibit mannequins. The museum's principal mannequin supplier, Ralph Pucci International, needed to design and fabricate an entirely new series of figures to fit the Dior designs.

AFTER COMPLETING THIS CHAPTER, YOU SHOULD BE ABLE TO

- Explain how the mannequin is used as a communication tool
- Identify resources for mannequins and mannequin alternatives
- Evaluate criteria for matching mannequins to store brand image
- Follow guidelines for dressing and maintaining mannequins
- Develop strategies for placing mannequins in departments

"Mannequins are the high-octane gasoline that fuel the throbbing of my window-dressing Lincoln Continental. No matter how groovy your window concept is, a dreary mannequin can reduce it to the level of suburban dinner theater."
Simon Doonan,
Confessions of a Window Dresser

"Mannequins in their fiberglass silence both whisper and shout at potential customers, using their own brand of body language to reach passersby. Frozen in time and space, mannequins constitute statements to be interpreted, each decade in their development a testimonial to the era and society that produced them."
Marsha Bentley Hale,
vmsd, *August 1983*

Figure 13.0a and b Ralph Pucci's "The Art of the Mannequin" exhibition explored the innovative mannequin designs that reflected cultural trends over three decades. MAD, The Museum of Art and Design in Manhattan, 2015. Installation photo of "Ralph Pucci: The Art of the Mannequin"' 2015. Photo by Butcher Walsh. Courtesy of the Museum of Arts and Design.

form   …

Figure 13.9 Dynamic mannequin alternative forms by Silvestri California. Silvestri California. Courtesy of Sylvestri California.

can be positioned almost anywhere a retailer needs them—atop a fixture, on a ledge, or flying through the air like trapeze artists. They may be very obvious in bright colors or dazzling white coverings, or they may seem to disappear into scenes made in colors that match backdrops. Again, as long as they fit a store's image, these are less expensive mannequins with indefinite life spans.

Puppet Cutouts

Puppet cutouts can be fabricated of corrugated cardboard, foam core, plywood, plexi, metal, or any other stiff material and articulated with bolts and wingnuts or other hardware fasteners to create entertaining, informal two-dimensional action figures. Toy-like in appearance, they adapt well to children's fashion and merchandising. They can be purchased, commissioned, customized, or built in your own prop shop. Versatile and novel alternatives to three-dimensional mannequins, these are not for every store image but, for the budget-conscious, they can brand the store as well as entertain.

■ MANNEQUIN ALTERNATIVES

In Chapter 5, you read about mannequin alternatives designed specifically for wall system merchandising. The alternatives described here are designed for selling floor use, on or near fixtures. Alternatives may be simple and very utilitarian, or they may be more elaborate, in designs that reinforce other aspects of store fixturing and décor. Look at the artful collection of forms by Silvestri California in Figure 13.9, and imagine the variety of store environments that they would complement.

   Mannequin alternatives are economical for four reasons:

- You can focus shopper attention on merchandise fashioned for specific parts of the body without having to dress the rest of a form.
- You do not have to pay for a full-size mannequin so it is more cost effective.
- You can place alternatives in display areas and strategic spaces that cannot accommodate a full figure.
- You add brand image and visual interest for shoppers at minimal cost.

Hosiery Forms

Hosiery forms may be right-side up or upside-down; they may be one-, two-, or three-dimensional in design (flat, half-round, and fully round). To show fashion from the toes up, there are:

- Shoe and foot forms
- Sock forms
- Knee-high forms
- Stocking leg forms
- Pantyhose forms

Innerwear Forms

Fashion is not limited to outer garments. Underwear and intimate apparel mannequin alternatives are available in varying sizes and skin tones, fabrications and finishes, for both genders and all ages. You will find:

- Brief and boxer forms
- Panty forms
- Corset forms
- Lingerie forms
- Swimwear forms
- Bra forms

As an alternative to innerwear forms, one creative retailer used simple white hangers to display bras and panties (Figure 13.10).

Combined with artfully arranged gift boxes, this series of shadow boxes delivered an eye-catching statement in a cost effective way. You might also consider working with an established manufacturer like B Free Hangers in New York to design custom hangers. They are available in a wide variety of colors and materials. You can even add retail store logos or messages to make them entirely unique and strengthen your store's brand image (www.bfreehangers.com).

Ready-to-Wear Forms

To accommodate layering and accessorizing ready-to-wear, these alternative forms are designed for both genders and all ages. They may be mounted on flat bases for table- and fixture-top presentations or on bases and pedestals for floor display (Figure 13.11). You could purchase:

- Shirt forms
- Blouse forms
- Bust forms
- Swimwear forms
- Suit forms

Figure 13.10 Creatively displayed lingerie on simple white hangers at Journelle, New York City. Ericksen / WWD / © Conde Nast.

BOX 13.1

Designers' Pet Peeves

If you just read "Selecting Garments for Mannequins", what do you think of the mannequins' outfits pictured here? If you were approaching this display would it grab your attention? Would you want to find the items and try them on? Would you want to attend an event dressed like these mannequins? Their outfits may not be your personal style, but if you did dress in this conservative manner would you walk out your door dressed like this?

The goal of the visual merchandiser when dressing mannequins is to inspire and educate shoppers with the best fashion looks. Effective presentation of accessories can teach shoppers how to accessorize fashionably and trigger additional purchases. Let's take a careful look at the photograph here and make a list of the visual merchandising "Don'ts" and suggest ideas on how to elevate this vignette.

1. The bright red blouse and the mauve sleeveless tank are from two different color groups: brights and midtones. Instead, use just one color group for both so that the outfits complement each other. You could replace the red blouse with another midtone for example, and a softer color skirt rather than black.
2. The photo was taken in the winter months in a very cold climate. The mannequin in the mauve sleeveless outfit looks cold. Offer her a jacket or soft cardigan sweater in a coordinating or neutral color.
3. The red blouse is too large for the mannequin. The sleeves almost cover her thumb! The collar of the shirt is sliding back and the shoulders sit too low.
4. The mannequin with the red blouse is leaning to the right—she may tip if given a nudge. You need to readjust the stand so that she stands upright with a strong core.
5. There is only one lonely white belt as an accessory, and it is slung loosely around the waist in a manner not appropriate for the conservative skirt and blouse.

You could select a different belt (not white!) and fit it at the waistline, not below.
6. What other accessories could you add to either outfit? Perhaps classic necklaces and bracelets. A clutch under one arm?
7. As a final step, you can see that a fixture is positioned immediately adjacent to the mannequin platform. Fill it with the apparel items that the mannequins are wearing to make shopping easy.

Which of these two outfits would you choose to try on? Neither? Why not? Judy Bell

mannequin dressers work in pairs to do this step and may also fit the shoes onto the form at the same time they stand the form back on the base.

Option 2 Remove the rod from the mannequin and the base. Then fit the rod back down the leg after the mannequin is back on its feet. Tighten the set screw at the buttocks and then tighten the screw into the base plate.

If you're using a standing or striding mannequin, the pant leg may not hang properly with the rod in place (Figure 13.16). If the pant leg is pulled taut by the rod, don't use that pant. Or you can carefully slit the back seam and insert the rod through the opening.

Action figures and mannequins with longer strides generally have one bent leg that must be removed for dressing and undressing. Treated like an arm, it is inserted through the waistband before the straight leg attached to the hip section has been inserted. Holding the bent leg and pant in one hand and balancing the inverted form between your feet, you'll slide the empty pant leg over the straight leg's foot. As the pant slides nearer the hip section, you'll be able to snap or lock the bent leg in place. This task is easier for two people to accomplish.

Because of all this maneuvering you may decide to select a larger size than the mannequin usually wears and pin any excess fabric away after the garment is on the figure. There is no simple way to describe this procedure; you'll simply have to do some hands-on experimenting until you know the mannequin well.

4. Slip on the mannequin's shoes. Be sure that the shoe you've chosen has the proper heel height. Measure the mannequin as shown in Figure 13.17. If the heels are too low, the mannequin will tip backward; too high, it will tip forward.

    Be sure that the shoe is properly fitted to the mannequin's foot. Shoes with gaping sides or shoes that slip off the figure's heel are never acceptable because customers won't buy or wear shoes that look as if they will fit poorly. Ill-fitting shoes left on mannequin's feet for long periods of time in hot windows tend to form in position,

Figure 13.13 Pantyhose and pants may be easily pulled onto a mannequin's legs while you are seated on the floor. Fairchild Books/ rendered by Craig Gustafson Art.

Figure 13.14 In Option 1, the mannequin's lower half is removed from its rod, dressed, then returned to the base by lifting the form and easing the pant leg down over the rod. Tighten buttocks screw when the form is standing on its base once more. Fairchild Books/ rendered by Craig Gustafson Art.

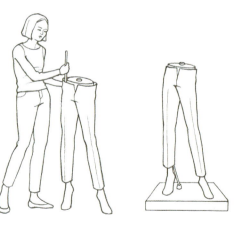

Figure 13.15 In Option 2, the rod is slipped down the pant leg and the mannequin's legs are fitted onto the base. Fairchild Books/ rendered by Craig Gustafson Art.

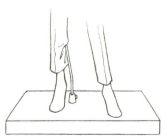

Figure 13.16 This pant is too narrow for the rod to be fitted through and the pant is pulled taut in an unnatural manner. Fairchild Books/ rendered by Craig Gustafson Art.

10. Accessorize neck and ears. Mannequins have pierced ears, but some models are too rigid or their ears are set too close to the head to accept French wires and some hoops without bending them badly out of shape. Posts aren't always long enough to accept their backs. Clips generally do not stay on at all. Tacky gum (the kind used to hang posters) will hold pierced and clip earrings in place. If you can't hook the French wires or hoops correctly, avoid them for that particular mannequin. You'll soon learn which figures can wear certain accessories.

11. Adjust hands and arms to natural positions (Figure 13.20). Add any handbags or bracelets before twisting hands into place at the wrist joints. To make the handbag seem more a natural part of the mannequin's costume, it should be tucked under an arm or held by the mannequin in the same way that a model might carry it on a fashion show runway.

12. When the mannequin is in place and properly lit, step away (outside if this is a window mannequin) and check the figure from head to toe. Make any necessary adjustments. Make sure that all mannequin bases, risers, and window floors or pedestals are dust free.

■ MAINTAINING MANNEQUINS

Mannequins are among your store's most visible fashion fixtures. They are also among the most frequently handled. The fact that they attract attention is good, but the fact that they may be disturbed by customer handling is not—unless you maintain their appearance and grooming daily.

Watch for:

- Exposed price tags
- Improperly positioned wigs, hands, and accessories
- Missing accessories or items of clothing

safety concern!

In-store mannequins placed on pedestals or riser platforms must be removed from their safety glass or metal bases and bolted directly to the units where they'll stand. This prevents them from being bumped or tipped accidentally by curious shoppers.

◀ BOX 13.2 ─

- Substitutions (resulting from sale of the original garment)
- Shopworn garments
- Dirty-looking skin
- Hosiery with runs or sagging wrinkles
- Dusty risers
- Trash on the riser or in the area of the display

■ SCHEDULING CHANGES

Shoppers should never have to search out selling stock for merchandise that they've seen on editorial mannequins. Since editorial mannequins should always be positioned with adjacent two-way or four-way selling fixtures with stock of the displayed garments, sell-down will often dictate your schedule for changes.

Other retail practices also require the visual department to change the store's mannequins frequently:

- Management's expectation that regular weekly shoppers will see something new each time they come to the store.
- Strategies that schedule quick, significant markdowns to keep stock turning through a department.
- Aggressive weekly advertising schedules that include backup floor displays in key editorial positions.
- Transfer and consolidation of groupings to facilitate sell-through.

POSITIONING AND PROPPING MANNEQUINS

Positioning mannequins with props in a triangular shape is more effective than positioning them in a straight line. If you look at Figure 13.21, you'll see a mannequin grouping in a triangular format that creates a three-dimensional presentation with more depth and greater visual interest than would have been accomplished if the mannequins were all at the same height.

The triangle is also a useful way to analyze the positioning of fixtures, props, and mannequins arranged on a floor or platform.

Used as you see illustrated in Figure 13.22, the triangle forces mannequin and prop into better optical balance with the prop and sign relating more closely to the form after repositioning.

Probably the most important thing to realize is that grouped mannequins, frequently used in odd multiples (3 or 5), must relate to each other in theme, in color story, and in physical proximity. The group must also relate to the props selected in exactly the same ways. They should all touch somewhere—either physically or optically. The correct view in Figure 13.22 shows an optical relationship. The potted plant isn't really touching the mannequin; she is positioned behind it. But the two elements appear to touch; lending depth and texture to the composition, causing it to feel tight, or closely related.

If you use two mannequins in an editorial platform grouping, a single larger prop will probably be all that the space can carry. Try to work in odd numbers if you can, because they are more pleasing to the eye.

Mannequin positioning, with or without props, can tell stories and set tone. Multiple window mannequins can be positioned so that one is standing alone while the others are positioned in a conversational grouping—causing viewers to wonder what's going on.

Mannequin positioning can also focus attention precisely where you want it. Imagine mannequins lined up in military file diagonally across a window floor, all wearing purple garments, except for one mannequin dressed in brilliant red. A dramatic presentation with a point of emphasis is created without the use of a single prop.

Figure 13.21 A triangular format is implemented in this mannequin grouping. Fairchild Books/ rendered by Craig Gustafson Art.

CORRECT   INCORRECT

Figure 13.22 The three-dimensional arrangement of mannequin, prop, and sign in the correct example has more visual interest than the incorrect example, where they are arranged in a straight line. Fairchild Books/ rendered by Craig Gustafson Art.

CYCLING AND REFURBISHING MANNEQUINS

In fashion retailing, an industry with continual visual change, mannequins are going to become outdated after a time and will have to be replaced. Expensive as they are, mannequins are still the best way to help customers visualize garments. Sometimes you can update a mannequin series with new wigs and prolong the inevitable need to update.

Cycling

Some retailers cycle their mannequins, saving their newest, trend-right figures for prime window presentations and rotating last season's mannequins into the store for interior editorial and departmental use. Eventually, outdated mannequins are either sold, sent to the mannequin factory for refurbishing, donated to a school or a thrift store, or discarded.

Refurbishing

Mannequins don't always age gracefully, and some are accident-prone. This gives rise to an important visual merchandising support system that can extend or restore a mannequin's usefulness. Frank Glover is one of the top US companies in mannequin refinishing and repair. Clients have included Bloomingdales, Macy's, Saks Fifth Avenue, Hermes, Kate Spade, Ralph Lauren, Tory Burch, and many more (www.frankgloverproductions.com).

"My exposure to mannequins began in London . . . servicing the likes of Harrods and Selfridges and traveling the country refinishing and spraying mannequins. In 1978 Adel Rootstein hired me to go to New York and in 1982 I left and established my own company. The experience from relationships with mannequin manufacturers and suppliers worldwide is what my service offers, in addition to rentals with over 2000 mannequins in stock."
Frank Glover

Shoptalk "Innovation Grows a Business" by Ralph Pucci, President, Pucci International, Inc.

In spite of differences in generation and location, I think that you, the reader, and I probably have much in common. When I started my career in this industry, it was with an established company that had an interesting history, rich traditions, and exacting quality standards. It was a business dedicated to serving its customers beyond their expectations.

I started out in my family's business, and you may be starting out in one that belongs to someone else's family. As I once did, you may feel alternately challenged and hemmed in by the company's traditions and standards. But at the heart of it, you'll probably end up doing those things that best serve your company's mission and its customers, just as I did.

I helped grow the business I'm in today. From exclusively doing mannequin repair in the 1950s, we turned to mannequin design and manufacture in 1976 when it was my turn to lead the firm. We set ourselves apart by anticipating trends and doing things that differentiated Pucci from its competitors.

First, we took a rather innovative approach and let our mannequins recline and relax on the job. Then we painted them brilliant colors. Having done all that, it was necessary to keep our vision fresh in other (and sometimes surprising) ways. I came to believe that display mannequins can (and should) do more than simply wear clothes. In Pucci's reach to lead the industry, we've commissioned well-known people from other creative fields—a pop artist, an interior designer, a fashion designer, an architect, and an illustrator—to push the parameters of mannequin design for us. Our vision is to create an identity for our products that will help you do the same for yours in whatever retail business you join.

Would you agree that a mannequin ought to communicate with customers, whether they be young, trendy, sophisticated, or chic? Do you think a mannequin should enhance the total visual environment and be your company's most efficient salesperson? Do you want the mannequins you use to add a unique point of view, a certain freshness, and a creative element to an item traditionally made purely with function in mind? If you're nodding your head "Yes," we do have a lot in common.

I want what you want—to have people lined up on the sidewalk to see your windows and to see shoppers throng the aisles to view fashion in your selling departments where art and fashion have come together to create history, tradition, and high, high quality.

I wish you well in your work.
www.ralphpuccimannequins.net

BOX 13.3

DESIGN GALLERY: RALPH PUCCI: THE ART OF THE MANNEQUIN, MUSEUM OF ARTS AND DESIGN, NEW YORK

Ralph Pucci, the iconic and renowned New York designer, is highly regarded for his innovative approach to mannequin design. In 2015, an exhibit at MAD (Museum of Arts and Design) was the first to explore his work. MAD's (*www.madmuseum.org*) online description reads: "As Pucci was building his business in the 1970s the notion of the 'super model'—the living model with a personality—emerged. Pucci captured this catalytic moment in his work, finding inspiration from sources as varied as Greek and Roman statues and the performance costumes of the New York Dolls. More than commercial armatures or sculptural forms, his mannequins became agents of change in our attitudes to the body, to fashion, and to individual identity . . . having collaborated with luminaries such as Diane von Furstenberg, Patrick Naggar, Andree Putnam, Kenny Scharf, Anna Sui, Isabel and Ruben Toledo and Christy Turlington."

"Most people think you go to the Yellow Pages, call and order two white, two black mannequins, and it's over. We wanted to show that great mannequins are works of art," said Ralph Pucci in an interview with Zoe Zellers for *design:retail* magazine (April/May 2015). Zellers writes, "Pucci believes this show will shine a light on the entire industry—the creativity, excitement and energy that the visual world has to offer, but often has been overlooked. 'It should make you think, it should make you smile, it should challenge you,' Pucci says, adding: 'Obviously having a show at MAD is our proudest moment.'"

Silent Selling author Judy Bell attended the exhibition and was most impressed that it covered every stage of the mannequin process, including a re-creation of

Installation photo of 'Ralph Pucci: The Art of the Mannequin' 2015. Photo by Butcher Walsh. Courtesy of the Museum of Arts and Design.

the studio workshop, complete with a workbench, sketches, and tools. (Go to www.madmuseum.org for photos and a fabulous video.) Over thirty of Pucci's most important mannequins were displayed; you can see a representation pictured here. Also look at the colored molds shelved along the wall, used in production of Pucci's artful and innovative mannequins.

Chapter 13 Review Questions

1. List three ways that mannequins reflect the historical times when they are designed.
2. List three major sources for mannequin purchasing.
3. What are the most important aspects that a visual merchandiser should think about when selecting mannequins for a particular store?
4. Give three mannequin alternatives and state how they are used.
5. What are the proper steps for dressing a mannequin?
6. Discuss how triangles are used in positioning mannequins within a display.

Outside-the-Box Challenge

Window Review

LOOK

Make six copies of the mannequin checklist in Figure 13.23. Take the forms with you as you visit three stores with enclosed windows showing mannequins and three stores with interior mannequin displays. Fill out the charts with all the required information.

COMPARE

Compare the presentations—windows to windows, interior displays to interior displays.

INNOVATE

Choose the one presentation from each chart that you believe needs the most improvement.

- What changes would you make?
- Explain why you think your changes will improve each presentation.

Critical Thinking

Sourcing and Selecting Mannequins

Directions: This exercise will help you make the important connections between store image, merchandise, and mannequin selection and send you off into cyberspace to source mannequins.

SCENARIO

You have been hired by your favorite retail store to purchase new mannequins or body forms for all of their stores. You must present this to the company's president and vice-presidents for approval.

1. Identify your favorite retail store.
2. Select three fashion outfits that you'd like to present in the store window from fashion publications or online resources. The threesome should have some connection in theme, season, color story, and/or attitude. Cut them out and mount them on a sheet of printer paper. Add appropriate accessories to the page. Don't be concerned about the size or scale of the pictures. Just be certain that the look meets the text's general requirements for selection—end use, fabrication, style, and color.
3. Describe your favorite retail store's fashion brand image and explain how the fashions and accessories you've chosen fit that image.
4. Now show what they are currently using as their store mannequin or body form. Visit several mannequin manufacturers' websites or scan recent issues of *vmsd* to select the mannequin (or series) that would be most appropriate to wear the garments you've chosen for your store window. Print a photo of the mannequin or series that you've chosen.
5. Describe the types and kinds of mannequins that you saw and excluded. Explain your reasoning.
6. Assemble your report. Justify your mannequin choice using criteria from this chapter and present your findings in a group discussion.

Case Study

Selecting Mannequins

THE SITUATION

Assume that you are an account manager at a marketing firm who has challenged you with

MANNEQUIN CHECKLIST

1. Mannequin fully dressed?	Y	N
2. Garments properly adjusted?	Y	N
3. Garment tags hidden?	Y	N
4. Mannequin fully accessorized?	Y	N
5. Accessory tags hidden?	Y	N
6. Exposed "skin" is clean, print-free?	Y	N
7. Wig is brushed and styled?	Y	N
8. Arms and hands positioned properly?	Y	N
9. Hosiery in good condition, properly fitted?	Y	N
10. Shoes in proper position, fitted properly, dust-free?	Y	N
11. Mannequin base clean, dust-free?	Y	N
12. Riser/platform clean, dust-free?	Y	N
13. Mannequin secure on base or platform?	Y	N
14. Supporting stock of merchandise nearby (if interior display)?	Y	N
15. Signing in place and current?	Y	N

Location: _____

Date: _____

Observer: _____

ActionRequired: _____

Figure 13.23 Mannequin check list. Fairchild Books/ rendered by Elaine Wencl Art.

creating a presentation to demonstrate the firms' expertise in selecting mannequins for a variety of retail stores.

YOUR CHALLENGE

Prepare a brief presentation using appropriate mannequin (or mannequin alternative) photographs or drawings for six of the following clients:

- The Club—an upscale exercise enthusiast shop for men and women
- **Just Like New**—a consignment shop featuring infant and children's clothing
- **The Pantry**—a kitchen and cooking enthusiast's shop that carries chef's garb
- **Sagebrush**—a Western-themed clothing boutique chain operating in Arizona, Colorado, and Montana ski-country resort areas
- **Artisan Alley**—a wearable art apparel shop and gallery
- **Tween Scene**—a national trendy clothing chain for girls aged nine to thirteen
- **CEO**—a conservative menswear apparel store specializing in high-quality suits, shirts, shoes, leather goods, ties, and other accessories
- **Fairchild's**—a national moderate-price department store chain specializing in clothing for the entire family
- **Getaways**—an upscale resort wear boutique for men and women
- **Expeditions**—an adventure sport clothing and gear store for men and women, which also carries camping, climbing, and diving gear
- **Underworld**—a specialty shop that sells natural fiber underwear for men, women, and children
- **Abondanza**—a women's clothing shop that specializes in business apparel and special-occasion dressing for plus-size women

Assume that each of these stores has a display window. Go to any of the following websites (or other websites or trade magazines) to find photos or drawings of at least one appropriate mannequin or alternative to fit each store's image and justify your choice in a written paragraph. You may add any necessary details about the store's image to strengthen your presentation. If possible, include budget figures for purchasing two or four mannequins and explain why you might prefer to have more than one.

Mannequin Websites:

- Bernstein—www.bernsteindisplay.com
- DK display corp—www.dkdisplaycorp.com
- Fusion Specialties—www.fusionspecialties.com
- Genesis Mannequins USA—www.genesismannequinsusa.com
- Greneker—www.greneker.com
- Hindsgaul—www.hindsgaul.com
- Hans Boodt—www.hansboodtmannequins.com
- New John Nissen—www.new-john-nissen.com
- Manex USA—www.manex-usa.com
- Mondo—www.mondomannequins.com
- Patina-V—www.patinav.com
- Ralph Pucci Mannequins—www.ralphpuccimannequins.net
- Seven Continents—www.sevencontinents.com
- Siegel & Stockman—www.siegel-stockman.com
- Silvestri California—www.silvestricalifornia.com
- Universal Display & Design—www.universaldisplay.co.uk
- Window France—www.windowfrance.com

14 Building a Visual Merchandising Department

Organizing Your Professional Work Environment

Attention to detail makes the difference between a good visual merchandiser and a great one. The way you handle detail on your job determines your working brand identity. Whether you're presenting mannequins in windows or presenting yourself in the way you dress and act, you are expressing your personal identity. When a visual merchandising executive can look at a display you've done and instantly recognize that you did the work, you'll know that you've established your own unique, personal brand. That brand should stand for excellence and a regard for detail.

The late retail observer Peter Glen, longtime writer for *vmsd* magazine, always offered astute, career-level advice in his monthly columns. In one, he offered a powerful idea that could have direct bearing on establishing your working brand identity and putting its indelible stamp on your career in a fast-paced industry. Glen's topic for the column was multitasking—a word coined to describe people routinely attempting (but not always succeeding) to juggle many tasks at once. Glen wrote that concentration cuts through chaos and changes it to clarity, and then he added, "A composed mind is a confident workshop." Glen's remarks seem apt as you as you get started in the fast-paced field of visual merchandising. His point was that focusing on whatever project you are working on without interruption is the best way to get to the finish line. With a ringing telephone as his example, Glen advised,

> "I will try every day to never say, 'What difference does it make,' remembering that no detail is small."
> *10 Years of Peter Glen: One Hundred Essays for the Improvement of Work, Life and Other Matters of Consequence*

AFTER COMPLETING THIS CHAPTER, YOU SHOULD BE ABLE TO

- Set up a visual merchandising office with basic supplies
- Organize tools for visual merchandising tasks
- Develop a visual merchandising resource center
- Plan a productive market trip
- Write a purchase order
- Plan a visual merchandising budget
- Create an idea board for presentations to executives

Figure 14.0 Uniqlo's dazzling holiday window encourages colorful gift giving. 5th Avenue, New York.

Finish what you're doing. The assumption here is that whatever you are doing when the phone rings, you are already doing something. You have decided what is most important, which gives you clarity and concentration, and presupposes order and even planning. So with that in mind, when the phone rings, keep doing what you are doing. Do it right. Do it until it's finished and then go on to the next (predecided) priority and concentrate on that. Answer the telephone when it's the highest priority, not when it rings. . . . You have to believe that without control you'll be multitasking helplessly, and that only concentration leads to your best effort at anything.

If you're going to be a visual merchandising manager—and the assumption here is that you will be—you'll need a strong resource center to back up your work. Your powers to prioritize, to organize, and to pay attention to detail will be critical to your success. Being focused and operating efficiently will lead directly to increased productivity, and productivity is what's going to get you noticed. Something as simple as having the right supplies within reach will free more of your time for activities that will build your visibility and reputation (your working brand image) in your department and

your store. Never forget that the first product you'll ever market on the job is yourself!

This chapter is dedicated to providing survival strategies, effective practices, and useful tips that organize the environments in which visual merchandising professionals labor—their workshops, toolboxes, offices, suitcases, briefcases, and calendars.

Becoming the Go-To Person

Visual managers need well-organized workspaces with accessible, easy-to-find information—contact names, emails, and phone numbers for product-line vendors, up-to-date and accurate budget reports, idea files, resource files—to support their work routines. Maintaining a professional, well-planned workspace, and becoming the person others go to for information, can lend credibility to your working brand, or style, and the ideas you express. When people in your department begin to say: "Go to [insert your name here] for that," you'll know you're on your way to wherever it is you plan to go in your career.

In the book, *Be Your Own Brand, A Breakthrough Formula for Standing Out from the Crowd*, authors David McNally and Karl Speak offer a theory that everyone has a brand:

Your brand is a reflection of who you are and what you believe, which is visibly expressed by what you do and how you do it. It's the doing part that connects you with someone else, and that connection with someone else results in a relationship. In reality, the image of your brand is a perception held in someone else's mind. As that perception, through repeated contacts between you and the other person, evolves and sharpens, a brand relationship takes form.

retail realities

Competitive retailing exists behind the scenes in the office as much as it does on the selling floor or out in the mall. Just as stores compete for business, departments in corporate offices compete to gain company resources for their projects. The more professionally visual merchandisers present themselves and their work environment, the easier it will be for them to gain credibility and secure positions as essential and productive partners in the retail operation.

Setting Up Your Toolbox

If you've accepted a position as a visual merchandiser with display responsibilities, don't be surprised to discover that the only place you have to call your own is your toolbox. After all, if you're doing what you were hired to do, you'll be out on the floor or in the windows doing your job, not planted behind a desk.

If that's the case, that toolbox will be your first resource center, holding everything you'll need to work efficiently and effectively. At the same time, you'll need to be able to lift and carry your "office" from place to place, so it can't literally hold everything an office usually contains. Start assembling your toolbox by reviewing your job description. Knowing what the company wants you to do will tell you what you'll need to do it.

An inventory of essentials for a fashion window toolbox might include:

- Large, lockable toolbox with lift-out tray/drawer
- Padlock
- Striking wire (20-gauge) metal
- Monofilament thread (50-pound test) plastic
- heavy sewing thread and needles with large eyes (yarn size)
- Diagonal wire cutter
- Pliers, adjustable and needle-nose
- Adjustable wrench
- Allen wrenches, hex wrenches
- Tack hammer
- Tack claw/staple puller
- Awl or hole punch
- Pin-pusher (brad driver)
- Assorted small screws, common nails, and brads
- Screwdrivers (Phillips and straight slot)
- Bank pins (#17), T-pins, dressmaker pins (#20)
- Wrist cushion or pin cushion
- Staple gun and staples
- Fabric scissors, small and large (very sharp)
- Paper scissors, not for fabric

- Razor blades, single edge
- Exacto knife, blades, safety cap
- Retractable utility knife
- Clear tape, masking tape, double-face tape
- Floral adhesive or foam tape tabs
- Velcro adhesive tabs
- Wood glue, rubber cement, epoxy glue
- Straight edge/metal ruler
- Measuring tape, steel and cloth
- Seam ripper and safety cap
- Whisk broom, disposable dusting cloth
- Assorted small bandages, antiseptic
- Pre-moistened towelettes
- Prepackaged dry-cleaning product

The list is extensive—and could be expensive as well. If you work for a corporation, your tools will probably be supplied, but if you have your own business, you will need to purchase tools. Before you buy every item, ask an experienced visual merchandiser for a guided tour of his or her working toolbox. Display routines vary and reviewing someone else's survival kit may help you edit the list to purely essential items.

Borrow a letter–M–from the SCAMPER model (see Chapter 1) and "minify" at every opportunity. For instance, elect to carry a reversible head screwdriver that stores one head in its handle when the other is in use; carry three or four bandages and a small tube of antiseptic in a resealable bag or container rather than full-sized packages.

The same toolbox for an interior fashion display person may not require striking wire, or wire of any kind. Instead, that person's toolbox may require a bag of ceiling clips compatible with the store's ceiling grid system, or a rubber mallet rather than a tack hammer. It may also require all of those items plus some that are not on the list. After a few days on the job, you'll learn exactly which tools you will need for your work.

Remember the padlock on the list? If you want to maintain a reliable set of personal

> "I knew I'd arrived as a 'go-to person' when I had to put a padlock on my toolbox."
> *A visual merchandiser*

tools, you will need a lock and a secure place to keep your tools overnight. Some seasoned merchandisers even color their toolboxes and hand tools with fluorescent spray paint so they can spot them when they've "strayed" or been left behind.

Setting Up Your Office

When you progress to the point where you have a space to call your own, you will need to think about your office setup. Your office will be an expression of your personal working style and brand identity.

■ BASIC OFFICE SUPPLIES

Know your work habits. If you're a spread-it-all-out person, you'll be happiest with a fair-sized work surface. If you're a filer and don't work well in clutter, you'll need filing cabinets, tote boxes, and open shelving. Try to provide yourself with a comfortable chair and the type of task lighting that helps you work efficiently. Whatever size, customize your workspace for function and comfort.

Your office fittings may be divided into priority tools that you use daily, like pens and markers, and those that you use occasionally, like manufacturer resource catalogs and price lists. You may find it helpful to have a small reserve of these items on hand and replenish them regularly. You'll soon discover other indispensable tools and develop a list of your own as your responsibilities become more defined.

Priority Office Tools
- Desk or wall calendar
- Business card file
- Sticky notepads
- Pens, pencils
- Art gum erasers
- Rubber cement
- Spray mount
- Pencil sharpener
- Ruler

- Steel and cloth tape measures
- Stapler and staples
- Tape and dispenser
- Paperclips
- Push pins
- Bulletin board
- Scissors
- Calculator
- Highlighters and/or sticky page flags
- Markers

■ BASIC DESK REFERENCES

There are additional essential and extremely useful priority supplies you'll need to keep your brand identity strong. Among the more important ones are the references that can guide your written communications and oral presentations. Rely on them so that your skills will grow stronger with each project.

- **Writing reference books**: Strunk and White's *The Elements of Style* or *The Chicago Manual of Style* for authoritative assistance with grammar, punctuation, and writing style issues.
- **Graphics references**: Pantone color specifiers (coated and uncoated chips for universally understood color choices) and International Paper's *Pocket Pal: The Handy Book of Graphic Arts Production*. www.internatiomalpaper.com, www.pantone.com
- **Company references**: policy and procedures manuals for signing and fixtures, and any additional proprietary presentation guidelines.
- **Professional references**: every visual professional has favorite dog-eared and much-used sources for expert opinion. This textbook can be a practical reference that you can take to your workplace. Then add *Your Idea Starts Here: 77 Mind-Expanding Ways to Unleash Your Creativity* by Carolyn Eckert, a virtual buffet of inspiration and colorful graphic images to inspire and delight. *Wake Up Your Creative Genius,* by

"Your mobile phone allows you to travel with everything you need to know about your business, from calendars and contacts to task lists to drawing pads for creative thinkers to e-mail, and even an alarm to remind you where you need to be when your calendar gets crazy! Just remember to back up the information because without it you may be lost."
Tony Mancini, chief executive officer at ThinkTank Retail Hospitality Group

Kurt Hanks and Jay Parry, is a refreshing paperback that can renew your energy and recharge your creative batteries. *Creative Whack Pack* by Roger Von Oech is a deck of cards that can easily be stored in a small tray on your desk. Choose one a day for a jumpstart to a creative day.

Organizing Your Work

■ BASIC ORGANIZER SYSTEMS

You will need in/out baskets for internal company mail; it will also be handy to have a bin on your desk for "hot" projects, and another bin for materials that arrive in the mail until you have time to file them. A planner of some kind is essential. The workplace is too fast paced for a manager to operate efficiently without an electronic and/or paper management system to organize time and activities. You may find it helpful to print out a paper copy of your weekly/monthly schedules with all activities visible at a glance as you move from meeting to meeting throughout the day.

A prioritized daily to-do list, where you can check off completed tasks, is a motivating tool. It can also be used as a record of what you've done to date, which will be useful at review time. A simple notebook or sketchbook can function as a daily journal of highlights from meetings that you attend. Book and stationery stores usually carry an assortment of notebooks and journals, some of which would be suitable for professional use. Choose a color and paper weight that you will enjoy working with and carrying with you every day. Consider a notebook color that matches the brand color of the retailer where you are working. For example, some team members at Target carry thick, red leather covered journals to all of their meetings. Choose your journal carefully— it will become part of your personal brand image. Your colleagues' appreciation that you value their ideas and opinions enough to write them down will help to build your brand as a serious professional.

In your office, you'll have to maintain a few files in a nearby cabinet for materials related to company operations, general information, and user information for company communication tools like e-mail and voice mail. If you manage a staff, you'll need to establish a file folder for individual staff members with information on their weekly projects, concerns, and requests. Any personal staff-related information, from performance reviews, for instance, must be kept in a locked file.

■ MAINTAINING YOUR OFFICE

The work in any retail organization moves at a fast pace. Sometimes multitasking without multi-filing results in near-avalanche conditions. It is all too easy for project files to stack up, mail bins to overflow, and desks to become overrun (if not totally obscured). The appearance of your desk and office is part of your brand. Make it a rule to file documents from meetings and samples from vendors, etc., at the end of every day before you leave. It's a good practice to block the last hour of your day on your calendar as "office hours," so you are guaranteed that personal time at the end of most days. You'll be grateful for the reward from that action when you enter your office in the morning.

Many creative individuals work best with their work spread out around them. If you are one of them, remember to put everything back in its place after your projects are completed. An organized office is the sign of an organized individual, a quality that is critical for handling a large number of projects and people. In short, if you want more responsibility, prove that you can handle what you already have.

retail realities

Building a Multimedia Resource Center

There are resources and ideas everywhere you go, and you must be prepared to capture them, even if you are not on the time clock. If you remember only one idea from this text, may it please be this: look (take a picture or do a sketch), so that you can later compare and innovate.

■ CAPTURING IDEAS

There are four key items you should never be without so that you are always ready:

- Smartphone for photos
- Tape measure
- Pen
- Small notebook

If you see a great storefront in your travels, you'll want a photo to remind you why you thought it was so effective. If you discover a unique fixture, you may want to sketch its features and record its dimensions accurately. You can record any notes on your phone, and eliminate the need for a pen and notebook, but for some, a physical pocketbook of exceptional ideas is preferred. These are the subtle tools of the comparison shopper, and as you use them, be a discreet observer. The sketches and photographs, along with things you make note of, become the basis for building a multimedia resource center in your office that will support your work (and the work of your department) for years to come.

▌GATHERING INSIGHTS AND INSPIRATION

Sometimes we simply need to look to others for fresh or unusual perspectives on our industry. Today consultants, marketing firms and visual merchandisers actively write about their craft; their views on retailing; their take on consumer issues; or the way art, science, current events, or economics affect their work as marketing practitioners.

The following insightful books geared to our business concerns are an excellent starting place:

- Paco Underhill, *Why We Buy: The Science of Shopping—Updated and Revised for the Internet, the Global Consumer, and Beyond* (2008); *Call of the Mall: The Geography of Shopping* (2004); and *What Women Want: The Global Market Turns Female Friendly* (2010)
- Jason Harris, *The Soulful Art of Persuasion: The 11 Habits That Will Make Anyone a Master Influencer*, by the CEO of the power house agency Mekanism. "It is about engaging rather than insisting; it is about developing empathy and communicating your values" (2019).
- David Kepron's *Retail (r)Evolution,* "takes the reader through the ways the human brain has traditionally responded to retail environments, and how recent technological innovations are changing everything" (2014).

If you're looking for something outrageous and funny and often inspiring, you might try

- Simon Doonan, *Confessions of a Window Dresser* (2001)

▌READING ABOUT THE INDUSTRY

You can begin to build a visual merchandising resource center by subscribing to trade magazines specific to the visual merchandising and store design industry. Purchase plastic or corrugated magazine files to store back copies of your magazines. Keep two years' worth on file and after that recycle them. Today most magazines have moved to an online-only format.

Three resources that relate directly to your work in visual merchandising are: *vmsd*

(Visual Merchandising and Store Design), *Retail TouchPoints*, and *Retail Environments*. All three are online resources, while *vmsd* also offers a print magazine.

- *vmsd*—www.vmsd.com
- *Retail TouchPoints*—www.retailtouchpoints .com
- *Retail Environments*—www.shopassociation .org

The following list of other publications relates to manufacturing trends, product developments, retail operations, merchandising specialty areas, and specific merchandise categories that you'll be working with during your career. Understanding the factors that affect retail businesses in general will be a real advantage in your work. Once you know what's available, you can decide which publications will give you a competitive edge in terms of product knowledge and other insights that can advance your working identity and your position with your company.

Chain Store Age (www.chainstoreage.com), both a print magazine and online resource, is known as "the business of retail" among executive decision makers. A bi-monthly magazine with daily online updates, it provides readers with critical information on the retail industry. Departments include retail technology, operations and supply chain, store spaces, and real estate.

NRF Smartbrief (nrf.com) The National Retail Federation is the world's largest retail trade association and it offers five daily free newsletters: NRF Smartbrief, NRF SmartBrief: What's Next Edition, NRF SmartBrief: Global Edition, NRF SmartBrief: Retail on Main Street Edition, and NRF SmartBrief: Retail Recap.

WWD, Women's Wear Daily (www.wwd.com) is "The industry's leading publication since 1910. Every story, every insight, is backed by more than a century's experience in global fashion authority. With bureaus in Paris, New York,

Milan, London, Hong Kong and Los Angeles, WWD brings you first-hand expert reporting from the world's key fashion markets." *WWD* is written for retailers and manufacturers of womens' and mens' apparel, accessories, business and beauty. Free newsletters and paid subscriptions are available.

FN, Footwear News (www.footwearnews .com) is the "ultimate destination for industry insiders and shoe lovers alike. From power players to style stars, FN draws on seventy years of history to offer a feet first look at what's new and what's next in shoes." *FN* is available in both print and digital editions.

HFN, Home Fashion News (ww.hfndigital .com) is the "only source of Total Home Renovation and Inspiration. HFN is read by top-level executives across all retail channels that sell home products . . . housewares, tabletop, textiles and rugs, furniture, lighting and home décor." *HFN* is available in both print and digital editions.

Progressive Grocer (www.progressivegrocer .com) describes itself as "the voice of the retail food industry since 1922. *Progressive Grocer*'s core audience targets top management at headquarters and key decision makers at store level. From chain supermarkets to regional and local independent grocers, supercenters, wholesaler distributors, manufacturers, and other supply chain trading partners, rely on *PG* for authoritative, comprehensive, relevant, research-based editorial content and need-to-know news." *PG* is available in both print and digital editions.

Echo Chamber (www.echochamber.com), "We are retail enthusiasts who travel the globe in search of the new and innovative. Based in London and Paris, but always on the move, we can be found pounding the shopping streets of the world with camera in hand, tracking trends on the ground. We help our clients improve their businesses by showing them what great retail looks like." Echo Chamber offers monthly updates with the latest retail news.

GDR Creative Intelligence (www.gdruk .com) is a "retail trends consultancy and design intelligence providing inspiration, analysis, momentum and guidance. *GDR*'s services pinpoint where, why and how your business can achieve innovation." You can sign up for their weekly online insights and trends review.

WindowsWear (www.windowswear .com) is the world's largest and most comprehensive visual database of retail and e-commerce. Content includes best-in-class visual merchandising, retail design, social media, window displays, product packaging, e-commerce, advertising and more. The *WindowsWear* community includes leaders and creators of global brands, retailers, schools, and specialists worldwide. You can sign up for varying levels of subscriptions to explore what is happening in the global community today.

There are many other exceptional industry magazines and publications to round out your library, depending on the merchandising style and the product focus of your store. Ask your supervisor or the store's trend department about the magazines and newspapers the company relies on for its market and trend information. You may request to be added to the in-house circulation list for these publications. You may also want to subscribe to popular newsstand magazines for the general public or special focus magazines that have editorial content focused on your area of responsibility.

LEARNING ABOUT INDUSTRY ORGANIZATIONS

A direct path for visual merchandisers to both networking and learning about the business aspect of their jobs is through the organizations in the retail design industry. Some offer memberships and online newsletters, and some sponsor trade shows and awards events where networking abounds. There are often opportunities to volunteer your time on various committees. For example, extra hands are always welcomed with the set-up of events. Once you begin to volunteer, you'll be working alongside industry leaders and soon other volunteer opportunities will open up. By making your mark there, you may be invited to serve on industry design boards where you'll meet colleagues who may become lifelong friends. And who knows? Your most significant career advancement may emerge naturally from taking time to give back.

NATIONAL RETAIL FEDERATION

www.nrf.com

NRF is the world's largest community for retailers, "representing discount and department stores, home goods and specialty stores, main street merchants, grocers, wholesalers, chain restaurant and internet retailers from the United States and more than 45 countries." The organization has been "a voice for every retailer and every retail job" for over a century. Membership in NRF "gives retailers the opportunity to advocate on important policy issues, gain insights from industry leaders and visionaries and network with retail's best and brightest. 16,000 member companies find value in the matchmaking and networking opportunities designed to bring members together to collaborate, share ideas and stay connected."

NRF educates through their blogs, newsletters, podcasts, and videos to highlight industry insights and data on topics including: the economy, careers and leadership, consumer trends, holiday and season trends, retail technology and others. The group is frequently quoted in publications like the *Wall Street Journal*, posting their retail business forecasts and insights on the state of the industry.

In addition to partnering with the retail community in general, NRF also joins hands with universities. They currently have over seventy-five university members with more than 6,500 students. "In an effort to develop retail's future talent, NRF membership provides resources, tools and experiences to support and promote education, research and careers within the retail industry."

NRF also produces and supports events every year, including Retail's Big Show and NRF TECH New York.

◼ PAVE: PLANNING AND VISUAL EDUCATION PARTNERSHIP

www.paveglobal.org

The Planning and Visual Education Partnership, (PAVE) was founded in 1992, and is the retail design, planning, and visual merchandising industry's premier educational foundation. It began as a statement, "Paving the way for future students." It enables young talent to build successful careers in all aspects of the retail industry. Additionally, PAVE seeks to encourage retail management, store planners, visual merchandisers, architects, and manufacturers to interact with and support design students.

The Mission of PAVE is to provide students with financial support and industry exposure. Every year there is a PAVE student design competition that promotes real-world design experience. Sponsors of the competition create specific design challenges related to their own business needs. Entries are judged by the sponsors and the leadership team at PAVE. Awards are presented at the PAVE Gala in NY, attended by over 850 retail designers, marketing firms, and manufacturers in a dazzling fundraising event. There are additional opportunities to receive scholarships from design agencies: learn more about the PAVE-Bergmeyer Scholarship and the PAVE Ingenious Scholarship sponsored by Zen Genius on the PAVE website.

◼ RDI: RETAIL DESIGN INSTITUTE

www.retaildesigninstitute.org

The role of the Retail Design Institute is unmatched as they bring the retail industry's creative professionals together at both national events in New York and at the local level. Architects, graphic designers, lighting designers, interior designers, store planners, visual merchandisers, resource designers, brand strategists, educators, trade partners, trade media and students of design all meet at their local chapters for educational and social events. Chapters are international, meeting in cities including Atlanta, Chicago, Cincinnati, New York, Minneapolis, Los Angeles, Madrid, Hong Kong, Toronto, and many more. In another effort of the organization to bring talented design professionals together, job board postings are available on the website.

Founded in 1961, RDI was developed to be a "collaborative community where ideas, knowledge and passion would be shared." The organization is known and respected for its International Design Competition, which has been running for nearly fifty years. Members can attend the awards event and gala in New York or view the winners by downloading *Stores of the Year* books from RDI's website. Filled with lavish photos and drawings of floor layouts, and notations of goals and objectives and how they were realized, the books are an invaluable reference tool for designers. Other awards from RDI include a Retail Design Legion of Honor Award, Fellow of the Institute recognition, and the Mark V. Looper Award for Design Collaboration.

◼ SHOP!

www.shopassociation.org

Shop! is a global trade association established in 1956 which has evolved into a dynamic community. From their website: "Our Purpose: Empowering members to innovate at retail. Our Mission: From ideation through implementation, Shop will engage our diverse array of members with education, insights and events that enable them to co-create innovation that evolves retail worldwide. Our Vision: Shop's members will shape the evolution of retail."

One of the key publications is the Shop! Buyers' Guide, which features the products, capabilities, and services of nearly 850 providers of store fixtures, POP displays, retail design services, visual presentation products, signage, materials installation, and more. They also publish *Retail Environments* magazine, the go-to resource for business issues affecting the industry.

Shop! offers their members professional development through podcasts, webinars, and research reports. Their MaRC certification is the retail industry's only globally recognized credential that keeps individuals current on retail environments and experiences. MaRC candidates purchase and download the MaRC Exam Book, which is authored by subject matter experts and details best practices for the activities that drive shopper purchases at retail. (Chapter 1 of *Silent Selling: Creative Thinking*, is one of the featured chapters in the exam book.) After studying the material, candidates can sign up to take the exam online, the final step before becoming certified.

Shop! is also known for their Design Awards including OMA (Outstanding Merchandising Achievement Awards), Global Awards for the POP (Point-of-Purchase) industry, and the Shop! Design Awards for retail environments. Many of the design award winners from past years are featured throughout this textbook.

■ BUILDING A MANUFACTURERS' LIBRARY

Set up a manufacturer's product file to organize and store the materials you receive. First, purchase clear file tabs in a variety of colors. Choose a different color for each category you would like to include in your sourcing file, for example:

- Red for mannequins and mannequin alternatives
- Orange for display props
- Yellow for fixtures

- Green for sign holders, printing processes, photography
- Blue for lighting fixtures
- Purple for design resources

Create file labels with manufacturers' names. Arrange them in alphabetical order in your file cabinet. If the manufacturers build fixtures, insert the name in a yellow clear tab on a file folder. If they produce and sell mannequins too, insert the name in a red clear tab and add it to the same folder, etc. By the time your resource file grows to several drawers and cabinets, you will enjoy the convenience of being able to quickly pull out all of the red tabs in the file for an in-depth mannequin search. When you've finished, they can easily be filed back into the alphabetical system.

A few manufacturers and distributors provide their clients with large binder presentations that encompass all of their product lines. You'll need a bookshelf to store them in an orderly arrangement so that they are readily accessible when you need them.

■ BUILDING A PHOTO LIBRARY

There are professional people in our field who have faithfully photographed every window, documented every major rollout, cataloged every holiday animation, and logged every major promotion as proof of their endeavors. They are the meticulous record keepers and archivists of our field. Many examples of their work appear in this book and they have broadened our view of visual merchandising.

Where will your archive come from? Where will your portfolio come from? Photography can record how you've grown professionally and remind you of theme ideas you've tried, fixturing techniques that worked well, and props, mannequins, color stories, and lighting tricks worth remembering. You can become your own PR (public relations) agent and your own historian.

At the same time you're photographing ideas that inspire you personally, you must document your professional work for the company. Remember, as a company employee you're not just marketing yourself. You're part of a team. Later on, as a manager, you will be marketing your department and its projects, too. Here's how to do it:

- Build a photo library of every project your group completes. Don't overlook the value of "before" and "after" photographs to show improvements. This builds a departmental track record—a graphic history. At some point, you may need to justify your department's expense, demonstrate its effectiveness to the company, or document a body of completed work to gain new resources. Photographs are also helpful during progress reviews to remind your supervisor of your accomplishments.
- Date each project and include notes on the store location where the project was tested, its costs, and a list of stores where the project was adopted and installed.
- Archive proposals and supporting materials that didn't receive initial approval. Ideas that are not accepted the first time they are presented may be successfully resurrected at a later date.

BUILDING A MATERIALS LIBRARY

What's the latest trend in floor coverings for heavy traffic areas? Is there a local upholstery fabric store that will match the wallpaper we found in an antique store in New York? These are the kinds of questions that you may be asked in visual merchandising. They are also the kinds of questions that take valuable hours to answer if you do not have a materials library. How to build your library:

- Set up a system of clear bins to hold samples of trend materials such as laminates, plastics, fabrics, paint, and carpet samples, showing the most recent product entries available to planners and designers.
- Set up a system of clear bins to document materials and sources currently in use in the store. Label each sample to show its vendor and style number, where the materials are being used, and date of installation for each. This facilitates reorders in the event of damage or excessive wear.

BUILDING A TRAVEL LIBRARY

One of the benefits of retail employment is travel, provided you make a point of developing familiarity with the cities you visit. If you work for a national or international retailer, travel may be a part of your basic job description.

Building a travel library that includes information about cities where your company currently does business—or plans to open stores in the future—is a career booster. Companies send confident, competent people to represent them away from home base. By doing some research up front, you'll be better prepared to be that representative.

If you hold a management position and your budget allows, plan to attend all of the visual industry's markets and any other conferences or conventions relevant to your company's retail business.

In addition to EuroShop, which is held in Germany, there are US markets and conferences that offer a wide range of visual merchandising products. Generally, attendees at these major markets and exhibitions are retail and point-of-purchase design professionals, visual merchandisers, store designers, contract designers, and brand marketers.

The following ideas can get you started on a resource library that can either help you build a case for attending major market events or ease your transition from inexperienced work-related traveler to seasoned frequent flyer:

- Set up a travel file for each city you visit or plan to visit. Whenever you travel, collect informational guides, brochures, and maps from local tourism organizations.

- Contact convention and visitors' bureaus for the cities you'd like to learn more about and request materials and maps. You can usually find a website and tour its links to points of interest and make inquiries about materials at the same time.

- *Where Traveler* magazines are targeted exclusively to the visitor market, providing timely local information on the best shopping, dining, cultural attractions, and entertainment that cities have to offer their guests. Online, you'll find *Where Traveler* at www.wheretraveler.com. Make notes of favorite restaurants and hotels and add all of these to your travel file.

- *Mapeasy's Guide Maps* (www.mapeasy.com) are exceptional. Hand-drawn and lettered, they include landmarks that bring you right into the heart of a particular city. They are color-coded with hotels, restaurants, retail stores, and attractions. You can find these maps at your local bookstore and online.

- To check specific dates and look for other shows that may have meaning for your particular visual merchandising specialty, visit The Tradeshow News Network (TSNN) at www.tsnn.com.

Conferences and Markets

Descriptions and approximate schedules follow for the most popular trade shows and markets.

■ EUROSHOP

www.euroshop-tradefair.com
EuroShop is the World's #1 Retail Trade Fair. It is held every three years in February/March in Düsseldorf, Germany, attracting more than 2,300 exhibitors from fifty-seven countries and 94,000 visitors from over 140 countries. Attendees benefit because they can discover the best possible solutions and services available worldwide. Of EuroShop 2020, Michael Gerling, Chairman of the Euroshop Advisory Board said, "This high level of international interest clearly documents the dynamism of the global retail world and the exceptional position EuroShop enjoys as its economic engine."

EuroShop is now divided into eight dimensions: Retail Marketing, Expo and Event Marketing, Retail Technology, Lighting, Visual Merchandising, Shop Fitting & Store Design, Food Service Equipment and Refrigeration & Energy Management. These eight dimensions are color-coded on an overview sitemap on the website. It's worth a look to see the sheer size of this show, housed in seventeen warehouses, where you'll find it necessary to board shuttles to reach all of the destinations.

■ ICFF: INTERNATIONAL CONTEMPORARY FURNITURE FAIR

www.icff.com
The International Contemporary Furniture Fair is "where designers, retailers, developers and architects converge to exchange inspiration and ignite a competitive drive for contemporary residential and commercial interiors." Exhibitors from over thirty countries gather to showcase what's best in the contemporary landscape in this two–four day annual event at Javitts Center in New York City.

You can take a virtual walk through the ICFF show floor by clicking on "About the Fair" and watching the video. You will also find a list of the featured product categories: Furniture, Lighting, Seating, Outdoor Furniture, Contract Furniture, Kitchen & Bath, Wall Coverings, Accessories, Textiles, Fabricators, Carpets & Flooring, and Materials.

As a visual merchandiser, why is it beneficial for you to attend ICFF? It is important to see the latest trends in design across all disciplines; you may be inspired by the materials and colors you see in home and interior furnishings at the show for use in fixture design, or you may see new lighting techniques and technologies that may have an application in your retail stores. You may attend ICFF Talks, which are led by the most iconic names in the industry. You may make new connections with like-minded creatives from around the globe. A wide professional network is always an asset as you move through different dimensions of your career.

IRDC: INTERNATIONAL RETAIL DESIGN CONFERENCE

www.vmsd.com

IRDC is presented annually by *VMSD*. "This one-of-a-kind conference comprises two full days of design dialogue centered on best practices, evolving trends and fresh strategies for engaging shoppers and maximizing resources. IRDC is recognized as the premier educational and networking event for the store design and visual merchandising communities."

Through its roundtable discussions, interactive sessions, and receptions, IRDC attendees share perspectives that will spark actionable insights and ideas. The always highly anticipated Iron Merchant Challenge is hosted by Joe Baer, cofounder and CEO of ZenGenius. Teams are comprised of attendees from different companies, so that they can experience firsthand their best quick-thinking strategies as they compete in building visual presentations in a limited amount of time.

NRF RETAIL'S BIG SHOW: NATIONAL RETAIL FEDERATION

www.nrfbigshow.nrf.com

National Retail Federation members gather annually in New York City for Retail's Big Show, the NRF's flagship industry event featuring keynote speakers and inspirational sessions on the most relevant topics of the day. Attendees can explore over 600 exhibitors' big ideas and innovative solutions, learn about emerging tech from the industry's best start-ups, and visit an immersive innovation lab featuring visionaries from around the globe.

Attendees of the show can also sign up for guided retail store tours to see the newest cutting-edge spaces of global retail leaders. Not only will they witness firsthand how retailers are using technology and other strategies to enhance the customer experience, but they will walk side by side with industry colleagues for unique networking opportunities.

RETAILX

www.retailx.com

The RetailX conference is sponsored by RetailTouchPoints. As a "physical event and digital platform, retailX provides direct access to the technology and trends shaping the digital future of retail. Catering to omni-channel and ecommerce retailers and brands, retailX is the ultimate resource to advance the retail industry's evolution. We deliver year-round retail education and insight from industry leaders through webinars, blogs, research, videos, onsite events, virtual experiences and networking opportunities. Whether guiding your retail business to digital for the first time or expanding technology within an established online and in-store experience, retailX is your education resource and networking partner for the digital future of retail."

PLANNING A PRODUCTIVE MARKET TRIP

Always plan to spend a few additional days beyond the scheduled dates for the market or conference you are attending to allow time to visit new retail concept stores, flagships, and remodels. This strategy will double the value of your trip. Provide your supervisor with a detailed schedule to account for your request for additional travel time.

A sample schedule might look like this:

- **Monday**: catch an early flight to your destination city, check into hotel, visit new or leading retail stores afternoon and evening
- **Tuesday**: continue tour of new or leading retail stores
- **Wednesday**: attend opening day of conference and seminars, visit vendor booths, attend opening night reception
- **Thursday**: attend conference seminars, visit vendor booths and city showrooms
- **Friday**: attend conference and seminars and visit vendor booths

Planning a market trip well in advance of the actual show date assures you of hotel availability at the best rates. Many market and exhibition producers hold blocks of rooms for attendees and may even have arranged for reduced airfares, but all of these should be researched and booked as early as possible, preferably the very day marketing for the event hits your email.

Reserving Rooms

It's probably wise to make hotel reservations for the December Market Weeks in Manhattan up to one year in advance. This show is held during the holiday season. If you don't reserve a room until a few weeks before the market, your only option may be a room priced at over $600 per night. You may find accommodations in New Jersey or New York's other boroughs, but you'll need to consider the extra time necessary for the commute. Manhattan is especially busy during the holidays, and at times it may take as long as a half-hour to move a single mile in traffic. Learn to use the subway system for speedy transportation.

Reserving Workshop Seminar Tickets

Most market registration is free if you preregister (except for EuroShop, which

charges a fee for one-day tickets, two-day tickets, or season tickets). You may register to attend markets on the Internet. One of the most attractive features of the markets is their educational and professional development programs with timely topical seminars and special speakers. These events require tickets because of limited seating. They should be booked early because many of the sessions are sold out at show time.

Networking

Opening night receptions, award presentations, and other hospitality events are networking sessions with the bonus of entertainment, food, and drink. Book these important tickets in advance. There is usually a fee, but these dollars are well spent. Receptions provide relaxed opportunities for visual merchandisers to get to know manufacturers and suppliers personally rather than through email. An important function of your position, even if you don't see it in your job description, is developing cordial working relationships with reliable vendors. This ability is critical to your advancement in the field. Free of the pressure to sell and buy, you can both enjoy each other's company.

Manufacturers' showroom parties are by invitation only, but there is no charge. You may be invited because your company is a regular customer of the manufacturer. You may also be invited because your company has been identified as a potential customer for the manufacturer. Go. It's another opportunity to get acquainted with people in the industry.

Dressing the Part

By day business attire, workday casual, or unique trend looks are appropriate apparel for the market. Keep in mind that your business is fashion, even if you don't work in an apparel store, and that your own personal brand identity is reflected in your appearance. Take advantage of the opportunity to present yourself as a fashion industry professional.

BOX 14.1

▒▒ Designers' Pet Peeves

Author Judy Bell writes: When I was working at Target and regularly shopping the competition, I liked to look at the big picture of the retail scene. Some of my favorite places to find inspiration were in neighborhoods like Soho, Nolita, and Tribeca in New York. Even though I was working for a company with stores that averaged around 130,000 square feet, I believed that the smallest boutiques might hold gems of inspiration. That's where raw creative talent was unleashed, without the need for a lengthy approval process that is common in corporations. I would shoot photos in both large department stores and boutiques and assemble them into reports and presentations.

One day a marketing director who was a colleague at Target asked why I "bothered" to visit Soho every year. Why would I go there so often? This wasn't the first time I was asked the question and I'll admit it was getting to be a pet peeve of mine. I said that I would respond to her question, but I needed a little time.

I was also creating shopping maps of various neighborhoods for the corporation, highlighting the newest concepts for corporate merchants and designers on their trips to New York. I updated the maps every year to keep them fresh. I pulled out a few maps from previous years and counted the number of updates I made to the maps, due to retailers closing and new ones opening in their places, and discovered that every year there were dozens and dozens of changes. Clearly the ideas one could see were endless and ever-changing. And even though not every one of the boutiques stayed in business, it didn't mean that their ideas weren't valuable!

I showed the numbers of changes on my maps to my colleague. I explained that the unbridled creativity in these stores was exceptional and would provide inspiration for our teams—not to copy the ideas, but to expand their thinking and the scope of possibilities. She got it!

This experience is why I advise visual merchandisers to add days to their conference and market schedules to allow time to explore. For an example of an inspiring one-of-a-kind store, look at the photo of Minneapolis' MartinPatrick3. In 2020, *Design:Retail*'s annual holiday Winning Windows competition in New York was expanded to stores outside the city for the first time ever, to create the North American Judges Choice Award. MartinPatrick3 won! And why?

Consider what the experience was like for shoppers: Music from Tchaikovsky poured out into the street over seven stylish windows all dressed in alluring costumes set in captivating scenes to recreate Loyce Houlton's Nutcracker Fantasy. After fifty-five years of annual performances in Minneapolis, Covid restrictions required the Minnesota Dance Theatre to hold off on the show for the season—but the warm and caring team at MartinPatrick3 dedicated all of their display windows to support their community, Now, that's an inspiring story and why I believe visual merchandisers will benefit from looking at the big picture of retail that surrounds them, both in large and small venues.

MartinPatrick 3, a one-of-a-kind store in Minneapolis, takes the first-ever Winning Windows North American Judges' Choice Award. Courtesy of MartinPatrick3.

By night, depending on the fashion season and the occasion itself, trend looks are fine. You'll find that many market-goers wear travel basics that can be dressed up with accessory changes. If you are planning to attend a manufacturer's showroom party, ask in advance about appropriate attire. Although business attire is always acceptable, many attendees dress in cocktail attire, especially in New York City, where there may be multiple types of events to attend in one evening.

Comfortable shoes are a necessity no matter what else you wear. Bring at least three pairs of comfortable (not brand-new) shoes so that you are able to change each day, or even twice a day. Athletic shoes are too casual for showrooms and pavilions; a lower-heeled or flat shoe with support is recommended. You may be on your feet for ten or more hours each day. Do take a pair of athletic shoes or sneakers if you are planning a day or two touring retail stores.

Packing
Be sure to take along the following items to make your trip and your information gathering easier and more productive:

- **Business cards**. Bring at least fifty for your first trip. If you are just beginning to build a resource center, you will be collecting a great deal of information and will be asked for your business card in return. As an alternative, some trade shows will scan your entrance badge for your information. Business cards are still important because you may meet new colleagues on the showroom floor, at seminars, or in other networking events.
- **Crossbody bag with a wide carrying strap.** Catalogues and brochures are heavy, and a thin shoulder strap will become uncomfortable. Manufacturers will offer to send brochures or email information, but it is always best to collect them yourself, so that you will have a complete presentation to show your supervisor and colleagues when you return to your office.

- **Mini stapler**. You can use it to attach vendors' business cards to their brochures so that you can locate them easily when you want to contact someone about a particular product. A small stapler is a simple tool, but it is an easy way to organize your materials.

Shopping the Trade Shows
Some general guidelines to ensure your trade show trip will be as productive as possible are to:

- Look at the show as an essential opportunity to learn firsthand about your fast-paced industry—new technologies, new materials, new ways to do business.
- Make trade shows part of your business plan, not a perk of your job. You need the networking, the fresh perspectives, and the in-person look at products you've only read about. Keep an ongoing information shopping list on your desk all year and do the research in person during the show.
- Exhibitors participate in trade shows to sell; you attend to gather information and make purchases. It's your responsibility to gather information from a variety of sources before you make decisions about buying. Preplanning your buying agenda will help ensure that your company's needs are met.
- Plan your shopping strategy. Refer to your shopping list of informational needs and identify four or five must-see exhibitors. Prepare a short list of questions to ask each one. Make a list of would-like-to-see booths for your second pass through the exhibition halls. Network before, during, and after the show. When you enter an exhibit hall, look for colleagues who are exiting the show. Ask, "What exhibit should I be sure not to miss?" When you return home, be sure to share the information you've gathered with your staff and peers. The interest and enthusiasm you communicate to them helps ensure that you'll be thought of as a go-to person.
- Come equipped, mentally and physically. Start with the must-see businesses before you start picking up samples and literature from

other vendors. Use your floor map and mark your priority visits first. Wear a watch; budget your time. If must-see vendors are busy when you get there, move on and come back later. Keep asking questions and writing down answers. Revise your questions in response to what you learn during your vendor visits. Keep working at your priority list.

- Take advantage of trade show extras. Special events, promotions, and incentives may flow freely. Since trade shows are showcases for new products, you may see some launched there. You might get a chance to speak to the technicians and designers who've been directly involved in the formation of the new product or line.

- Follow up after the show. Go back to the office and confirm any deals you might have put into motion, record the names and phone numbers of new contacts you've made, sort your information and samples. Make three piles. One for action, one for future reference and reading, and one to pass along to colleagues in the store.

- Prepare a report for your supervisor. Get on her or his next staff meeting agenda. Start an information shopping list for the next trade show on your calendar.

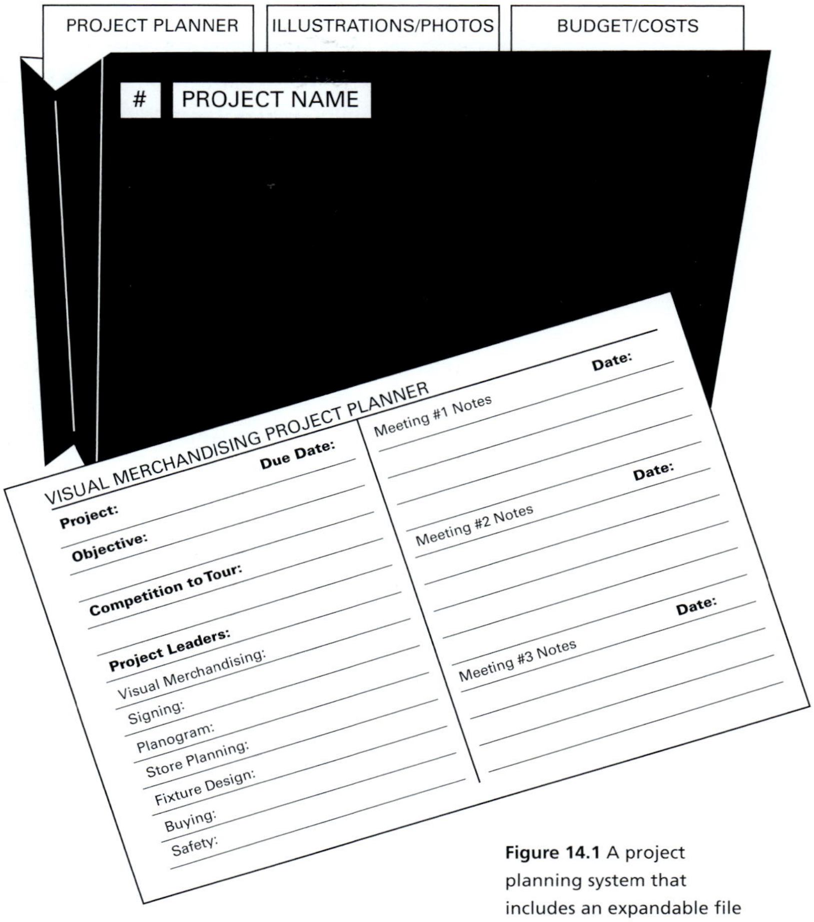

Setting Up Visual Merchandising Projects

Being a go-to person means that you have developed a reputation for being organized and being able to produce accurate documentation when it's called for. As your career develops, you will need to discipline yourself to become a respectable record keeper. Whether you work for a large corporation or have your own visual merchandising business, you will need a systematic method for recording and tracking information related to projects, contacts, and deadlines. This system may be set up online so that it may be easily be accessed by all members of the team. Smaller retailers may prefer a paper system as shown in Figure 14.1.

Figure 14.1 A project planning system that includes an expandable file with labeled folders and a project planner form. Fairchild Books/Rendered by Elaine Wencl Art.

- Write the project's name or title with bold marker on a white label and position it on the upper-left-hand side of an expandable pocket folder. Add a sticker with a project number.
- Develop a project planning form that lists information like the project name, its objectives, strategies, names of contact people, and due dates on its header. If the project involves fixture development, include a safety engineer as a contact. Under that, provide spaces to write consecutive, brief updates on all meetings related to the project. Then, if someone else must fill in for you at a meeting, that person can refer to the meeting updates and report on current project status.
- Place the project planning form at the front of the expandable file in a manila folder labeled "Project Planner."

- Label two more manila folders and title them: "Illustrations/Photos," and "Budget/Costs." Place these inside the expandable file to organize project paperwork.
- If a number of different people need access to project files, arrange them by number in an open file so that they are easy to find. Develop a multiple project master form that lists each current project, its current status, due date, and the name of the person in your area responsible for overseeing each one (Figure 14.2).

Setting Up and Managing a Visual Merchandising Budget

In a business environment, creative ideas must always have strong financial backbones. Even when they do, creative projects must do more than merely pay for themselves. They must generate income and contribute to profits.

Figure 14.2 A project list that may be reviewed weekly to ensure accountability of project leaders and timeliness of tasks. Fairchild Books/ Rendered by Elaine Wencl Art.

VISUAL MERCHANDISING PROJECTS

#	PROJECT	DUE DATE	CAPTAIN	STATUS
1	Valentine's Day Windows	January 15	Tracy	Waiting for design approval, need 10/15.
2	Private Label Cosmetic Event	November 15	Cheryl	Props due to arrive 10/30.
3	Cruisewear Kiosk	November 15	Jenny	Written instructions for stores due 10/15.
4				
5				
6				

TRACKING AND REPORTING SYSTEMS

To be considered a credible business manager as well as a creative merchandiser, you'll need to develop resource management skills that demonstrate your ability to use the company's resources wisely and bring resulting profits back to the organization. To accomplish that goal, you must be able to control your budget: You must know the exact dollar amount available in your budget at any time. Before you make purchases or hire any outside agencies or consultants, you have to know how many unencumbered dollars are available for spending.

Your working relationship with your company controller's office or its bookkeeping department is very much like your relationship with your personal bank. You trust the bank to handle your money correctly on your behalf. If you use your bank's Bill Pay system, it is a good practice to review your account once a month, when you receive your bank statements. If you find any discrepancies, you can work with the bank to explain and correct (reconcile) the differences between its records and yours. Tracking and managing your department's finances is really no different—at least from a record-keeping perspective.

If you're working in an established business, the mechanics of the company's financial system are already in place through the controller's office or the accounting department, but you must still keep your eye on the purchase orders you write from your department's account. In your personal checking account, although the bank has no control over your spending it can refuse payment on your overspending or warn you that you're exceeding your balance. In business, when you overspend your budget, you can count on hearing from the controller or your supervisor. Ideally, neither happens, but both scenarios depend on your paying attention to vital details.

Like any other system, an effective budgeting system is one that you actually use to guide your work (Figure 14.3). It will be a record-keeping system (like your personal check register) that accurately describes and allows you to track:

- The total amount (in dollars) available at the beginning of your department's fiscal year (or specific reporting period)
- The total amount already spent (bills that have been paid)
- The total amount outstanding (dollars already encumbered or bills that have not yet been paid)
- The total dollar amount that remains available in the budget

▇ WRITING PURCHASE ORDERS

To track what is being spent, your department will probably use a purchase order (PO) system. Most companies have these systems in place and expect you to use them and to follow guidelines for working with the established purchase order system. Many of these systems are accessible only through an in-house computer network. If you operate your own business, you may purchase a software spreadsheet system that tracks spending, generates purchase orders, and writes checks. If you're keeping your company books manually, you can buy generic accounting books and purchase order forms at an office supply store.

Purchase orders should have consecutive identifying numbers to facilitate orderly record keeping. You will want to track each document and, in many companies, you are

> Ability to maintain a balanced budget is an important criterion for advancement. It is a straightforward way to demonstrate your skills and business sense to your employer. It is also a great selling point for your résumé as you move on to other positions or companies. Employers value positive results.

retail realities

find it helpful to change your board styles and layouts to create new visual interest. For example, a standard plain black foam-core presentation board may be updated with a computer-generated border or sidebar for a fresh look.

Each presentation should feature a board that lists the project's objectives and strategies. Your idea boards will show renderings or printed photographs, enlarged on your printer to at least 8 ½ × 11. Position each printed photograph or rendering squarely on the board in grid fashion. Do not mount them at angles as shown in the incorrect example in Figure 14.5. It does not look professional.

Display your idea boards on floor easels in the presentation room. If you have samples or models, easels may be set up on tabletops with the samples displayed in front. If you are making a sizable presentation with several exhibits, prepare a brief agenda outlining key points and hand the agendas out to your audience as they enter the room. Do not post financial information on presentation boards. State it clearly and simply on 8½ × 11-inch paper, and hand it out only if your audience is interested in the project, after you have made your presentation.

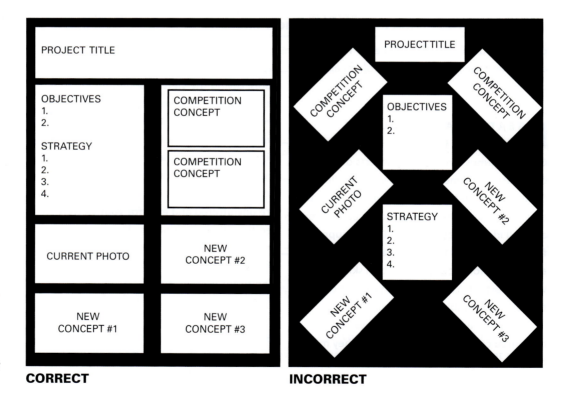

Figure 14.5 A project presentation board. In the correct example, all photographs and information sheets are laid out in a grid fashion. In the incorrect example, the items are pasted on at angles, resulting in an unprofessional look. Fairchild Books/Rendered by Elaine Wencl Art.

BOX **14.2**

DESIGN GALLERY: UNIQLO, 5TH AVENUE, NY

Uniqlo (pronounced "YOU-nee-klo" in the US) is so named because of its origin in Japan as "Unique Clothing Warehouse" in 1984. By 1994, there were 100 stores operating in Japan by parent company "Fast Retailing," a holding company for seven main brands, including Helmut Lang and Theory. Today there are over 2,250 Uniqlo stores in eighteen countries, from Australia to Indonesia to Russia, with more than fifty-one in the United States. Their flagship on 5th Avenue in New York City boasts an impressive design with a dominant staircase in the center of the store, a must-see architectural dynamo.

The massive success of this brand is due to providing a solid assortment of basics along with unique collections of high-end designer partnerships with the likes of Jil Sander and Christophe Lemaire. The quality and wearability of Uniqlo fashions are excellent, with all offerings at the lowest of prices. In addition, they have long been at the forefront of innovative high-tech fabrics, like their HEATTECH, AIRism, and UV cut (sun protection) styles. Their designer UT (Uniqlo t-shirts) is designed to "add fun to your everyday wardrobe with a collection of pop culture icons." This winning combination of innovative fabrics in their basic assortment and designer fashion partnerships have been the catalyst for this brand's massive expansion plans to solidify itself as a global brand. You can learn more about the brand's story and their commitment to community at both the local and global level at www .uniqlo.com by clicking on OUR STORY.

The window pictured in our Design Gallery encouraged holiday shoppers to "Give Color! Find your holiday gift" at their 5th Avenue flagship store in New

Copyright WindowsWear Inc., http://www.windowswear.com, contact@ windowswear.com

York. In support of this theme, a graphic backdrop with colorful photos of men, women, and children outfitted in indoor and outdoor fashions show the breadth of the assortment. Six mannequins are lined up at the front— notice the rhythmic pattern that is formed by positioning the mannequins in a short-tall-short-tall sequence. Balloons in primary colors and a variety of sizes add fun and holiday spirit to this engaging, delightful window.

Shoptalk "Letter to the Reader: Organization, Administration, and Credibility" by Eric Feigenbaum, Head of Workshops, WindowsWear

Retail is the showplace for new ideas, new concepts, and new products. As such, the store environment becomes a selling stage for the merchandise offerings of the day. The essence of retail is the ability to compel the prospective customer to stop, look, and buy. The question that confronts every retailer is: What encourages a customer to shop in one store rather than another? The answer: A well-planned, coordinated team effort that includes marketing, merchandising, store planning, store operations, and, of course, visual merchandising. Every endeavor that you undertake in the retail world will be a team endeavor. Every team member's contribution must be in sync with the established company image and stated company goals. Long gone are the days when a *display man* would emerge from a back area of the store with a multitude of props to present a single item. Today, the visual merchandiser is an integral member of a holistic selling team. The retail formula is simple: "Buy It, Show It, Sell It." Our role as visual merchandisers is to interface with all members of the team in order to show the merchandise to its best advantage.

Each team member has a defined role, bringing specific contributions and insights to the overall team effort. Beyond the obvious—creativity—the successful visual merchandiser will possess and consistently demonstrate the following three attributes and/or skills: organization, administration, and credibility. Visual merchandising is a 24-hour-a-day, 7-day-a-week occupation. You must be a sponge—soaking up all stimuli whether they are visual, literary, contemporary, traditional, popular, or offbeat. Read anything you can get your hands on, see movies, visit museums, and listen to music. All of this collected information is applicable to the art of visual merchandising. Remember, retail is a mirror of society and visual merchandising is the reflected image of life and culture within that society. The ability to have information, inspiration, and sourcing at your fingertips is essential. You must develop your own filing system for this information. Upon building a visual merchandising department, you must organize your workplace both physically and mentally.

As you ascend the organizational ladder, your administrative abilities will be called upon as often as your creative abilities. The running of a visual merchandising department is a multifaceted endeavor. You will be asked to manage multiple tasks and meet strict deadlines. A good administrator knows how to prioritize responsibilities. Moreover, documentation of what needs to be done, what has been done, and what will be done is essential.

The development of your administrative abilities will complement your creative energies and creative sensibilities.

You are an integral part of a team. As such you have specific responsibilities. Your teammates will depend upon you. Each teammate's performance and deliverance is vital to the success of the whole. Complete your assigned tasks in a professional and timely fashion. If you declare that a particular task will be complete by the first Tuesday of the following month—be sure that it is. Your team and your supervisors will soon know that you are reliable. You will become a go-to person. This is credibility. Don't drop the ball!

During the course of your visual merchandising career, you will make numerous trips to the various visual merchandising and store design markets. You will experience a change of roles—you will be the customer. What will compel you to shop one vendor rather than another? As any targeted customer, you will be inundated with a blizzard of stimuli and messages. Employ your organizational skills. Walk the entire market once for an overview, then a second time with focus. Zero in on what is important to you, on what will make your job easier, and on what will make your company more successful. Be a sponge, but a selective sponge.

With a professional sense of organization, administration, and credibility, you are now positioned for the center stage. The store environment is a critical medium in the selling mechanism. The store itself is the fulfillment of the customer's expectations. It's the delivering of every promise that was made to the customer through marketing and advertising campaigns. Visual merchandising is the "icing on the cake." It's the first tactile representation of projected merchandise that the customer will see. You've worked with the merchants, the marketing, with store design. You've interfaced with store management. Now is the time to execute. Be organized, be a leader, and deliver what you promised and what is expected. With a well-developed sense of OAC (organization, administration, and credibility), you will now be able to let your creativity loose.

Chapter 14 Review Questions

1. How does a visual merchandiser become the go-to person for their particular retailer or place of employment?
2. What are the priority tools for setting up your office? Your toolbox?
3. What types of libraries should you build for a visual merchandising resource center?
4. How would you organize a productive market trip?
5. What are the steps to writing a purchase order?
6. What must creative projects do in addition to pay for themselves?
7. How do you create an executive presentation?

Outside-the-Box Challenge

Creating a Resource Center

LOOK

Take a picture of your current office space (at home or at work) and describe how it functions as a resource center for you today. You need a photo to capture details (clutter) that you'd naturally edit out with a sketch.

1. Does your workspace meet all of your current needs? Describe what you actually do in that space.
2. What are its strengths? What works well for you?
3. What are its more challenging aspects?

COMPARE

Visit a store or an online resource that sells office organizers and desk and storage systems. Select a system that combines strong positive features that you already have in your current setup, with solutions to some of the challenges you noted above.

INNOVATE

1. Design an improved workspace or resource center for yourself based on your comparisons of your present-day reality and an improved, custom-designed ideal.
2. Present a photograph of your current workspace and compare it to your new design. Share your findings and results with classmates in a small group discussion.

Critical Thinking

Building Your Brand and Business Practices

DISCUSSION QUESTIONS

1. If you had to describe your working "brand identity" to someone in a job interview, what would you say about yourself? Pair up with someone in class and do this exercise together.
2. Is your working brand identity different from your personal brand identity in any way? Note: it isn't unusual for people to think that the two are different.
3. Describe what you think about the chapter's premise that being the go-to person is advantageous to career

advancement. Do you share that sentiment? Disagree? Explain.

4. Describe your current time-management system. Use an example to demonstrate how it currently works or does not work to keep your life operating smoothly.

5. Assume that you and some of your classmates are going to present a time-management workshop. As a group, create a list of ten useful ideas that you'd present at the workshop. Provide a real-life example to accompany each idea. Present your workshop in EuroShop for the first time. Go to the website www.euroshop-tradefair.com and do the following:

- List participating manufacturers that you would like to visit.
- Find a way to rationalize or justify your attendance at EuroShop.
- Prepare a presentation that could be made to a group of executives who control the funding for your first trip to EuroShop to get their endorsement of your venture. Show them your proposed itinerary, including visits to new, innovative, retail concept stores, flagships, and remodels.

Case Study

Setting Up a Professional Toolbox

THE SITUATION

You have been employed as a visual merchandiser in a large department store for nearly five years and feel that you are ready to strike out on your own as an independent contractor. There are a number of interesting shops, galleries, and restaurants opening in a revitalized section of a former warehouse district near the river that flows through your city, and you want to be part of the excitement. Your business cards and brochures are at the printer, and the only remaining item on your to-do list revolves around equipping yourself with a professional toolbox. You know that leaving your present position means leaving behind the tools that have been supplied for you up to this point.

YOUR CHALLENGE

Option 1—Use the tool list in this chapter and price the items to discover a bottom-line figure for a practical tool and accessory assortment that will prepare you to work independently.

Option 2—Invite an experienced freelance visual merchandiser to bring his or her toolbox to your classroom.

1. Ask your guest to compare the items in his or her toolbox to the items on your list and comment about the tools that person finds indispensable.

2. Prepare a list of questions you might ask relating to your guest's training and experience as a professional in the field. Possible topics:

- The creative process in day-to-day work
- All-time favorite or least favorite display project during career
- Sources of inspiration and fresh ideas
- Required (or helpful) technical skills or background (art, drafting, theatrical lighting, stage carpentry, electricity, etc.)
- Sources of product and technology information
- The importance of teamwork and collaboration with clients.
- Establishing an accounting system for expenses and earnings.
- A cost-effective way to develop a website to promote your services.

part five tools and techniques for merchandise display

This section of the project focuses on display windows (Chapter 12) and mannequins and mannequin alternatives (Chapter 13). Whether you have chosen to deal with fashion stores or to sell hard lines or food service, there is knowledge and strategies in those two chapters for any type of retail.

The logical conclusion for this creative project focuses on presenting your ideas to a decision-maker—perhaps your instructor—or to a creative team—perhaps a group of your classmates.

Personal presentation of an idea that's near and dear to you can be an exceptionally powerful selling strategy—provided that you're well-prepared. As Chapter 14 in your text says, "What you present and how you present it are expressions of your working brand identity. Your presentations should reflect your standards for a quality project and a quality presentation."

Section One

- Identify the type of window that you've chosen for your capstone store (open, closed, etc.). Show it from an overhead view.
- Explain how you expect your store's windows to routinely function (promotional, institutional, etc.).
- Identify a theme and write related sign copy.
- Specify colors, props, mannequins, alternatives, background materials (drop-down graphics, for example), and any other elements to be included.
- Sketch a front view of your display window concept.
- Select at least one area within the store to locate a related editorial display. Identify it on a floor plan. Sketch your editorial idea—front view. Explain its purpose and how it ties in with your planned window display.

Section Two

- Select a line of mannequins (if appropriate) or mannequin alternatives that fit your store's brand image. Explain your choices in terms of your store's brand image. Include photographs or drawings of your choices.

- Choose a line of mannequin alternatives to either replace standard mannequins or be used in conjunction with mannequins on the selling floor. Explain why you've chosen these alternatives—how they are a better choice for your unique circumstances, for example. Include photographs or drawings.

Section Three

Consult with your instructor to determine what kind of capstone presentation is expected.
- A PowerPoint presentation with illustrations and/or slides selected from various parts of the Capstone Creative Project.
- A series of presentation boards representing various parts of the Capstone Creative Project.

Section Four

- Prepare and produce a constructive critique form that can be used by members of your audience during your presentation to give you feedback on your capstone concept and its presentation. What do you think people should offer their comments on—your professionalism, your creativity, your attention to detail?
- Write a one-page reaction paper to be turned in to your instructor. It should include your frank comments on the capstone project's most positive as well as its most challenging aspects. For starters, you might want to touch on the following:
- What you learned about visual merchandising that surprised you
- What you learned about managing a major project over the course of a semester
- What you wish you had known at the very outset of the course

Part Six CAREER STRATEGIES

kate spade
NEW YORK

15 Visual Merchandising Careers

Beginning a Career in Visual Merchandising

Do what you love. As you begin to think about your professional career, consider that you want your work to bring you a psychological reward as well as a paycheck. If you are going to spend forty or more hours each week in the workplace, why not spend it in a career that is engaging and fun? Why not get involved in something that you have a passion for, and enjoy?

Since you are just beginning, you may not know exactly what you want to do. Sometimes hobbies and leisure activities are accurate career indicators because they represent things you enjoy. Let's assume that you've already narrowed the field to retailing. If you enjoy indoor and outdoor sports, you may want to look for employment at stores like Nike or REI. If you are happiest when you are entertaining in your home, you may want to check into opportunities at stores like Crate&Barrel, Pottery Barn, or Williams-Sonoma. If you read fashion apparel magazines and stay in tune with the latest trends, a position at stores like Zara and H&M may be a good place to start.

After a year or two of retail experience, try to connect with a major retailer for your next position. Aim as high as you can go in the retail community. The better known your earliest employers are, the better are your chances of moving up. **Fortune 500 companies** frequently hire people trained by other industry leaders, knowing they will benefit from the new hires' experience with those companies. Another plus is that companies of this stature usually provide the best benefits and opportunities for growth. A job with such a company will help you build a more impressive résumé and make you more marketable.

> "Visual merchandising has infinite opportunities. At one time it was mainly in retail. Today, it's how companies communicate their brand, and who they are—galleries, magazines, automotive showrooms, restaurants, architectural firms, etc. It's about how you pursue the options. Get out there and make a difference!"
> *Tony Mancini, chief executive officer, ThinkTank Retail Hospitality Group*

Fortune 500 companies are the 500 largest companies in the United States ranked by revenue (gross sales). *Fortune* magazine publishes the list annually.

AFTER COMPLETING THIS CHAPTER, YOU SHOULD BE ABLE TO

- Identify many visual merchandising career options
- Build a professional portfolio
- Prepare to interview effectively for a visual merchandising position
- Discuss constructive interpersonal strategies to advance your career
- Use networking skills to establish yourself in the retail community

Figure 15.0 Kate Spade's window is certain to bring smiles to chocolate lovers. Madison Avenue, New York. WindowsWear Photo. Copyright WindowsWear Inc., http://www.windowswear.com, contact@windowswear.com.

The top retailers in America for the year 2020 (www.fortune.com) were led by these ten:

1. Walmart
2. Amazon
3. Costco Wholesale
4. Home Depot
5. Target
6. Lowe's
7. Best Buy
8. TJX
9. Dollar General
10. Macy's

No matter where you begin your career, each path you try is part of your journey, but may not be your final destination. In other words, there is no need to think you are stuck in any one position or that you have not gotten off to the best start. If you discover that you are not well suited to a position that you were initially excited about, you have still made progress. The only way to find your professional niche is experimentation. Looking back, you'll find that no single experience was a waste of time because you learned something from each situation. Experienced people will tell you that figuring out what they didn't want to do eventually lead to the discovery of what they wanted to do passionately!

There are countless stories of personal interests that grew into great career successes. Here are several favorites that cover a wide variety of professions in the visual merchandising and store design industry. These stories illustrate the winding road and abundant opportunities these well-known adventurous travelers discovered along their career paths.

KEN ALBRIGHT, PRESIDENT, SEVEN CONTINENTS

After high school graduation with an honors diploma and college scholarship, I left home, finished a year of college, and then worked a summer with four overlapping jobs. Along the way, I discovered that I was "tapped out" on conventional education. At age twenty, I took my winnings, bought a motorcycle, and hit the road to experience life.

After a year in the cultures of Central America, Mexico, the United States, and Canada, I took a two-month break for more self-evaluation. That accomplished, I liquidated the bike and took more two years to see Europe, North Africa, Central Asia, India, Southeast Asia, Japan, and Hawaii. Now twenty-four years old, it was time—to take stock of my global interests, to choose an economic course for my life, to have fun, and to stay stimulated.

My business began with a parasol—found in my travels. In Northern Thailand I noticed a cottage industry fabricating decorative parasols of handmade paper with painted patterns. I bought some and they sold very well at retail for residential interiors, but they quickly migrated to furniture store windows. The parasols were serendipitously spotted by people in the visual industry—and my vision was realized!

Seven Continents was named for the places I'd been during that journey of self-discovery. It began as a firm retailing antique textiles and artifacts from Thailand, Indonesia, and Japan. Our focus was creating reproducible products using the indigenous materials and techniques from these locales.

We had barely broken into the Canadian market when America beckoned. Bloomingdale's bought in, and Saks Fifth Avenue followed. We were in business. We were a hit! We discovered the NADI show and booked the last available space. . . .

Fast forward twenty years: We had 250 on staff in Toronto, 150,000 square feet, sales of $35 million. I sold the firm but repurchased it in 2003. With over 100 staff in Toronto, we are chameleons. We continue to invent new proprietary products, using exotic and often unexpected materials, create custom branded visuals for our clients, and connect fashion and architecture to store design. From seed to reality, it's great! They call me Mr. Ken.

TOM BEEBE, CREATIVE CONSULTANT-STYLIST & WINDOW WIZARD

Tom Beebe, for many years creative director of Paul Stuart, New York City, began his career thinking he wanted to go into advertising. Instead, his father suggested that he look into display as a creative field that was growing at the time. He began at Gimbels, assembling fixtures and gathering as much product knowledge as he could from the retail side of the store. From there he travelled uptown to Bergdorf Goodman, then Neiman Marcus—each time moving into increasingly responsible positions until he was named regional display manager for Nieman's East Coast stores. Beebe found a home in Manhattan's Paul Stuart store windows in 1986 and remained there

for fourteen years—six of them as creative director—with more than 3,332 windows to his credit.

After a stint as creative director for Fairchild's *Daily News Record*, Beebe has come back to retail as a creative consultant. In 2010, Mr. Beebe was presented with the prestigious Markopoulos Award, an honor named after the late visual merchandising legend Andrew Markopoulos and given to one outstanding industry professional presented annually by *design:retail*.

CHRISTINE BELICH, FORMER VICE PRESIDENT, VISUAL MERCHANDISING, SONY

While studying art at Kent State University, Christine Belich, former executive creative director of Sony Style in New York, landed a part-time job at a local department store, a branch of the May Company known today as Kaufman's. On the job, Christine learned the basics—stapling pads, dressing mannequins, and rigging forms. "I learned some on my own (out in my little branch store) and some from the 'road crew' that visited me once a month supplying me with endless bolts of felt and piles of dried foliage. When I had learned enough, I joined that traveling team." Eventually she moved on to Texas and Neiman Marcus in Houston.

I spent years there, and then continued with Neiman's in Westchester, New York. I learned so much about display excellence—how to make the merchandise stand out and on its own without the clutter of props. There is an "old Neiman's" way of doing display that everyone who was part of it is still so proud of . . it's almost like a secret club. The standards I learned at Neiman's are with me today. They are what I try to teach to everyone else.

The teamwork theme is still strong with Belich:

I came to Sony when the company was just getting into the retail business and was part of a team that created and marketed the retail brand Sony Style. I had many exciting opportunities at Sony that go far beyond the traditional role of visual merchandising. I was part of the team that created several retail venues for Metreon, a Sony Entertainment Center in San Francisco—a huge and challenging project. We also reinvented the Sony Style store and connected it to e-commerce and Sony Style magazine.

▌LINDA CAHAN, INDEPENDENT VISUAL MERCHANDISING CONSULTANT, CAHAN & COMPANY

In my many years working in visual, I never once wished I had gone in a different direction. I have had amazing opportunities, fabulous travel, and have worked with and for great people.

My first job was working for an upscale department store in Syracuse, NY. I was a fine arts major at Syracuse University and saw a painting in a window with a mannequin. I loved art, fashion and dolls and saw an opportunity. My boss was a smart and talented man who taught me a lot. I went on to work for several other top department and specialty stores leading to Corporate Director of Visual Merchandising for a chain of stores in Connecticut and then for another chain in the NY metropolitan area.

In 1983 my book, "A Practical Guide to Visual Merchandising" was published by John Wiley & Sons, NYC. It gave me the impetus to go out on my own and that's when the fun began. I developed a Visual Merchandising Manual for the overseas division of Singer, an entire new visual look for AMEX TRS including a custom Visual Standards guide and a catalog of visual displays I designed for the offices. I did the same for United Rentals. At the same time, I was teaching VM at Parsons School of Design in NYC for 12 years, installing window displays for Intel throughout the NYC metro area and giving seminars on visual presentation around the world.

I also wrote Feng Shui for Retailers based on my interest in the practice and how it impacts retail success. From 1985 through 2015, I travelled to thirty-six countries, gave over 500 seminars, wrote hundreds of articles and columns for B2B retailer magazines, consulted for large and small stores and taught again, this time at The Art Institute of Portland (OR) where I moved in 2005. Currently, I consult for all types of retailers on how to improve the look of their stores and the customer experience. I also train VM teams and give one-on-one classes.

▌ROBB COOK, FORMER DIRECTOR OF VISUAL MERCHANDISING & STORE DESIGN, SHEA ARCHITECTURE

Robb Cook, former director of visual merchandising and store design for Shea, Inc., a Minneapolis architectural firm, began his career as a "trimmer" at Sears, moved on to become a visual manager for JCPenney, and was park-wide visual designer at Camp Snoopy in Bloomington, Minnesota's Mall of America. Cook believes that architectural firms will hire more visual merchandisers in the future because "they are finding that it enables them to offer additional services to their clients."

What did Cook enjoy most about his position with Shea? "I loved the variety. I worked on everything in softlines and hardlines from A to Z, cosmetics to haute couture, shopping centers to pet stores." He advises visual merchandisers beginning their careers to "take every opportunity that is presented to you to express your individual creativity. Keep a photo library of all your visual projects as a foundation for your portfolio."

Cook is thankful to those who have mentored him through the years. Early in his career during his internship at Sears, a mentor noticed his work and offered him a position in special projects at the corporate offices. "He continued to offer support and guidance throughout my career at Sears." Cook later found another mentor at Mall of America's Camp Snoopy. "Even though I did not have an entertainment background, he offered me a visual position which enabled me to make an indoor theme park come alive."

STEVE KAUFMAN, FREELANCE WRITER-EDITOR-CONSULTANT-CREATIVE SPIRIT

Steve Kaufman, former editor of *vmsd* (*Visual Merchandising + Store Design*) magazine explained how he got his start in visual merchandising communications. "I'd been a writer and editor long term, when I saw an ad in the *New York Times*, answered it, and became the editor of *Display & Design Ideas*" (eventually *design:retail*). He later joined the staff at *vmsd* as editor.

Kaufman earned a journalism degree from the University of Illinois. In college, he had planned to be a sportswriter, which might explain the advice he offers to people starting out in their careers: "Don't view life as a linear experience. Don't assume that if you start here you are going to get there. Life is full of curves and turns and even reversals, and you can't always plan for them, nor should you try to."

Although Kaufman didn't grow up in retailing, it didn't take him long to get to know and like his target audience. "The [visual merchandising] industry is filled with creative people who are on a mission. It's fun to spend time with them. I find it fascinating to see how they fit their creative impulses and ability into the business of retail." These same people pose Kaufman's greatest professional challenge: "Writing to people who know more about the topic than you do. It's a huge responsibility— you want to provide a service; offer them help in some way."

TONY MANCINI, CHIEF EXECUTIVE OFFICER, THINKTANK RETAIL HOSPITALITY GROUP

I started my career as a stock boy for the Anderson Little Company. One time I was in this store shopping for a suit for Easter, and someone asked me whether I worked there. Little did I know a couple of years later that I would indeed work there.

After stocking the store, I became involved in sales and suddenly had an opportunity to display product in the store. I loved it! That led to a regional merchandise position, to assistant director, to divisional director. Anderson Little was once owned by the Richman Brothers Company, a division of the Woolworth Corporation. I was promoted to corporate director, visual merchandising and store design for the Richman Brothers Company.

*After seventeen years, I moved
on to Herman's World of Sports in
New York as director, and within six
months became vice president of
visual merchandising and store design.
Then, the most exciting call of my
career came from the Walt Disney
Company. After one and one-half
years as a director, I was promoted to
a position where I was responsible for
store design planning, merchandise
presentation, retail project services,
special events display, fixture
manufacturing, and the sculpting
production division.*

*Along the way I have met
the most incredible people and
established friends and personal
relationships in this industry. I am
involved in four boards of directors.
Still, there's so much more to do! You
can absolutely have a phenomenal
career in this industry. It takes
creativity, business savvy, courage, and
most important—passion!*

ED SCHILLING, WEST COAST DIRECTOR AT RALPH PUCCI

Ed Shilling is a west coast sales representative for Ralph Pucci, which is based in New York City. Ed began his career as a "window trimmer" at George Muse Co., a men's store in Atlanta. He traces his career path from there: "Following that, I was an assistant director of display at Saks in Atlanta, then a visual merchandising director at August Max in New York City. After that, a creative director at Winkleman's in Detroit, and finally vice president of visual merchandising and store planning at Ivy's, Florida." If you charted Shilling's work history graphically, you'd see a career ladder.

Shilling also knows visual design work, having served as vice president of design at Niedermaier in Chicago, where the international manufacturer makes custom products for retailers, the hospitality industry, Fortune 500 companies, architects, and designers. His greatest challenge seems to fall in the category he calls "time frames." He most enjoys "the creativity . . . and the people." Shilling advises newcomers to the visual field, "Don't be afraid to move onto the next step, don't be afraid of challenge, and don't follow the rules!"

Twenty-One Visual Merchandising Careers

There has never been a better time to begin a career in visual merchandising. Once limited to "trimming" windows and in-store displays in apparel stores, the visual merchandiser's role has dramatically expanded—in the level of positions, in the scope of positions, and in earning capacity. Today, someone who began as a display specialist might become a vice president of visual merchandising in almost any retail-related environment—from a grocery chain to a group of automobile showrooms.

Trends indicate that today's consumers appreciate and expect good design in all of the products they bring into their lives and their homes, no matter what their income or spending capabilities. This shouldn't come as a surprise to you when you consider the myriad sources of lifestyle information that consumers can access online and onscreen. As a result, employment potential for someone with a "good sense of design" increases proportionately.

As design-related positions and responsibilities evolve, their exact titles and types vary among retail-related companies. A look at the following twenty-one job titles and job descriptions will give you an idea of what's available today.

1. VISUAL MERCHANDISER/ VISUAL PRESENTATION SPECIALIST

This person is primarily responsible for the hands-on construction of displays and product arrangement on fixtures. In many cases, that includes both initiating the original display and maintaining the presentation. Department stores often employ two or more visual specialists with departmental responsibilities, i.e., menswear or junior fashions. Depending on sales volume and size, specialty stores may have one visual position per store, or a single visual specialist may be responsible for weekly or biweekly visits to a group of stores. This is an excellent entry-level position.

2. CORPORATE VISUAL DESIGNER

A visual designer creates new presentation techniques, develops fixtures for product displays, and may also do graphic design. The designer, who works with manufacturers and printers to build prototypes to be used in the corporate stores, is responsible for testing them before they are adopted companywide. The visual designer presents testing results to management to facilitate corporate decision making. When the fixtures or techniques are rolled out, the designer works with a visual communication specialist to write simple instructions for installation and use of the fixtures. This position requires a seasoned visual professional, often with five or more years of experience, including attendance at national markets.

3. PRESENTATION SPECIALIST/ ADJACENCY SPECIALIST

These specialists work closely with store merchants to develop planograms and floor layouts showing placement of products and fixtures. This position requires excellent written communication and computer design skills. In some retail organizations, walls are set in one store, then photographed. With an accompanying set of directions (identifying specific products and suggested placements), the photographs are sent to all of the other stores, ensuring uniform implementation chain-wide. This is largely an inner office (corporate)

position, but it is essential that specialists have had hands-on experience merchandising wall and floor fixtures in a store environment.

4. VISUAL TRAINING SPECIALIST

Visual training specialists train sales associates in multiunit chains to coordinate and present merchandise with brand image in mind. They use videos, visual merchandising guides, and update bulletins provided by visual communication specialists. Training specialists may travel from store to store or use vehicles like Zoom or Google Meet. An outgoing personality with excellent interpersonal communication skills is required because a large part of the job is motivating sales associates to follow company standards and create effective presentations. A teaching or training background is desirable, but not necessary. A clear sense of the company's vision, mission, goals, objectives, and brand image is essential.

5. VISUAL COMMUNICATION SPECIALIST

This individual writes copy for the visual merchandising guides and visual merchandising update bulletins and develops the videos that corporate visual training specialists use as communication tools to support training efforts. In addition to being effective in a directive sense, this specialist's writing must be as descriptive and imaginative as any ad copy and must motivate as well. Moreover, because the work requires so much attention to detail, this person's organizational skills are critical for successful employment.

6. VISUAL ART DIRECTOR

Art directors sketch graphic designs or develop layouts on computers, hire photographers and models, and oversee photo shoots. They also select the photos to be used in graphic signing and pass them along to the marketing

to one year of training, especially in a smaller retail operation where staff size is limited. Here are additional strategies to use as you enter the next natural phase of your career:

- **If you are in a management position, hire people who appear to be practicing the same ten strategies you've just learned about.** They are exactly the kind of workers you'll need on your team. They can carry the department (and you) to great achievements.
- **Make it your goal to build a strong identity for your department within the company.** If you put the department's progress high on your priority list, your career will take care of itself.
- **Invite your entire team to write a mission statement that describes what your department has to offer the larger organization.** For example, "We turn ideas into reality." Your department is a part of the corporate culture, but it's also a microculture of its own. Ask yourself what kind of culture you want to work in and what kind of culture will foster the results you want for the larger organization.
- **Invite your entire team to develop goals for your department.** For example, "Our goal is to train store associates to employ engaging presentation strategies to increase sales." Retail goal statements should always include the words "increase sales" or words to that effect. If there are no profits, there is no company. If there is no company, there are no jobs. If your team understands that, it will have little trouble embracing the goals it has set for itself.
- **Market your department to the rest of the company.** Consider developing a logo and a tagline for your department. Use them on printed interoffice memos, T-shirts and other tools to help familiarize the rest of the company with your departmental goals.

Treat your department like an important product and sell it to your internal customers.

- **Once you launch a visibility campaign (or any other internal program), revisit it regularly and reinforce its value to the group.** If the campaign fails through lack of support from you, your team will question your leadership credibility and be skeptical about other motivational techniques you use.
- **Visit stores in your organization on a regular basis, even if the majority of normal working hours are spent in a corporate office.** In addition, work in the stores occasionally. Store associates will clearly understand that you're accessible and that you appreciate their expertise and opinions on what works and what doesn't.
- **Model behaviors you want store associates to use and establish standards for performance.** Demonstrate something you want them to do in a specific way—how to set a floor according to a planogram, for instance. Then ask them to set the floor in another area. Next, ask them to train others to do the task they've just completed successfully. The "see one, do one, teach one" strategy accomplishes several useful tasks for a manager:

1. It communicates to associates that you're a real working partner.
2. It sets standards for acceptable performance.
3. It shows associates that the tasks they're being asked to do can be accomplished and are worth doing well.
4. It helps associates internalize (learn) an important task and empowers them to take ownership of it.

WORKING WITH VARIOUS PERSONALITY AND THINKING STYLES

Individuals are not all motivated in the same way. Whether managing a group of creative thinkers or working alongside them, this is critical to understand. Anneli Rufus in her book *Party of One* explains:

> Some of us appear to be in, but we are out. And that is where we want to be. Not just want, but need, the way tuna need the sea. Someone says to you, "Let's have lunch." You clench. What others thrive on, what they take for granted, the contact and confraternity and sharing that gives them strength leaves us empty. After what others would call a fun day out together, we feel as if we had been at the Red Cross, donating blood.

Many companies require employees to display team spirit. When one US retailer opened stores in Europe, some employees were found hiding in the restroom to avoid doing the company cheer at the start of the business day. We do not all respond to the same stimulus. If you are managing a team of people, recognize that you may need to modify activities to get the best results for your team.

Creative individuals are by nature not followers of the pack. This is what gives them their edge and ability to think outside the box. Take time to learn about your colleagues' preferred personal style. Ask them questions about how they like to interact and listen attentively to their answers. Do not assume you "know" what they are thinking, or what they prefer. If you understand them better, you will be less likely to judge them.

Generously giving creatives the space and freedom to work in their own style, at their own pace, will bring out their best. And if you are the creative individual with a stomach that churns when you see others join in with company cheers, respect their need for a different kind of motivation. Diverse personalities working together, allowing each other to operate with their own personal style, will create the most amazing innovations of all.

NETWORKING

Networking is the all-important human connection. Whether you know it or not, each time you interact with another human being and exchange even the smallest bit of information, you are building your network, expanding your world by practicing a vital interpersonal skill.

You already have active networks in your life:

- Family and friends
- Coworkers, business group members
- Fellow volunteers, church members
- Accountants, attorneys, doctors, dentists
- Former workmates, classmates, roommates
- Meet-up acquaintances

What binds you to these people is some common interest, concern, opinion, or mutual connection. It can be an occasional now-and-then sort of relationship, or a long-lasting thick-and-thin friendship. Each person you know is part of your "circle of influence"—maybe a hundred people or more. Each of them has a circle, too, so you can imagine how far your networking may reach.

There are as many ways to network as there are interactions between humans in a day. To make networking strategies effective in your professional life, however, you really have to keep your goals and your specific needs in mind all the time—just in case. After all, you're managing a career, and networking is a great way to give and receive, to build your reputation as a person who is always in the loop. Your company has resources and

BOX 15.1

🪢 Neuroscience Pop-Up!

In *Silent Selling*, you've learned about design principles, signing, floor layouts, and window displays. When you begin to use this information in a workplace setting, to put it into action, the concepts will begin to come alive for you. But what will you offer that is unique, your personal brand identity? Is there a way to invite in a taste of wisdom that will turn the key to your own one-of-a-kind signature?

Dr. Sanjay Gupta, when interviewed about his book, *Keep Sharp: Build a Better Brain at Any Age,* promoted the effect of exercise when he said a walk with a friend is like Miracle-Gro for the brain. "Exercise helps me think better and consolidate new information. With my brain on exercise, I find that I am more likely to have truly novel thoughts . . . ."

Exercise in nature has other benefits. Shinrin Yoku, which translates to Japanese Forest Bathing, was developed in 1978, in an effort to explore the results of time spent in nature. An engaging book on the subject, *Forest Bathing: How Trees Can Help You Find Health and Happiness* by Dr. Qing Li, is the result of eight years of scientific study. Dr. Li explores the effects of the secretion of phytoncides from trees and plants on our health and immune systems. He found both physical benefits like lowering blood pressure, decreasing anxiety and fatigue, along with breaking through creative blocks. "Spending time in nature can boost problem solving ability and creativity by 50 percent. Plenty of research substantiates what leaders, poets and philosophers have known since the days of Aristotle: walking in the forest clears our minds and helps us to think."

Dr Qing Li writes further: "In nature, our minds are captured effortlessly by clouds and sunsets, by the movements of leaves in the breeze, by waterfalls and streams, by the sound of the birds or the whisper of the wind. These soothing sounds give our mental resources a break. They allow our minds to wander and reflect, and so restore our capacity to think more clearly."

As a visual merchandiser, with creativity at the core of your work, a simple daily walk in nature will allow you to reach into your subconscious and bring all you have learned together in your own unique way. Your way, your brand. Build it with confidence and boldness and heart.

A walk in nature is a clear path to creative insights. Eloise Butler Wildflower Garden, Minneapolis. *Judy Bell*

you're one of them. You can use other people's resources, and you can be one of theirs.

There are global networking possibilities for you through social networks like LinkedIn, Facebook, Instagram, and Twitter. A note of caution: Be careful how much personal information you post in any public place, the

Internet included. Check out the sources of emails from individuals or companies you are not familiar with before you interact.

How do you get started as a networker? You communicate. First, you need to really look at people you pass in the halls. If you say, "Hi! how are you?" to each person you see and then move down the corridor without waiting to hear the answer, you've just wasted an opportunity to network. Of course you can't stop and visit at length with every person you pass, but you can stop asking empty questions of people when you have no intention of listening to their answers. Smile and nod, say "hi!" but save extended conversations for networking and make them meaningful. Networking is not about a popularity contest. Networking is about developing a strategy for delivering your personal brand. You can begin by listening. When you listen, you become important to the speaker. Be selective. Keep your goals and specific needs in mind when you seek out the people who need to know you're alive and a contender. If you want to market your department, build a network of people who can help you do it. If you want to market yourself, build a network that can help you do that. If you want to enhance your resources, become an expert networker.

CONNECTING WITH THE INDUSTRY

Some professional organizations offer special services to their subscribers. University professors view WindowsWear not only as a trend subscription service, but as an opportunity for students to network in the industry. WindowsWear's Mentorship Program invites students to share their concepts involving retail, design, marketing, and technology strategies with a specific retailer every year. The top ten student finalists celebrate at the retailer's headquarters. See videos from the events at www.windowswear.com

Trade magazine *vmsd* features a career tab on their website, www.vmsd.com, where you can post the type of job you are seeking and also find available positions. *vmsd* also hosts the annual IRDC (International Retail Design Conference), a two-day event where you can meet with other retailers from around the globe. The conference is held in a different city every year to share insights, get ideas, and network, largely through roundtable discussions and other events like the Iron Merchant that promote peer interaction. Recent cities found the conference in Montreal, New Orleans, Seattle, and Boston. Visit www.vmsd.com to learn more.

GETTING YOUR FOOT IN THE DOOR

Once you have identified positions that you want to learn more about, you can develop a strategy to meet, and even work side by side with, individuals in the workplace.

Informational Interviews

One way to meet industry professionals is to try to set up brief, informational interviews. Because most of these people are extremely busy, you may only be able to get in by networking. If you know anyone working for the company, for instance, ask for help connecting with someone in the visual department. Encourage your school to invite a panel of professionals working in the visual industry to answer questions during a class session.

Internships

An internship is an excellent way to take a step inside a company and learn more about it. Many college programs offer credit for school term internships; some allow them only during breaks, interim sessions, and summer vacations. Internships often lead to permanent positions. Treat each opportunity very seriously because it could launch your career.

Independent Contracting

Many companies will hire a visual contractor to work on a specific short-term project. A permanent position may be created if the need for the contractor's work extends to a longer period of time. Even if the new position has to be posted for all applicants, the experienced contractor has an excellent chance of securing the permanent position. This is often the easiest way to make your way into an organization, even though it may mean spending some time as an independent contractor.

DOCUMENTING YOUR PROFESSIONAL QUALIFICATIONS

You are preparing for a career in a visual industry, so you will eventually develop a **portfolio** with examples of your professional work. Until then, a good cover letter and a simple but professional-looking résumé are all you need. Simple is better. There is a certain amount of ritual to job seeking. You do not need to reinvent the process.

Portfolios

No portfolio at all is preferable to a weak one. Do not include photographs of your work from fine arts or any other projects you have done in school unless the work is truly exceptional and has won national awards or has appeared in a national publication. Photos from retail displays you've executed are acceptable. In any case, when you are just starting out, keep the portfolio presentation brief. Editing your own presentation is as important as editing any visual presentation you'll do. If you're not sure about the quality or effectiveness of a display photograph, ask someone from a retail visual merchandising department to analyze its merit as a portfolio item. This is just like asking another person to proofread what you've written in your résumé. You need an objective opinion.

Invest in a simple black portfolio case with clear pages and a zipper closure. Place your résumé (a single sheet with your name, contact information, educational highlights, and job experience) in the first sleeve and follow it with all of your favorite displays and floor or wall fixture presentations. If the photographs

don't completely fill the sleeve, mount them on good quality paper. Slip thin cardstock into the sleeves between paper documents to give them more body. As your career progresses, edit your photographs to a dozen of your best. Also include any awards or recognition certificates that you receive.

INTERVIEWING EFFECTIVELY

You can prepare yourself for your interview by learning all you can about the company, by learning what to do at the interview, and by planning answers to the questions that you may be asked at the interview.

Pre-Interview Strategy

Candidates who've done their homework impress interviewers. Implement a pre interview strategy. Here are a few ideas that have worked for others:

- **Research the organization's website.** You'll find company history there, and often its mission statement, lists of products, locations, and other information that you can later use in conversation with the interviewer. Print the pages and insert them into the notebook that you'll be taking to the interview. Invest in a professional-looking cloth or leather-covered version rather than the usual college spiral or three-ring binder.
- **Pay a visit to the store where you will be interviewed.** This special trip will help you become familiar with the company's current promotions and strategies. Bring your notebook along and make a note of the store's strengths.
- **During your store visit, analyze how the employees are dressed**. Take your clothing cues from them, but plan to take it up one level for your interview. A quote to interview by: "Dress for the job you want, not the one you have."

A **portfolio** is a visual résumé, a portable case for presenting photographs, drawings, graphic designs, certificates, letters of recommendation, and other documentation of a person's professional experience.

- **Next, visit the company's competitors, so that you are able to have a discussion if the interviewer goes in that direction.** The more knowledgeable you are, the greater your level of confidence will be. If the topic comes up during your interview, describe competitors objectively, never negatively.
- **Select clothing that is appropriate for the environment where you would be working.** Even if the company is having a casual dress day on your interview date, dress in business attire. Clean the outfit, if necessary, and always press it. Check the heels on your shoes; they should not show wear. Clean and polish them. This is the fashion industry. Dress as if you understand that. Look in the mirror, at least twice. You're the one on display today!

Your Interview

Here are some suggestions for a successful interview:

- **Arrive at least ten minutes before your appointment on the day of your interview.** Turn off your cell phone and put it away. A few minutes at rest in the waiting room will help you to compose your thoughts.
- **Sit up straight.** Excellent posture is a plus; it helps you radiate confidence—and allows more air into your lungs, which will send more oxygen to your brain and help you to think clearly.
- **Make eye contact.** Smile. Let your interviewer offer his or her hand to shake. When you respond, your grip should be brief and gently firm.
- **Wait to be offered a seat.** Once seated, do not handle anything on the interviewer's desk or help yourself to the candy dish.
- **Answer questions thoughtfully and clearly.** If you don't know the answer to a question, say so. See the list of typical interview questions that follows.
- **Speak articulately.** It should go without saying that you need to "watch your language" when you interview. Good grammar is essential. Statements including "her and I" rather than "she and I", will not make a good impression. Avoid using regional slang and common interjections such as, ". . . like . . . you know . . ." repeatedly in your conversation.

- **Once the interviewer has had the chance to ask you questions,** indicate that you also have a few and open your notebook to your list of questions so that you can take notes. Not only will you have a record for yourself, but the interviewer will perceive that you are serious about the job opportunity.
- **After the interview,** shake the interviewer's hand again (if offered) and thank her or him for the opportunity to learn more about the company.
- **Send a thank-you note** the next day and again express your interest in the position and the organization. Consider adding how helpful the interview was in gaining a clear understanding of the position responsibilities and challenges, and how your experience has prepared you for the opportunity.

Common sense says that you should be appropriately groomed and dressed when you present yourself for interviews, but you'd be amazed to know how many applicants arrive chewing gum and wearing wrinkled clothes and unpolished shoes. It's true: you have only seconds to make a good first impression.

retail realities

Now that you have a sense about your interviewer's style, you can be creative with your thank-you note. If your interviewer was strictly professional, your thank-you note should be the same. If the interviewer was casual and creative, respond accordingly. One candidate for a graphic design position sent his interviewer a pair of work gloves with a computer-designed label that read, "Ready to Work." His name, phone number, and "Thank You" were also imprinted on the label—and yes, he got the job!

retail realities

Typical Interview Questions

You should be prepared to answer these typical questions:

- Why are you interested in a position with our company?
- What are your short-term career goals?
- What are your long-term goals?
- What are your strengths?
- What are your weaknesses? (Neutralize the negative in that sentence and rephrase it by responding with something like "My greatest opportunity for growth is. . . .")

A list of questions you would like your interviewer to answer might include:

- What are the most critical responsibilities for this position?
- What positions could someone working in this area grow into?
- What are the company's expansion plans?
- What is the company's philosophy or mission?
- How would you describe your organization's culture?
- What benefits do you offer to your full-time employees? (Save this question for after you have been called back for a second or third interview, if this will be one of your first positions in the field.)

■ FUTURE CAREER GOALS

The visual merchandising industry has a wonderful history of recognizing leaders in the retail design field and there is a very prestigious award offered each year:

The Markopoulos Award. This award was established in 1996 by *design:retail* magazine, in honor of the late Andrew Markopoulos, who was the senior vice president of visual merchandising at Dayton Hudson's department store. In the April/May 2016 issue of *design:retail*, Jenny S. Rebholz writes of the twentieth anniversary of the award:

An Emmy, a Grammy, an Oscar, these are prestigious awards for their respective industries . . . in the retail design industry, the Markopoulos Award is celebrating twenty years. The recipients are nominated by peers and selected by The Markopoulos Circle of previous recipients based on their lifetime achievements and overall career accomplishments, their ability to innovate and inspire, their contributions to the success of a particular retailer or company, their ability to nurture and mentor young talent, and their ongoing contributions and support of the retail design and visual industries. The recipients are admirable role models on both a professional and personal level.

In May of 2016, *design:retail* celebrated twenty years of the Markopoulos award with an event in New York. All former recipients were invited to attend the presentation of the award to the twentieth winner. This same event recognized the forty under-40 winners, the up-and-coming leaders of the industry. Prior to the award ceremony, The Markopoulos Circle participated in roundtable discussions with the forty under-40 group. Each table was given a topic to discuss, and after twenty-five minutes everyone moved to a new table. The event provided the optimum in networking opportunities—before each discussion started, everyone at the tables introduced themselves with their name, business, and headquarters location.

One of the requirements for The Markopoulos Award is to serve the industry by participating on boards and committees, speaking at conferences, etc. There is no better way to get involved than to volunteer to help in whatever way you can. Opportunities abound in the visual merchandising and store design industry where you can express your interest to volunteer on committees for organizations like PAVE. See www.paveglobal.org to learn more.

Here is a list of recipients, with the positions they held at the time of their awards.

Markopoulos Award Winners

- **1996**: Andrew Markopoulos, senior vice president of visual merchandising, Dayton Hudson
- **1997**: Ignaz Gorischek, vice president, visual planning and presentation, Neiman Marcus
- **1998**: Tony Mancini, vice president, global retail store development, Walt Disney Imagineering and Walt Disney Parks and Resorts
- **1999**: Judy Bell, group manager of innovation, Target, and author of *Silent Selling*
- **2000**: James Mansour, founder, Mansour Design
- **2001**: Linda Fargo, vice president, visual merchandising, Bergdorf Goodman
- **2002**: Chuck Luckenbill, vice president, visual merchandising, Kohl's
- **2003**: Simon Doonan, creative director, Barney's
- **2004**: Christine Belich, executive creative director, Sony
- **2005**: James Damian, senior vice president, experience development group, Best Buy
- **2006**: Michael Cape, vice president and director of brand marketing at JCPenney
- **2007**: Jack Hruska, executive vice president of creative services at Bloomingdale's
- **2008**: Alfredo Peredes, executive vice president of global creative services, Polo Store Development and Home Collection Design Studio at Polo Ralph Lauren Corp.
- **2009**: Ralph Pucci, president of Pucci International
- **2010**: Tom Beebe, creative consultant at Paul Stuart
- **2011**: Dennis Gerdeman, principal & CEO, Chute Gerdeman

- **2012**: Eric Feigenbaum, chair, visual merchandising, LIM College
- **2013**: Joseph Feczko: senior vice president of integrated marketing, broadcast services and innovation strategies, Macy's
- **2014**: Harry Cunningham: senior vice president, store planning, design and visual merchandising, Saks Fifth Avenue
- **2015**: Ken Smart: artistic design director, Ralph Pucci, Intl.
- **2016**: Bill Goddu: chief brand officer and ambassador, Brand Value Builders: Fleetwood Fixtures
- **2017**: Linda Lombardi: head of global store design for Godiva Chocolatier
- **2018**: Anne Kong: program coordinator for visual presentation and exhibition, design associate professor at FIT
- **2019**: Dan Evans, managing partner and executive vice president marketing and business development for Wests Designs.

Photograph your work. It is the best way to record the professional displays you've done and sell your design skills to future employers. It also shows that you have ambition, determination, and initiative—all good qualities for a job candidate to have.

retail realities

One of the most effective ways to network is to join a professional group or a service organization, like a downtown council or mall merchant's association. You can become your company's ambassador to the retail and creative community. (Never leave your office without business cards.)

retail realities

The Planning and Visual Education (PAVE) partnership holds an annual student design competition judged by leaders from the visual merchandising industry. Winners travel to national markets for formal recognition and an opportunity to meet executives from nearly every retail operation in the United States. Check out www.paveglobal.org for details on the competition.

retail realities

BOX 15.2

DESIGN GALLERY: KATE SPADE, MADISON AVENUE, NY

Kate Spade, the late cofounder of the iconic brand, began her career as an accessories editor at *Mademoiselle*, the perfect background for her path to designing some of the most stylish and easily recognizable handbags in the world today. Her first shop opened in New York in 1996 and the business has grown to over 175 retail shops and outlet stores internationally. Kate Spade products are also featured in more than 450 stores around the globe.

The website www.katespade.com describes the artful product line:

> *Crisp color, graphic prints and playful sophistication are the hallmarks of Kate Spade New York. From handbags and clothing to jewelry, fashion accessories, fragrance, eyewear, shoes, swimwear, home décor, desk accessories, stationery, tabletop and gifts, our exuberant approach to the everyday encourages personal style with a dash of incandescent charm. We call it living colorfully.*

The Kate Spade and Company Foundation "inspires women to be the heroines of their own stories. The foundation gives away $1 million annually to causes that support women's economic empowerment, access to opportunity and pathways to mental well-being to underserved communities of women in NYC and beyond."

Kate Spade's Madison Avenue store pictured here is a delightful traffic stopper, certain to bring a smile to chocolate lovers (and maybe even a quick trip to the nearest chocolate shop!). Mannequins, side by side, dressed in chocolate-and-cream–colored outfits, mimic the gold foil-wrapped chocolate candies on their heads. Notice how the bold graphic pattern on the first mannequin's skirt repeats the pattern on the second mannequin's candy topper, and cleverly draws your eye from left to right and up.

Copyright WindowsWear Inc., http://www.windowswear.com, contact@ windowswear.com

The solid vest on the first mannequin and the solid skirt on the second mannequin help to create a balanced look in the display. To emphasize the repetition of the candy toppers, notice that both mannequins are wearing blouses with matching bows. Repetition is also demonstrated by using two identical mannequin forms, each with a clutch under their arms. It is easy to see the careful planning that went into the design of this window, even to the final wink of the sentence lettered on the glass: "She always did have good taste."

Shoptalk "A Visual Merchandising Career in Publishing" by Janet Groeber, Managing Editor at RE:Media

I can't ever remember a time that I wasn't involved in some kind of publication. My family still laughs about the newspaper I started, *The Groeber Gazette*, which was designed to inform my mom and dad, brother and sisters about our activities. I guess I got the idea from my dad—a reader of several daily newspapers, myriad magazines, and editor of a union newsletter. I had a rubber stamp set; he had a typewriter. From grade school through college, I worked on newspapers, yearbooks, and magazines.

In college, I took a job doing layout for the student newspaper, which helped pay for expenses. My coursework as a communications and journalism student included news reporting, writing, editing, and law, and I rounded out the communications portion to include art and theater history, mass media, stagecraft, music appreciation, literature, public speaking, psychology, politics, geology, geography, and business. In short, a liberal arts education. As an upperclassman I landed an associate editorship on the quarterly student magazine—and that cemented my desire to work professionally for a magazine.

Interestingly, I was working summers in a local department store as well as between breaks at the same time. There, I was exposed to visual merchandising, formerly called the display department. And, though I was working in the bargain basement, another young college part-timer and I put together our first presentation. It was a fully accessorized outfit pulled together from merchandise on our floor and presented in the bottom half of an old wooden showcase. I was hooked! I can remember visiting the store's attic filled with fixtures, displayers, and props and thinking, "What a world."

After college, I worked for a textbook publisher. My job was to research photography for business textbooks for high school and college students. Among our references and resources were publications such as *Stores* and *Visual Merchandising and Store Design*. Later, I learned *VMSD* was based in Cincinnati. Eventually I met someone who worked at the company, and that person introduced me to the right people. When I was hired as an assistant editor, my friends and family thought I'd died and gone to heaven. I was working in my two favorite passions! Within eight years, I was named editor and later took on the additional duties as associate publisher.

Next, I did a stint on the other side with two retail interior design and architectural firms. I helped gain new business for one and handled media relations for the other. I actually got to see another side of the process that I'd only been reporting on, and, of course, it was a wonderful addition to my professional education. And, when I could (and it was appropriate), I accepted assignments with other retail and design-oriented trade magazines. Several years ago I returned to publishing to help launch a new section on design, planning, and visual merchandising with the editors of *Chain Store Age* magazine. Once again, I used both my new-found and long-term experience and skills in my chosen profession.

Today, I'm using my editorial skills as director of the Retail Design Institute, a nonprofit association for design professionals. The position requires not only writing and editing for our newsletter, but for our website which reaches all of members in North and South America as well as Europe. I look forward to connecting with our members and learning more about the retail industry with every interaction. One of the most exciting projects on the horizon is the Institute's upcoming anniversary since its founding in 1961. Not only will we look back at our history, but we will be asking our members to make predictions about the future of retail design.

Chapter 15 Review Questions

1. Identify a visual merchandising career that appeals to you. What are the main job skills you will need for this position and why?
2. What are the steps in preparing for a successful interview?
3. What are the key interpersonal strategies you will need to advance your career?
4. How can you network to get new jobs in the retailing community?

Outside-the-Box Challenge

Personal Brand Identity

LOOK

Name two people you admire in the business world. List the traits you find admirable.

COMPARE

Compare their traits with your own.

INNOVATE

How can you improve the way you present yourself? What are you doing to sell yourself?

Informational Interview

LOOK

Set up an informational interview with a visual professional. Assess the traits and interests this person possesses that contribute to his or her success in the visual field.

COMPARE

Compare this person's traits and interests with your own.

INNOVATE

How can you improve on the skills that are necessary for success in the visual field?

Leadership Skills

LOOK

Examine the culture of your classroom. Which students seem to be most successful at getting their ideas implemented? Who are the class leaders?

COMPARE

Compare the techniques they use with your own current leadership skills.

INNOVATE

What do you think you need to do to further develop yourself as a leader? This could become an action plan for you.

Critical Thinking

Department Brand Identity Building

Your goal is to start an internal marketing program for your own visual merchandising department as a motivational tool for coworkers and also to raise your group or team's corporate visibility (stressing your department's potential to contribute to the company's bottom line). Create an identity for your department by completing these two projects.

BRAND IDENTITY BUILDING

1. Design a logo that a visual merchandising department might use as its marketing symbol.
2. Write a tag line (motto) to accompany the logo. For example: "Creative Solutions That Increase Sales."
3. Write a departmental goal statement in twenty-five words or less. For example: "To train store teams to execute the latest techniques in product presentation."
4. Design an interoffice memo form using your logo.

BUILDING YOUR OWN BRAND IDENTITY

Use the following questions and assignments to develop a strategy to market yourself:

1. What position would you like to hold as you begin your visual merchandising career?
   - List your long-term career goals. For example: what do you want to be doing five years from now?
   - List your short-term employment goals: things that must happen in the next year or sooner in order for you to reach those long-term goals.

2. Name two potential employers in your area.
3. Whom do you know right now who might be able to help you connect with those potential employers?
    - Name the people you know right now.
    - Describe your networking plan to meet more people connected in some way with the employers you've identified.
4. Write a brief script that you could use for contacting each company to arrange an informational interview.
5. Describe your plan of action for a pre-interview on-site visit. List the elements that you would be looking for as you visit each store prior to an informational interview.
6. What would you need to know in order to determine which company might have the better opportunity for your career development and employment goals? Write down at least five possible interview questions to ask each potential employer. Include questions about working culture, mentoring opportunities, and so on.
7. Think about the things you know about yourself and what you've learned about the visual merchandising field that would make you a good fit as an employee for each company. Envision each of the potential employers you've identified for this activity as "shoppers" and yourself as a branded "product." Write a short paragraph that explains why either of them would want to hire you. Describe the unique talents, interests, and skills that make up your personal brand identity and make you a truly value-added individual.

Case Study

The Next Step

THE SITUATION
You have graduated from your training program, and you are ready to look for work in a retail setting as an entry-level visual merchandiser. You realize that you don't have a great deal of (or, perhaps, any) experience in the field. Nevertheless, you are determined to work for one of the following types of stores:

- A large national chain with hundreds of stores. You'd like to explore several parts of the country before settling in one area.
- A mom-and-pop operation in the city where you live. This company doesn't have a visual merchandising staff, but you'd like to create a position.
- A retail company selling merchandise that you've purchased to pursue your favorite outdoor sport. It has a number of regional stores in the area and also has a very busy Internet site that reaches out to specialized shoppers all over the world.
- Any store that has a bank of closed display windows. You want as much experience as you can get to build a portfolio for a position in New York City a few years from now.

YOUR CHALLENGE
Working with your present resume and educational experience, design a job strategy that will give you the experience you need to take your next professional step and then do the following:

1. Modify your current resume to emphasize the skills, work experience, work habits, and personal accomplishments that you currently have.
2. Set long-term and short-term goals.
3. Examine your interests and experiences outside of work.
4. Think about your personal characteristics in terms of strengths to capitalize on and weaknesses to overcome, as you set about this task.

Glossary

A

accent lighting describes lighting effects designed to emphasize certain wall areas, merchandise displays, or architectural features in a retail setting.

adjacencies are thoughtfully planned layouts that position same "end-use" products next to each other. Example: shoes and hosiery positioned side by side.

ambient lighting describes general, overall lighting.

analogous schemes consist of two or more colors that are next to each other (adjacent) on the color wheel. Example: yellow with yellow-green.

artificial intelligence refers to computer systems' ability to perform tasks that normally require human intelligence.

atmospherics are multiple décor elements (lighting effects, sound levels, aromas, etc.) that appeal to our five senses and contribute to the brand image and overall environment of a store.

augmented reality is the real-time use of text, graphics, and other virtual elements to integrate with real-world objects.

B

balance refers to an equality of optical weight and relative importance that creates a unified presentation.

basics—the bulk of the stock in any department—are a department's core merchandise.

bid is an estimate of manufacturing costs to produce something (e.g., a fixture) or perform a service and a formal offer to do so. Once the bid and all its terms have been accepted, a contract is awarded. This formal agreement between the buyer and the manufacturer becomes the official basis for actual production, delivery schedule, and terms of payment.

bin is a term for a container often used interchangeably with *cube*, although many retailers define cubes as containers that are open on their sides and define bins as containers that are open from their tops.

branded groupings are formed when merchandise from a single designer or manufacturer is brought together for display and merchandising purposes—for example, Nike or Tommy Hilfiger.

brand image is the shopper's perception of a retailer's identity. It encompasses not only merchandise, but also store environment, reputation, and service. In some cases, the retailer employs the store's name or another branded element on its private-label products, like Hermes signature "H" pattern on handbags, rings, belts, pockets squares and dog collars.

broken merchandise refers to assortments with missing sizes, styles, and colors after sell-down.

C

capacity fixture holds large quantities of merchandise, usually showing a single style in several colors and in a complete range of sizes.

catwalks are narrow walkways. In theatrical productions, they are the bridge over the stage lights in the "fly" area that allows technicians to reach, change, and aim spotlights. In fashion, it's the narrow runway that extends beyond the stage that allows fashion show patrons unobstructed views of models and garments.

color rendition is the degree to which lighting allows colors to be viewed under conditions that are closest to those offered by natural light. The lighting industry uses the term CRI (color rendering index) when listing specifications on each lamp.

color story describes a color-coordinated or color-keyed product grouping that shows consumers how to use a season's trend colors. Creates visual impact when showing otherwise unrelated items.

colorways are the assorted colors or groups of colors a manufacturer has chosen for its line of fashion products. A manufacturer's representative might tell a store buyer that a polished cotton skirt comes in three different colorways: jewel tones, pastels, and earth tones.

combination floor layout employs the best features of several selling floor layouts in an overall plan that suits a retailer's specific merchandising strategies.

complementary schemes consist of two colors that are directly opposite each other on the color wheel. Example: yellow and violet.

contrast refers to extreme differences between objects or items: light-colored merchandise compared to very dark items, for example, or huge items shown with miniscule items.

CRI (color rendering index) is the measure of the ability of a light source to reveal the colors of various objects faithfully.

cross-merchandising refers to moving merchandise across traditional department or classification lines to combine elements in a single department or display. For example, books of poetry, romantic novels, candles, bath salts, terry-cloth robes, and over-sized bath towels could be brought together in a single spa-like display.

cube is a term for a container often used interchangeably with *bin*, although many retailers define cubes as containers that are open on their sides and define bins as containers that are open from their tops.

D

decorative lighting creates atmosphere, enhances retail branding, and can also influence a customer's mood.

design strategy is a plan of action to achieve retail goals and create a welcoming place where shoppers will purchase goods and services.

design thinking is a human-centered approach to innovation that integrates three considerations: inspiration, ideation, and implementation.

direction describes the design element or tool that leads the shopper's eye from one place to another. A directional arrow that points to a particular destination within the store and leads the shopper from one space to another is one example.

double-complementary schemes consist of four colors—two colors plus their color wheel complements. Example: yellow with violet plus green with red.

E

emphasis is the special focus or stress placed on an item to highlight it in a presentation. This can be achieved by using contrast, lighting, color, placement, repetition, and so on.

endcaps are valuable display and stocking spaces at the ends of gondola fixtures. They may be used to feature a sampling of the merchandise on either side of the gondola, for new merchandise offerings, for value-priced products, or for advertised specials. They may be stacked, pegged, or shelved.

F

face-outs are hardware for hanging merchandise so that the full front of the item is visible. Face-outs may utilize straight arms or slanted arms that create cascading waterfall effects.

fashion editorials are displays in strategic locations within a store that reflect retailers' support for merchandise and trends in the form of strong fashion statements. Editorials are always positioned in high-traffic areas like store entrances, department entrances, escalator platforms, main aisles, and at the ends of aisles on sight lines. They may incorporate mannequins, signs, t-stands, and/or props to support the featured items. Other names used by retailers for these locations include strike-points, hot zones, focals, visual impact areas, and interior windows.

faux pas, a phrase taken from the French for "false step," describes an error in fashion judgment or a mistake in coordination techniques.

feature fixtures typically hold smaller merchandise assortments, allowing presentation of two styles (on a two-way) or a coordinate grouping (on a four-way). They are intended to spotlight items or bring together coordinated outfits rather than show full category assortments.

flagship stores display the highest ideals of a company's brand image. Every detail, from fitting room hooks to floor coverings, reflects the company's brand. Stores built after the flagship is developed are usually modified for cost effectiveness. Examples of flagship stores include Uniqlo and H&M on 5th Avenue in Manhattan.

flat metal crossbars are basic fixture components used to show large quantities of goods on hangers along walls.

fluorescent lamps are sealed glass tubes filled with mercury vapor. Their inner surfaces are coated with a mixture of phosphor powders. When electricity arcs through the gases in the lamps, the gases produce ultraviolet energy that is absorbed by the coating and causes the powder to become fluorescent, emitting visible light.

formal balance occurs when two items of equal size or optical weight are balanced equidistant from a center point. Also called *symmetry*.

Fortune 500 companies are the 500 largest companies in the United States ranked by revenue (gross sales).

four-ways, also called *costumers* or *four-way fixtures*, feature hanging coordinate groups or small quantities (24–48 items) of separates presented as coordinated outfits.

free-flow layout describes a floor plan that has selling fixtures arranged in loosely grouped, informal, nonlinear formations to encourage browsing.

functional groupings are formed when merchandise is segmented or grouped on a fixture or in a display presentation according to its end use.

G

gondola is a versatile four-sided capacity fixture that may be shelved for folded or stackable products or set with garment rods to show apparel on hangers.

grid layout is a linear design for selling floors in which fixtures are arranged to form vertical and horizontal aisles throughout the store.

gridwall is a wall system of metal wire in a vertical and horizontal pattern that accepts brackets and display accessories with gridwall fittings.

H

harmony is an art element that creates visible unity. It is a careful selection of complementary, interwoven elements that create a unified whole in keeping with a store's overall brand image.

home meal replacement (HMR) foods are complete take-home, ready-to-warm-up and ready-to-eat meals like nutritious salads, hearty pasta dishes, and protein and veggie combinations.

hue is another word for the name of a color family—the reds, blues, browns, and so on. It is also used in nontechnical speech as a synonym for color.

I

informal balance occurs when items or objects are positioned so that a single larger object is counterbalanced by two or more smaller objects on the other side of an optical center point.

institutional windows are display windows devoted to intangible ideas and causes; they promote an image for the store as an institution rather than feature merchandise. An example would be a congratulatory window for a championship sports team.

intensity is the brightness, purity, and degree of saturation of a color.

K

key items are proven sellers purchased in depth for the department and offered at competitive prices. They can be found in trend or basic areas and in shops.

kiosks are freestanding selling units, open on one or all sides.

L

lamp has at least two distinct meanings. In the lighting industry, lamp is another word for light bulb. In common terms, it applies to a lighting fixture complete with a bulb, a power source, a base, and a shade that is either decorative or purely functional.

lead time is the amount of time it takes to complete products from receipt of order through production and delivery.

lease lines are the boundary lines where store space begins and a mall's common area ends.

LEDs (light-emitting diodes) are tiny semi-conductors, similar to incandescent bulbs, that give off light when electric current passes through them. With no filaments to burn out, they are cooler and more durable than incandescent lamps.

leveraging, used as a verb, describes gaining a mechanical advantage or adding impact, power, or effectiveness—adding impact to a store's brand identity by using an interactive display window, for example.

lifestyle center is a mixed-use commercial development that combines the traditional retail functions of a shopping mall with services like shared workspaces and leisure amenities including table service restaurants, multiplex cinemas, and fitness clubs. In addition, other services may be introduced, like medical and dental offices and license bureaus.

line guides the eye to a feature or is a linear element that sets a mood. Long horizontal lines can suggest calm and stability, for example. Jagged diagonal lines can convey a sense of excitement and movement.

M

minimal floor layout, gallery-like in its simplicity, shows small selections of handcrafted or very exclusive merchandise.

mom-and-pop store is a term that comes from early retailing when many retailers were in family businesses and often lived in apartments above their stores. Today, it refers to small, independent retailers.

monochromatic schemes consist of a single color in different values and intensities (more white or gray blended into the basic color). Example: navy blue shown with medium blue and light blue.

multiple sales are transactions in which two or more items are purchased at one time. For example, a shopper buys a necklace to wear with a blouse.

N

niche marketing means identifying a very specific market segment and offering products or services that research has shown the segment wants or needs and can afford to buy.

O

open sell is fixturing that makes most merchandise (even items traditionally kept in locked cases) accessible to shoppers without the assistance of salespeople.

operational signs relate to the day-to-day business of a store, listing store hours, return policies, emergency exits, locations of help phones, department locations, and fitting-room policies.

optical center of a sign is its focal point, where the eye naturally comes to rest, just above the center point (roughly a third of the way from the sign's top edge).

optical weight is how important, large, or heavy an object appears to be (which may be different from how much it really weighs or how large it is in actual scale).

outriggers are decorative or functional elements mounted to a wall at right angles in order to define, separate, and frame categories of merchandise presented on shelves or display fixtures. Outriggers often include signs that call out categories of merchandise for easy navigation.

P

pegwall is a system that has a backer panel with a grid pattern of holes into which pegwall hooks and other specialty fixtures may be inserted.

pivot pieces are the dominant apparel items that dictate the direction (end-use, fabrication, style, and color) for all subsequent pieces used in coordinated outfits.

planograms are drawings that show how merchandise and selling fixtures should be placed on selling floors, walls, freestanding displays, and window displays. They are planning tools that make it possible to communicate consistent store layout and décor directives to multiple locations, thereby creating a strong identity for the retailer.

portfolios are visual résumés carried in portable cases to present photographs, drawings, graphic designs, certificates, letters of recommendation, and other documentation of professional experience.

price points are the actual numbers (for example, $12.99) used on signs to inform shoppers of prices.

primary colors are yellow, red, and blue. They are the starting points on the color wheel. Other colors are formed from them.

promotional mix is a combination of marketing communication tools—online, print, broadcast special events, and in-store visual merchandising, as well as personal selling—that tells targeted customers about stores and their merchandise.

proportion describes the relationship between the apparent size, mass, scale, or optical weight of two or more objects.

props (stage properties) are items or objects other than painted scenery and actors' costumes that are used on a stage set. The term has migrated to the visual merchandising vocabulary to mean decorative items or objects other than merchandise and signs used in a display.

prototype is the original model upon which later types are based. For example, before rolling out a dozen retail stores, a prototype is built so that design features may be tested and refined. The same process is used in the development of custom merchandise fixtures and visual fixtures.

R

racetrack layout exposes shoppers to a great deal of merchandise as they follow perimeter traffic aisles with departments on the right and left of circular, square, rectangular, or oval "racetracks."

repetition is achieved when recurring design elements like size, color, or shape create a visual pattern that establishes a sense of order and emphasis in a presentation.

retail mobile units, commonly called RMUs are promotional or product displays that are usually freestanding and moveable. They are commonly located in shopping malls, airports, and at fairs and expos.

retrofit is to add architectural features, fixtures, or other elements after the original structure is completed.

rhythm refers to the repetition of design elements to create visual cadence or emphasis for the viewer. The eye travels along the paths of repeated items, and the merchandising message is reinforced.

riser is a display unit used to elevate merchandise in a composition so that the overall presentation has added visual interest and variety.

round garment rods are basic fixture components used to show large quantities of goods on hangers along walls.

round rack (rounder) is a capacity fixture fabricated in several diameters and adjustable heights for stocking quantities of basic apparel items on hangers.

S

secondary colors are formed by combining pairs of primary colors. Red and yellow merge to become orange; yellow and blue become green; blue and red become violet.

sell-down, also called *sell-through*, is the period during which an item or grouping is on the selling floor, from introduction at full price through the markdown stage.

sequence refers to the particular order in which items are presented for viewing. In addition to numerical order, a presentation might also rely on gradation of items from small to large, or large to small, to stress that a particular item is available in a variety of sizes.

shade refers to a single color that is darkened by adding varying amounts of black or gray to it.

shape refers to a standard or universally recognized spatial form, like a circle or a triangle, that helps the viewer identify various objects; it can also refer to an irregular contour of an object or part of an object. The shape of a three-dimensional object is also called a *form*.

shops are created when similar types of merchandise are bought in depth (sufficient to fill six to ten selling fixtures) and are pulled together into one area of a department.

sight line refers to the area a person can see from a particular vantage point—the view at the end of an aisle, or at the top or bottom of an escalator, for example.

signature fixture is an attention-getting, one-of-a-kind unit positioned at store and department entrances that reflects stores' brand images.

slatwall is a wall system of horizontal backer panels with evenly spaced slots that accept brackets and display accessories with slatwall fittings.

soffits are long ledges, permanent arches, or boxes reaching down from a store's ceiling to its top shelves or usable wall space. They are often used to mask nondecorative (functional) lighting fixtures that illuminate merchandise displayed on store walls.

soft aisle layouts are floor sets with fixtures arranged in groups, creating natural aisles without any change in floor covering to designate separate aisle space.

sourcing (or resourcing) describes the process of finding resources for use in a business.

split-complementary schemes consist of three colors—one central color plus the two colors on either side of its color wheel complement. Example: yellow with red-violet and blue-violet.

straight arm is a display arm affixed in a perpendicular manner to a wall standard, slatwall, gridwall, T-stand, or other selling floor fixture to show small quantities of hanging merchandise.

striking a mannequin means removing its support rod and base plate in order to secure it to the floor of a store window or display platform with wire so that the figure appears to stand on its own.

strip malls contain side-by-side stores with parking lots immediately outside their doors. Some strip malls may have enclosed walkways, but they are not configured under one large roof as conventional covered malls are.

superquad is a four-armed capacity floor fixture with adjustable height used for showing items purchased in depth or coordinate groupings of pants, skirts, blouses, and sweaters or jackets.

T

target markets are identified (targeted) segments of the population that research indicates are good fits for retailers' products or service offerings. These are the groups at which retailers aim all of their stores' promotional communication efforts.

Chapter 5

Gorman, Greg M. *The Visual Merchandising and Store Design Workbook*. Cincinnati, OH: ST Publications, 1996.

Underhill, Paco. *Why We Buy: The Science of Shopping*. New York: Simon and Schuster, 1999.

Chapter 6

Doonan, Simon. *Confessions of a Window Dresser*. New York: Penguin Group, 1998.

Eisman, Leatrice. *Pantone Guide to Communicating With Color*. Sarasota, FL: Grafix Press, Ltd. 2000.

Chapter 7

Eagleman, David and Brandt, Anthony. *The Runaway Species: How Human Creativity Remakes the World.* U.S: Catapult, 2017.

Glen, Peter. *10 Years of Peter Glen: One Hundred Essays for the Improvement of Work, Life and Other Matters of Consequence.* Cincinnati, OH: ST Publications, 1994.

Underhill, Paco. *Why We Buy: The Science of Shopping*. New York: Simon and Schuster, 1999.

Chapter 8

Glen, Peter. *10 Years of Peter Glen: One Hundred Essays for the Improvement of Work, Life and Other Matters of Consequence.* Cincinnati, OH: ST Publications, 1994.

Linden, David A. *Think Tank: Forty Neuroscientists Explore the Biological Roots of Human Experience.* New Haven and London: Yale University Press, 2018.

The Vomela Companies. www.vomela.com.

Chapter 9

Hera Lighting. www.heralighting.com.

Underhill, Paco. *Why We Buy: The Science of Shopping*. New York: Simon and Schuster, 1999.

Chapter 10

Collins, Terry. "We Really Are What We Eat, and There's Cause to Celebrate." *Star Tribune*, October 8, 1999.

Cobb, Matthew. "Smell, A Very Short Introduction." Oxford, United Kingdom, 2020.

EuroShop. www.euroshop.de.

Food Marketing Institute. www.fmi.org.

Kantar. www.kantar.com.

Pikes Place Market. Pikeplacemarket.org.

Redmond, Russell. "Online Groceries Sales to Grow 40% in 2020." *Supermarket News*, May 11, 2020.

Wahl, Michael. *In-Store Marketing: A New Dimension in the Share Wars.* Winston-Salem, NC. Wake Forrest University Press, 1992.

Whole Foods Market. www.wholefoodsmarket.com.

Yoon, Eddie. "3 Behavioral Trends That Will Reshape Our Post-Covid World." *Harvard Business Review*, May 26, 2020.

Chapter 11

International Live Events Association (ILEA). http://www.ileahub.com/.

Special Events. www.specialevents.com.

Chapter 12

Albrecht, Donald and Livenstein, Barbara. *Cooper-Hewitt National Design Museum Program Notes for the Window Show,* May 14—21, 1999.

Doonan, Simon. *Confessions of a Window Dresser*. New York: Penguin Putnam, 1998.

Gorman, Greg M. *The Visual Merchandising and Store Design Workbook*. Cincinnati, OH: ST Publications, 1996.

Kepron, David. *Retail (r)Evolution: Why Creating Right-Brained Stores Will Shape the Future of Shopping in a Digitally Driven World.* Cincinnati, OH: ST Books, ST Media Group, 2014.

"The Window Show: A Groundbreaking Exhibition by Cooper-Hewitt, National Design Museum, Spotlights Window Design and Designers." *Retail Ad World*, October 1999.

WindowsWear—www.windowswear.com.

Chapter 13

Bentley Hale, Marsha. Interview. Photographs from personal archive collection. August 1983.

Doonan, Simon. *Confessions of a Window Dresser*. New York: Penguin Putnam, 1998.

Ola, Per and d'Aulaire, Emily. "Mannequins, the Mute Mirrors of Fashion History." *Smithsonian*, April 1991, 61–75.

Redstone, Susan. "Adel Rootstein." www.fashionwindows.com, August 8, 1998.

Sipe, Jeffrey. "Adoring Dior's Haute Couture." *Insight on the News*, December 16, 1996, 37.

Tobias, Tom. "I Sing the Body Inanimate." *New York*, June 28–July 5, 1999, 177.

Chapter 14

The Chicago Manual of Style: For Authors, Editors and Copywriters, 16th edition, rev. and exp. Chicago: The University of Chicago Press, 2010.

Doonan, Simon. *Confessions of a Window Dresser*. New York: Penguin Putnam, 1998.

Eckert, Carolyn. *Your Idea Starts Here, 77 Mind-Expanding Ways to Unleash Your Creativity*. North Adams, MA: Storey Publishing, 2016.

Glen, Peter. *It's Not My Department*. New York: William Morrow and Company, Inc., 1990.

Glen, Peter. *10 Years of Peter Glen: One Hundred Essays for the Improvement of Work, Life and Other Matters of Consequence*. Cincinnati, OH: ST Publications, 1994.

Glen, Peter. "ADD: Attention Divided Disorder." *Visual Merchandising and Store Design*, November 1999.

Harris, Jason, *The Soulful Art of Persuasion: The 11 Habits That Will Make Anyone a Master Influencer*, New York: Currency, 2019.

Hanks, Kurt and Parry, Jay. *Wake Up Your Creative Genius*. Menlo Park, CA: Crisp Publications, 1991.

Kepron, David. *Retail (r)Evolution*: *Why Creating Right-Brained Stores Will Shape the Future of Shopping in a Digitally Driven World*. Cincinnati, OH: ST Books, ST Media Group, 2014.

Kondo, Marie. *The Life-Changing Magic of Tidying Up: The Japanese Art of Decluttering and Organizing*. Berkeley: Ten Speed Press, 2014.

McNally, David and Speak, Karl D. *Be Your Own Brand*. San Francisco: Berrett-Koehler Publishers, 2002.

Strunk, W., Jr. and White, E. B. *The Elements of Style*, 3rd edition. New York: Macmillan, 1979.

Tindell, Kip. *Uncontainable: How Passion, Commitment, and Conscious Capitalism Built a Business Where Everyone Thrives*. New York: Grand Central Publishing, 2014.

Underhill, Paco. *Why We Buy: The Science of Shopping*. New York: Simon and Schuster, 1999.

Underhill, Paco. *Call of the Mall*. New York: Simon and Schuster, 2004.

Von Oech, Roger. *Creative Whack Pack*. Stamford, CT: United States Game Systems, 1992.

Chapter 15

Gupta, Sanjay. *Keep Sharp: Build a Better Brain at Any Age*. New York: Simon & Schuster, 2021.

Li, Qing. *Forest Bathing: How Trees Can Help You Find Health and Happiness*. New York: Viking, 2018.

Rebholz, Jenny S. "The Markopoulos Circle." *design:retail*, April/May 2016, 40–45.

Rufus, Anneli. *The Party of One: The Loner's Manifesto*. Marlowe and Company, 2003.

Useful Websites

Chapter 1

Echochamber—www.echochamber.com
GDR Creative Intelligence—www.gdruk.com
Shop! Association—www.shopassociation.org
WindowsWear—www.windowswear.com
Forbes—www.forbes.com

Chapter 2

Capsule—www.capsule.us
Census Bureau—www.census.gov
Evereve—www.evereve.com
Nordstrom—www.nordstrom.com
Target—www.target.com

Chapter 3

Color Marketing Group—www.colormarketing.org
Dwell—www.dwell.com
Elle Magazine—www.elle.com
M. Grumbacher—www.grumbacherart.com
Pantone—www.pantone.com
Vogue—www.vogue.com

Chapter 4

B & N Industries—www.bnind.com
Betsey Johnson—www.betseyjohnson.com
The Center for Universal Design at North Carolina State University—www.2.ed.gov
Envirosell—www.envirosell.com
Loft Girls—www.theloftgirls.com
Sephora—www.sephora.com
Shop!—www.shopassociation.org
Silvestri—www.silvestricalifornia.com
Swatch—www.swatch.com

Chapter 6

Women's Wear Daily—www.wwd.com

Chapter 7

ABC Carpet & Home—www.abchome.com

Crate&Barrel—www.crateandbarrel.com

Fishs Eddy—www.fishseddy.com

IKEA. www.ikea.com

MartinPatrick3—www.martinpatrick3.com

RH—www.rh.com

West Elm—www.westelm.com

Williams Sonoma—www.williams-sonoma.com

Chapter 8

Allbirds—www.allbirds.com

Dwell—www.dwell.com

Signs of the Times Magazine—www.stmediagroupintl.com

SignWeb—www.signweb.com

Under Armour—www.underarmour.com

West Elm—www.westelm.com

Williams Sonoma—www.williams-sonoma.com

Chapter 9

American Lighting Association—www.alalighting.com

BÄRO—www.baero.com

Envirosell—http://envirosell.com

International Association of Lighting Designers (IALD)— www.iald.com

Chapter 10

Byerly's—www.lundsandbyerlys.com

Epicurious—www.epicurious.com

Food Marketing Institute—www.fmi.org

Fred Meyer Stores—http://www.fredmeyer.com

Progressive Grocer Magazine—www.progressivegrocer.com

Publix—www.publix.com

Real Simple Magazine—www.realsimple.com

Supermarket News—www.supermarketnews.com

Supervalu—www.supervalu.ie

Trader Joe's—www.traderjoes.com

United States Department of Agriculture—www.usda.gov

Whole Foods Market, Inc.— www.wholefoodsmarket.com

Chapter 11

Chandler Industries— www.chandlerindustries.com

RCS Innovations—www.rcsinnovations.com

Triad—www.triadmfg.com

Chapter 12

Cooper-Hewitt National Design Museum—www .cooperhewitt.org

Fashion Display Website—www.fashionwindows.com

Tiffany & Co.—www.tiffany.com

VMSD—www.vmsd.com

WindowsWear—www.windowswear.com

Chapter 13

Bernstein—www.bernsteindisplay.com

DK display corp—www.dkdisplaycorp.com

Fusion Specialties—www.fusionspecialties.com

Genesis Mannequins USA—www.genesismannequinsusa .com

Greneker—www.greneker.com

Hans Boodt—www.hansboodtmannequins.com

Hindsgaul—www.hindsgaul.com

New John Nissen—www.new-john-nissen.com

Manex USA—www.manex-usa.com

Mondo—www.mondomannequins.com

Patina-V—www.patinav.com

Ralph Pucci mannequins—www.ralphpuccimannequins.net

Seven Continents—www.sevencontinents.com

Siegel & Stockman—www.siegel-stockman.com

Silvestri California—www.silvestricalifornia.com

Universal Display & Design—www.universaldisplay.co.uk

Window France—www.windowfrance.com

WindowsWear—www.windowswear.com

Chapter 14

Chain Store Age—www.chainstoreage.com

EuroShop—www.euroshop-tradefair.com

Footwear News—www.footwearnews.com

Home Fashion News—www.hfndigital.com

ICFF: International Contemporary Furniture Fair—www.icff .com

IRDC: International Retail Design Conference—www.vmsd .com

MapEasy's Guide Maps—http://www.mapeasy.com

National Retail Federation—www.nrf.com

NRF Retail's Big Show—www.nrf.com

PAVE—www.paveglobal.org

Progressive Grocer—www.progressivegrocer.com

RDI, Retail Design Institute—retaildesigninstitute.org

Retail Environments—www.shopassociation.org

RetailTouchPoints—www.retailtouchpoints.com
RETAILX—www.retailx.com
Shop!—www.shopassociation.org
NRF Smartbrief—www.nrf.com
Trade Show News Network—www.tsnn.com
Where Magazine—www.wheremagazine.com
WWD, Women's Wear Daily—www.wwd.com
vmsd—www.vmsd.com

Chapter 15

IRDC: International Retail Design Conference—www.vmsd
    .com
PAVE: Planning and Visual Education —www.paveglobal.org
vmsd—www.vmsd.com

Retailers

Abercrombie & Fitch—www.abercrombie.com
American Eagle—www.ae.com
Andrei Duman Gallery—www.andreidumangallery.com
Anne Fontaine—www.annefontaine.com
Ann Taylor—www.anntaylor.comApple—www.apple.com
Athleta—www.athleta.com
Banana Republic—www.bananarepublic.com
Bergdorf Goodman—bergdorfgoodman.com
Brooks Brothers—www.brooksbrothers.com
Bulgari—www.bulgari.com
Calvin Klein—www.calvinklein.com
Converse—www.converse.com
COS—www.cosstores.com
Costco Wholesale—www.costco.com
Crate & Barrel—www.crateandbarrel.com
Diane Von Furstenberg—www.dvf.com
Dillard's—www.dillards.com
Dolce&Gabbanna—www.dolcegabbana.com
Eataly—www.eataly.com
El Palacio de Hierro Polanco—www.elpalaciodehierro.com
Evereve—www.evereve.com
Ferragamo—www.ferragamo.com
Five Below—www.fivebelow.com
Gap—www.gap.com
Guy Laroche—www.guylaroche.com
H&M—www.hm.com
Harrods—www.harrods.com
Hickey Freeman—www.hickeyfreeman.com
Issey Miyake—www.isseymiyake.com

J.Crew—http://www.jcrew.com
JCPenney—www.jcpenney.com
Kate Spade—www.katespade.com
Kohl's—www.kohls.com
Lands' End—www.landsend.com
Loft Girls—www.theloftgirls.com
Louis Vuitton—www.louisvuitton.com
MAC—www.maccosmetics.com
Macy's, Inc.—www.macys.com
Marni—www.marni.com
Merrell—www.merrell.com
Neiman Marcus—www.neimanmarcus.com
Nike—www.nike.com
Nordstrom—www.nordstrom.com
Old Navy—www.oldnavy.com
Printemps—www.printemps.com
Pottery Barn—www.potterybarn.com
RH—www.rh.com
Saks Fifth Avenue—www.saksfifthavenue.com
Sears—www.sears.com
Sony—www.sony.com
Sonia Rykiel—www.soniarykiel.com
SuperValu—www.supervalu.ie
Target—www.target.com
The Broad—www.thebroad.org
T.J. Maxx—www.tjmaxx.com
Tory Burch—www.toryburch.com
Under Armour—www.underarmour.com
Uniqlo—www.uniqlo.com
Valmont Gallerie Gastronomique—epicerievalmont.ca
Versace—www.versace.com
Victoria's Secret—www.victoriassecret.com
Walmart—www.walmart.com
Whole Foods Market—www.wholefoodsmarket.com
Williams-Sonoma—www.williams-sonoma.com
Zara—www.zara.com

Index